Civil Society under Authoritarianism

The China Model

Despite the dominant narrative of the repression of civil society in China, *Civil Society under Authoritarianism: The China Model* argues that interactions between local officials and civil society facilitate a learning process, whereby each actor learns about the intentions and work processes of the other. Over the past two decades, often facilitated by foreign donors and problems within the general social framework, these interactions generated a process in which officials learned the benefits and disadvantages of civil society. Civil society supports local officials' efforts to provide social services and improve public policies, yet it also engages in protest and other activities that challenge social stability and development. This duality motivates local officials in China to construct a "social management" system – known as consultative authoritarianism – to encourage the beneficial aspects and discourage the dangerous ones. Although civil society has not democratized China, such organizations have facilitated greater dialogue between citizens and the state as part of politics in an authoritarian system that normally lacks such channels for participation.

Jessica C. Teets is an assistant professor in the Political Science Department and Jeanne Epp Barksdale '48 Junior Faculty Fellow at Middlebury College, Vermont. Her research focuses on civil society, governance, and policy diffusion in authoritarian regimes, with an emphasis on Chinese politics. She is the author, most recently, of "Let Many Civil Societies Bloom: The Rise of Consultative Authoritarianism in China" (*The China Quarterly*, 2013) and "Reforming Service Delivery in China: The Emergence of a Social Innovation Model" (*Journal of Chinese Political Science*, 2012). Dr. Teets was recently selected to participate in the Public Intellectuals Program created by the National Committee on United States–China Relations.

Civil Society under Authoritarianism

The China Model

JESSICA C. TEETS
Middlebury College

CAMBRIDGE
UNIVERSITY PRESS

CAMBRIDGE
UNIVERSITY PRESS

32 Avenue of the Americas, New York NY 10013-2473, USA

Cambridge University Press is part of the University of Cambridge.

It furthers the University's mission by disseminating knowledge in the pursuit of education, learning and research at the highest international levels of excellence.

www.cambridge.org
Information on this title: www.cambridge.org/9781316507919

First published 2014
First paperback edition 2015

A catalogue record for this publication is available from the British Library

Library of Congress Cataloguing in Publication data
Teets, Jessica C.
Civil society under authoritarianism : the China model / Jessica C. Teets.
pages cm
ISBN 978-1-107-03875-2 (hardback)
1. Civil society – China. 2. Authoritarianism – China. I. Title.
JQ1516. T44 2014
300.951–dc23

2013043766

ISBN 978-1-107-03875-2 Hardback
ISBN 978-1-316-50791-9 Paperback

Contents

Figures

Preface and Acknowledgments

This book was conceived of serendipitously during my dissertation fieldwork in China during the 2006–2007 academic year. I was interviewing a local official at the provincial Poverty Alleviation Bureau (PAB) in Chengdu about partnerships between civil society organizations (CSOs) and local government to provide public services. When I met him at a local teahouse for our interview, he began by lecturing me in a raised voice about why foreigners always romanticize civil society and denigrate government: "everything that civil society can do, the government can do better." After I explained that my research focused on the complementary nature of civil society and government work, I asked him to walk me through the process of forming one of the PAB's projects with a civil society partner. He described how he initially did not want to work with the group because he thought CSOs had low capacity, but he was forced to because of the foreign donor's requirements for project funding. However, after completing this project, he reevaluated his original view of CSOs and admitted to me that the group actually helped the PAB develop a very effective and innovative plan, and that in the future he would partner with this group and others like it. Although this information did not fit into my dissertation, his comments stayed with me long after I defended the dissertation.

In political science in general, but especially in the field of comparative political institutions, most scholarship characterizes state actors' preferences and institutional rules (whichever way you view the causal arrow between the two) as remarkably stable and only changing as a result of exogenous shocks to the system. However, this official's comments illustrated another more gradual and endogenous mechanism of change – learning. All other things constant, my interviews revealed that interactions over time between local officials and CSOs in China were facilitating a learning process whereby each actor learned about the priorities, work processes, and intentions of the other. In addition to highlighting a social feedback mechanism, this process of learning illustrates agency on the part of CSOs despite power asymmetries. Much that is written about CSOs in China, whether in academic journals or the popular press, focuses on state repression. However, this victim narrative disregards the many ways in which CSOs effectively navigate the authoritarian state and even more importantly change state officials' views of these organizations. This altered perspective is evidenced through changing formal policies governing CSOs such as registration and fundraising, but also informally by the number of local agencies partnering and contracting with CSOs. In this book, I seek to demonstrate the power of learning and the agency of CSOs in creating these learning opportunities. I argue that ongoing interactions with CSOs over the past two decades, often facilitated by foreign donors and the political economy of local social service delivery, generated a process whereby local officials learned the benefits and disadvantages of CSOs. In many ways, CSOs support local officials in providing social services, improving public policies, and alleviating social unrest. These experiences encouraged officials to continue to partner with CSOs, much as the PAB official described. However, CSOs also engage in protest and other activities that challenge social stability and economic development. These benefits and disadvantages motivated local officials to construct a social management system that seeks to encourage the beneficial aspects and discourage the dangerous aspects of civil society: consultative authoritarianism.

Civil society activity in China has not catalyzed democratization, much to the disappointment of the "foreigners" to whom the PAB official referred. However, CSOs have facilitated greater consultation and social advocacy as part of normal politics in an authoritarian system that lacks these channels. In addition to all of their innovative projects aimed at improving the environment, delivering social services, and serving vulnerable groups in society, CSOs participate in improving governance in China. CSOs should be praised for this amazing progress in policy participation, not criticized for not toppling the government. CSOs persevered (and continue to do so) through an adverse environment, and they regularly improve governance and daily life for many in China. In addition, many local officials are committed to these same goals and serve as advocates for CSOs and their programs inside of the party-state. In order to accurately portray this learning process and the active engagement of both CSOs and local officials, I relied on more than a hundred interviews with scholars, civil society practitioners, local officials, and expatriates who served as pioneers in the development of the civil society sector in China. Although there are too many people to thank in the limited space I have here, I wanted to acknowledge my debt of gratitude to at least a few. It goes without saying that all mistakes are of course my own.

First, I would like to thank my advisors (both formal and informal) for challenging my thinking and providing support throughout this process: Margaret Pearson, David Leblang, and Andrew Mertha. These three are impressive scholars in addition to being excellent advisors, and my work benefited greatly from their example. Now I am lucky enough to count them as friends as well. I also must thank my professors and classmates at the University of Colorado–Boulder for the rigorous methodological education and constant feedback. Orion Lewis, Erica Chenoweth, and Michael Touchton graciously discussed this project throughout its duration and continue to provide intellectual support. I remember the long days spent in the basement office of Ketchum Hall fondly. After 2009, my colleagues at Middlebury College and in the small academic field of Chinese civil society offered suggestions on many chapters: Erik Bleich, Anthony Spires (a fellow PIP III), Shawn Shieh, Jennifer Hsu, and Karla Simon. I also would like to thank the two anonymous reviewers and Cambridge University Press editors Eric Crahan and Robert Dreesen for helping to improve this project.

Second, I would like to express my gratitude to my colleagues and friends in China who made this project possible: Zhu Feng, Shi Xiaoqin, and Yuan Ruijun at Peking University; Xiaojing Wang and her colleagues at Tsinghua University's NGO Research Center; and numerous other academics across the country who met with me over the past seven years to explain the development of civil society in China and changing local state–civil society relations. I must also thank the civil society practitioners and local officials who met with me repeatedly over the years with many eventually becoming my friends: Angela (Yanfang) Cun, Shawn Shieh and Fu Tao at CDB, and Andy Wilkes, Chen Yunzhi, Hu Zhongming, and Tan Jingzheng. Without the generous amounts of time and information they shared, this project would be sorely lacking. Many studies examining civil society in China interview only civil society practitioners, so the numerous interviews with local officials balanced and strengthened this research and are greatly appreciated.

Lastly, and most importantly, I want to thank my family and friends for their unwavering support while I was researching and writing this book, especially the Teets and Lewis clans: Sharon, Joshua, Sarah, Angie, Hiram, Nancy, and Adriane. My father, Charles Teets, was seriously ill and passed away while I researched and wrote this book, and my friends and family helped me balance my professional responsibilities with grieving for my father who believed the true test of intellect is the ability to make a good pun. The first time I could do so in Chinese, he pronounced me fluent and ready for fieldwork! Finally, I must thank my husband, Orion Lewis, for maintaining my sanity and always pushing me to dig deeper and think harder. I could not have written this book or accomplished any of my professional achievements without you, especially after the joyous arrival of our son Draco. I dedicate this book to you.

INTRODUCTION

Civil Society in China

Better Governance under Authoritarianism

THE PUZZLE: WHY IS GREENPEACE IN CHINA?

While conducting research in China in 2006, I was surprised to see the Greenpeace office in Beijing. With its anti-state rhetoric and dramatic whaling interventions, this seemed to be the last group that the Chinese Communist Party (CCP) would allow to operate. The presence of a group such as Greenpeace raised the question of how we understand the relationship between an authoritarian state and civil society. Most scholarly and policy analyses describe an environment in which all types of associations are either directly state controlled or highly incorporated into state bureaucracy.[1] However, clearly the story is not simply one of state control and repression, of a David civil society opposing a Goliath state; otherwise, why would the CCP allow a prominent independent group such as Greenpeace to exist?

In the following chapters, I examine this puzzle of why an associational revolution is occurring in authoritarian regimes such as China. Given the participatory goals and past role in democratization experiences in various countries including

[1] See the following authors for this discussion about the autonomy of groups in China: B. Michael Frolic, "State-Led Civil Society," in *Civil Society in China*, Timothy Brook and B. Michael Frolic, eds. (Armonk, NY: M.E. Sharpe, 1997); Heath Chamberlain, "Civil Society with Chinese Characteristics?" *The China Journal* no. 39, January 1998: 69–81.

Poland and the Philippines, why are authoritarian leaders allowing these groups to form and proliferate? I contend that local Chinese officials have learned through direct experience and observation of the experiences of other authoritarian regimes that civil society groups may both assist and threaten nondemocratic governments. On one hand, civil society generates reliable information about citizen dissatisfaction that authoritarian states are unable to access through formal institutions, and it meets these demands through social innovation, thus improving governance and increasing satisfaction with the regime. On the other hand, civil society advocates for more citizen participation in policy making and an expansion of democratic political ideals such as transparency and accountability. This advocacy challenges the opaque and concentrated nature of authority in an authoritarian regime. In seeking to retain the benefits of civil society while mitigating the dangers, Chinese local officials developed a new model of state–civil society relations that combines the pluralistic aspect of democratic governance with the state control mechanisms prevalent in authoritarian regimes.

This new model of consultative authoritarianism (CA) encourages the formation and development of an autonomous civil society while creating new, more indirect methods of state control. Thus, the growth of civil society under authoritarianism is not a unidirectional march toward political liberalization, but rather an interactive and dynamic process whereby government officials and civil society leaders learn from experiences with each other to build a new state-society model that emphasizes *both* pluralism and control. As I discuss in more detail at the end of this chapter, the normative implications of this new CA model are also nuanced and complex. The more cooperative relationship existing between local state and civil society generates better development outcomes and improves governance through increasing transparency and pluralism in policy making; however, this same relationship also decreases the ability and likelihood of these groups to challenge authoritarian rule and mobilize citizens to resist nondemocratic governance. Although proponents of democratization might be disappointed in this outcome, I argue that the improvement of human welfare in authoritarian regimes around the world is non-trivial and should not be dismissed in favor of a focus only on sweeping revolutionary change.

Greenpeace-China offers an instructive example of this dynamic process of policy learning that is driving the development of the CA model. Greenpeace-China's first office opened in Hong Kong in 1997, followed by expansion to Beijing in 2002. One of Greenpeace's first mainland projects in 2004 was shut down after conflicts with Yunnan provincial leaders over its direct methods to oppose logging; however, in response to the Yunnan campaign, Greenpeace pursued a more collaborative relationship with Beijing officials and the Beijing office continued to operate.[2] This learning process flowed both ways, as officials also learned how the group could assist with state goals, such as using technical expertise to help draft a renewable energy law in 2006.[3] This variation in Greenpeace's experiences questions the dominant understanding of the oppositional model of state-society relationship described by liberal civil society theories, and it illustrates that this relationship in authoritarian regimes is much more nuanced than previously thought. I find that the relationship between the state and civil society changes from corporatism in the 1990s to a more independent one in the 2000s through a process of policy learning by local officials occurring through two mechanisms: (1) direct experience with emerging civil society groups and (2) observing state-society relationships in other provinces and states.

Interestingly, I also find this process of learning, or policy diffusion, occurring in other authoritarian regimes. In fact, Greenpeace's experience in China is mirrored around the world, with the rise of a fairly autonomous civil society in authoritarian

[2] "Greenpeacers in China and Australia Target Illegal Logging," *Research and Environment News from China*, Embassy of Switzerland in Beijing, November 2004: available at http://www.eda.admin.ch/beijing

[3] Greenpeace-China, "China Has Potential to Be World's Biggest Wind Energy Market by 2020," press release, November 6, 2005: available at http://www.greenpeace.org/eastasia/press/releases/climate-energy/2005/20051106-wind-force-12-china/

regimes. In this book, I focus on local government learning in response to an emerging civil society in China and then briefly extend this analysis to illustrate policy diffusion in other authoritarian regimes, such as Russia. Whereas this analysis was motivated by the changing state-society relationships I observed in China, I also noticed that China, although unique in many ways, has increasingly converged with other nondemocratic regimes in developing a new relationship with civil society – one that allows more participation in the policy process while creating new tools of state control. In the following chapters, I explore the factors leading to this convergence to understand why China and other nondemocratic regimes would allow, and in fact welcome, civil society organizations like Greenpeace.

This analysis challenges much of the current understanding of civil society in authoritarian regimes, namely by asserting that cooperation, not opposition, is possible between the two and that each side learns from experiences with the other. First, I develop a new hybrid model of state-society relationships merging the ideas of pluralism and autonomy in liberal theories of civil society with the idea of state control over group activities in corporatist theories. This model, which I call "consultative authoritarianism," challenges traditional liberal theories by finding that civil society needs less autonomy from the state to accomplish goals of advocacy and service delivery and in fact increasing channels of interaction with the state might help these groups have more impact on policy making. This is not to suggest that civil society does not need space from the state to accomplish these goals, but that operationally autonomous groups cooperate with the state to provide services and policy advocacy, creating a new state-society model that is not a dichotomous choice between total independence and total cooption. This model of consultative authoritarianism is increasingly being adopted by authoritarian regimes as a way to enjoy the governance benefits of autonomous groups but still control certain activities that might challenge the regime, and by civil society groups as a way to influence policy making in authoritarian regimes.

As a result of this cooperation, I find that civil society might play a role not in challenging authoritarian governments, as liberal theories predict, but rather in making them more durable. Civil society plays an important role in good governance especially under authoritarianism. Authoritarian regimes do not maintain formal channels for receiving citizen feedback about policies, and thus officials often do not know which policies are ineffective or which might be causing grievances to build up that might eventually challenge the regime's authority. By transmitting information about policies and needs to the government and helping provide goods and services to citizens, civil society improves governance in these regimes, which might serve to extend authoritarian rule. Although my findings challenge the democratic opposition role ascribed to civil society by liberal theories, the role played by these groups in creating better governance should not be overlooked. This is a vital role that directly increases the well-being of the world's population in meaningful ways.

Second, my analysis highlights the role of learning in the changing relationship and policies toward civil society that reveals an endogenous mechanism for authoritarian institutional change. The existing literature on endogenous institutional change examines the use of feedback loops as the primary mechanism of change; however, authoritarian regimes do not have mechanisms for participation in the policy process, making receiving feedback slow and difficult.[4] So how do authoritarian institutions lacking social feedback mechanisms change without regime overthrow? Much of the current literature examines how these regimes alter formal institutional structures such as legislatures and political parties to access information.[5] However, I argue that change in these regimes is most commonly a result of a process of authoritarian learning,

[4] Avner Greif and David Laitin, "A Theory of Endogenous Institutional Change," *American Political Science Review* 98, 2004: 14–48; James Mahoney and Kathleen Thelen, eds., *Explaining Institutional Change: Ambiguity, Agency, and Power* (Cambridge, UK: Cambridge University Press, 2010); Orion Lewis and Sven Steinmo, "How Institutions Evolve: Evolutionary Theory and Institutional Change," *Polity* 44, 2012: 314–339.

[5] Jennifer Gandhi, *Political Institutions under Dictatorship* (New York: Cambridge University Press, 2008); Jason Brownlee, *Authoritarianism in an Age of Democratization* (New York: Cambridge University Press, 2007).

whereby policy makers' experiences and observations serve as a feedback mechanism leading to endogenous institutional change.

Although the policy learning literature focuses on this process in democracies, I find that a similar learning process occurs in and across authoritarian regimes as well and in fact that the role of civil society in this process is strengthened in nondemocracies that lack institutional mechanisms for the transmission of information about policy. In democracies, civil society organizations offer only one perspective (or voice) on policy and compete with many other actors, such as lobbyists and media, whereas in nondemocracies, civil society might be the only non-state actor advocating for policy change and sharing information about failed policies. As I find in the case of China, local officials' learning about the emerging civil society appearing in the early 1990s led to a new state–civil society relationship at the local level first in Yunnan and then in Beijing before spreading to other provinces. In the final section of this book, I trace the process whereby the consultative authoritarianism model diffused to other authoritarian regimes as policy makers observed this seemingly successful model of balancing the benefits and dangers of civil society developing in China.

THE ARGUMENT: THE PROCESS OF POLICY LEARNING

Dominant theories of civil society depict a state-society relationship of autonomy, whereby civil society operates in a separate social sphere from the political one of the state.[6] In democracies, these liberal theories of civil society depict an independent and often conflictual relationship with the state. In authoritarian regimes, these theories predict repressive or incorporated state-society relationships as a result of social threats to state authority.[7]

[6] Michael W. Foley and Bob Edwards, "The Paradox of Civil Society," *Journal of Democracy* 7, 1996: 38–52.

[7] Philippe C. Schmitter, "Still the Century of Corporatism?" *The Review of Politics* 36, 1974: 85–131.

Corporatism is a state-society model that incorporates all societal groups into state organizations as "transmission belts," transferring information between state and society. For example, all labor associations would be incorporated into one mass labor organization that is funded and staffed by the government. The characteristics of corporatism are that all social organizations operate as government entities and as such depend on government funding and employees to meet goals outlined by the state. Additionally, there is a lack of competition among organizations for each constituency: "at the national level the state recognizes one and only one organization (say, a national labor union, a business association, a farmers' association) as the sole representative of the sectoral interests of the individuals, enterprises or institutions that comprise that organization's assigned constituency."[8] The intention of corporatism is to integrate interest articulation into state agencies to control it and not allow social mobilization that might possibly be used against the state. Independent grassroots groups in this system are not allowed to exist, but as in the case of China when these groups began to form in the 1990s, corporatism can adapt by requiring that all groups register and operate under a state agency.[9] However, I argue that during the 2000s, state–civil society relationships in China have changed from corporatism to a hybrid model of consultative authoritarianism that combines the autonomous civil society found in liberal models with mechanisms of state control found in corporatist models. Although corporatism still exists in China, CA is increasingly becoming the dominant model, as seen in recent regulatory changes such as easing registration requirements for groups.[10]

[8] Jonathan Unger and Anita Chan, "Corporatism in China: A Developmental State in an East Asian Context," in *China after Socialism: In the Footsteps of Eastern Europe or East Asia?* Barrett McCormic and Jonathan Unger, eds. (Armonk, NY: M.E. Sharpe, 1995), pp. 95–96.

[9] Kenneth W. Foster, "Associations in the Embrace of an Authoritarian State: State Domination of Society?" *Studies in Comparative International Development* 35, Winter 2001: 84–109; Jennifer Hsu and Reza Hasmath, eds., *The Chinese Corporatist State: Adaption, Survival and Resistance* (London: Routledge, 2013).

[10] Zhuang Pinghui, "Guangdong to Allow Some NGOs off the Leash," *South China Morning Post*, November 25, 2011: available at http://www.scmp.com/article/985858/guangdong-allow-some-ngos-leash

In contrast to corporatism, consultative authoritarianism is a state-society model that allows for fairly independent social organization of many competing groups but seeks to control these organizations through a system of state management. However, in contradistinction to the direct tools used in corporatism, those used here are indirect and consist of positive and negative incentives that seek to punish certain activities while encouraging others. This term "consultative authoritarianism" is my adaptation of Li Junru's term "consultative democracy (*xieshang minzhu* 协商民主)."[11] Li argues that an increase in public participation in policy making indicates a process of democratization in China. However, I argue that growing consultation does not indicate a process of democratization, but rather the creation of a new model that encourages independent civil society groups to participate in policy but also seeks to guide that participation through a system of indirect positive and negative incentives. Kang Xiaoguang and Han Heng also contend that this system of incentives, which they call "differentiated controls," indicates changing state–civil society relations whereby the government uses different tools to control varying types of groups.[12] Groups that are deemed "safe," such as those formed by government cadres or primarily interested in service delivery, are treated differently from those that might deal with issues of human rights advocacy. This has led to an explosion of civil society groups in China since 2000 – an associational revolution composed of both independent grassroots groups and those with close ties to government agencies.

[11] 李君如 (Li Junru), *Dangdai Zhongguo zhengzhi zouxiang (Trends in Contemporary Chinese Politics)* (Fuzhou: Fuzhou renmin chubanshe, 2007), pp. 143–146.

[12] 康晓光与韩恒 (Kang Xiaoguang and Han Heng), "分类控制：当前中国大陆国家与社会关系研究 (Differentiated Control: Current State and Society Relationship Research in Mainland China)," 社会学研究 *(Sociology Research Journal)* 6, 2005: available at http://www.chinareform.net/2010/0116/8243.html; for another conception of growing consultation, see Orion Lewis, "Net Inclusion: New Media's Impact on Deliberative Politics in China," *Journal of Contemporary Asia*, 2013: http://www.tandfonline.com/doi/abs/10.1080/00472336.2013.769387#.Ul2k7VCko_4

In contrast to corporatism, this CA model is characterized first by a more autonomous civil society, such as grassroots groups or formerly government-organized groups gaining more operational autonomy (i.e., designing projects, securing diverse sources of funding, independent hiring). Second, this model is characterized by a set of positive and negative incentives designed to indirectly control group activities, rather than the direct methods utilized by corporatism such as control over budgets and hiring. Positive incentives include government grants, capacity-building programs, pilot project permits, and access to policy making. Negative incentives include tax fraud charges, volunteer or staff intimidation, and seizure of documents or lengthy questioning of staff by police (喝茶).[13] As seen in the case studies analyzed in later chapters, repression is the most extreme of the possible negative incentives but does still occur. Many groups focusing on controversial topics or those led by prominent activists in areas such as HIV/AIDS, legal advocacy, and human rights have been closed or had members arrested. Despite a changing political economy in China, local officials are still powerful and able to repress groups if necessary. In fact, the 2012 budget prioritized spending on social stability above that on national defense. However, local officials have developed a toolkit of indirect incentives that make outright repression less necessary.

I contend that the state-society relationship in China is evolving from corporatism to CA in response to a process of learning by local officials. As a result of a changing political economy during the 1990s in which they were expected to deliver public goods and increase development with little control over fiscal policy, officials were searching for ways to achieve expanded goals with less funding. As they learned through direct experience with civil society and observation of other provinces' and countries' experiences, one

[13] Yaxue Cao, "Drinking Tea with the State Security Police – Components of a He Cha Session," *Seeing Red in China*, available at http://seeingredinchina.com/2012/03/01/drinking-tea-with-the-state-security-police-components-of-a-hecha-session/

emergent policy solution was to partner with civil society groups receiving funding and innovative policies from abroad. The CA model grew out of a desire by these local officials to reap the benefits of allowing the formation of an independent civil society that assists with development and governance goals, while minimizing the danger of these groups mobilizing citizens to pressure the state for political change. As I discuss later, civil society played a large role in shaping perceptions of these benefits and dangers.

THE GLOBAL ASSOCIATIONAL REVOLUTION

The associational revolution experienced in China beginning in the early 1990s was shared as volunteering and associational activity grew rapidly all over the world. As Lester Salamon argues,

> We seem to be in the midst of a "global associational revolution," a massive upsurge of organized private voluntary activity, of structured citizen action outside the boundaries of the market and the state, that I am convinced will prove to be as momentous a feature of the late 20th century as the rise of the nation-state was of the late 19th century.[14]

This global associational revolution is led by voluntary citizen organizations, such as nonprofit organizations (NPOs), nongovernmental organizations (NGOs), charities, sports clubs, and other interest-based organizations. Scholars often use the term "civil society" to represent this diverse associational life, ranging from large groups such as The Nature Conservancy or Doctors Without Borders to smaller, local groups such as soccer or book clubs.

The civil society sector is a major economic force in the world. In fact, NPOs as early as the mid-1990s accounted for $1.2 trillion in expenditures and 31 million full-time workers.[15] In the United States alone, the country's more than 76,000 grant-making foundations gave an estimated $45.7 billion in 2010, in addition to

[14] Lester Salamon, "The Third Sector and Volunteering in Global Perspective," presentation at the 17th Annual International Association of Volunteer Effort Conference, Amsterdam, The Netherlands, January 15, 2001.

[15] Lester M. Salamon et al., *Global Civil Society: Dimensions of the Nonprofit Sector* (Baltimore: Center for Civil Society Studies, 1999).

grants of $10 million or more in 2009.[16] These resources have continued to increase, expanding the influence of these groups especially in the developing world. Whereas the majority of these organizations are based in the United States and Europe, many Western international nongovernmental organizations (INGOs) conduct projects in the developing world and fund the further development of indigenous groups through capacity-building projects. For example, of the ten largest grants in the United States in 2009, five were awarded by the Gates Foundation mainly for overseas health and education programs, and international giving accounted for nearly 24 percent of total grant dollars awarded.[17] In large part, the ability of local groups to link to international groups increases the strength and capacity of grass-roots organizations in developing countries.[18]

Additionally, and perhaps more interestingly, this global associational revolution is occurring regardless of regime type. For example, in democracies such as France, analysts see rapid growth in the formation of new associations from 10,000 per year in the 1960s to between 50,000 and 60,000 per year in the 1980s and 1990s, but also in more authoritarian regimes such as Russia, with more than 100,000 organizations organized in the late 1990s alone.[19] In China, registered organizations increased from approximately 5,000 to 500,000 since 1990, and unregistered organizations far exceed these reported numbers. Although the scale and group resources of this explosion of civil society activity in nondemocracies trail behind those of industrialized democracies, this is truly a global associational revolution.

The associational revolution is widely hailed as a transformative force in domestic and international politics, as many scholars credit a vibrant civil society with positive economic and political

[16] *Foundation Growth and Giving Estimates*, Foundation Center, 2011: available at http://foundationcenter.org/gainknowledge/research/nationaltrends.html.

[17] *Foundation Giving Trends: Current Outlook*, Foundation Center, 2011: http://foundationcenter.org/gainknowledge/research/nationaltrends.html.

[18] Margaret Keck and Kathryn Sikkink, *Activists beyond Borders: Advocacy Networks in International Politics* (Ithaca, NY: Cornell University Press, 1998).

[19] Salamon, *Global Civil Society*.

outcomes such as the overthrow of dictators, greater participation in democratic politics, economic development, and increased social trust.[20] President Bill Clinton describes the political power of the global associational revolution in the following way: "We have, as private citizens, because of the rise of democracy, the rise of the Internet, and the rise of the NGO in the developing as well as the developed world, we have more power as private citizens to do public good than at any time in world history."[21] Dominant liberal theories of civil society contend that associational activity influences these outcomes by encouraging citizen participation and is thus a prerequisite for democratization. For example, Alexis de Tocqueville argued that voluntary associations in the United States served to articulate the interests of broader society while serving as a check on the tyranny of government power.[22] In order for associations to limit government power, it is thought that these groups must be autonomous or independent from the state.[23] Thus, liberal theories of civil society depict an autonomous and oppositional relationship between associations and the state.[24] In an authoritarian context, liberal theories of civil society depict a state-society relationship predicated on conflict as the regime attempts to incorporate civil society into the state apparatus and represses any groups that resist. In short, in authoritarian

20 Robert Putnam, *Making Democracy Work* (Princeton, NJ: Princeton University Press, 1993); A. Hadenius and F. Uggla, "Making Civil Society Work, Promoting Democratic Development: What Can States and Donors Do?" *World Development* 24, no. 10, 1996, 1621–1639; Deepa Narayan and Lant Pritchett, "Cents and Sociability: Household Income and Social Capital in Rural Tanzania," World Bank Working Paper, May 1997: http://econ.worldbank.org/external/default/main?pagePK=64165259&theSitePK=475520&piPK=64165421&menuPK=64166093&entityID=000009265_3971023104038

21 William Jefferson Clinton, "Finding Our Collective Voice," *InterAction Annual Forum*, April 12, 2006: http://www.kaiserhealthnews.org/health_cast/uploaded_files/041206_interaction_clinton_transcript.pdf

22 Alexis de Tocqueville, *Democracy in America* (New York: Harper & Row, 1969). Originally published in 1835.

23 Jürgen Habermas, *The Structural Transformation of the Public Sphere* (Cambridge, MA: MIT Press, 1989).

24 Jürgen Habermas, "Three Normative Models of Democracy," *Constellations* 1, 1994: 1–10.

regimes, we should not observe independent civil society, only organizations acting as societal arms of the state.

Although this liberal approach to civil society dominates both the academic and policy discourses, many debates exist over which types of groups belong in this category and how to define civil society.[25] These debates center on the role of public participation and autonomy from the state, and they question the distinction made by liberal theorists that groups included in this category have voluntary membership and independence from the government. For example, groups with non-voluntary members or state employees would be excluded. Many scholars question this definition, especially the autonomy criterion, and ask how much and what kind of autonomy from the state are necessary for civil society to achieve political participation, economic development, and increased social trust.[26] As Gordon White, Jude A. Howell, and Shang Xiaoyuan argue, "in brief, the extent to which a specific social organization embodies the defining qualities of 'civil society' – autonomy, separation and voluntariness – is a question of degree rather than either/or."[27] In fact, despite liberal theorists' claims that civil society in democracies is autonomous from the state, Lester Salamon's Nonprofit Sector Project finds that Western European groups on average receive approximately 56 percent of their funding from the government or public sector, whereas groups in the post-communist states of Eastern/Central Europe receive 33 percent, and those in newer democracies in Latin America receive approximately 15 percent of funding from

[25] Larry Diamond, "Rethinking Civil Society: Toward Democratic Consolidation," *Journal of Democracy* 5, July 1994; Michael W. Foley and Bob Edwards, "The Paradox of Civil Society," *Journal of Democracy* 7, 1996: 38–52; Antonio Gramsci, *Letters from Prison*, Raymond Rosenthal, translator, and Frank Rosengarten, editor (New York: Columbia University Press, 1994).

[26] Neera Chandhoke, "A Critique of the Notion of Civil Society as the 'Third Sphere,'" in *Does Civil Society Matter? Governance in Contemporary India*, Rajesh Tandon and Ranjita Mohanty, eds. (New Delhi: Sage Publications India Ltd, 2003), pp. 27–58.

[27] Gordon White, Jude A. Howell, and Shang Xiaoyuan, *In Search of Civil Society: Market Reform and Social Change in Contemporary China* (Oxford, UK: Clarendon Press, 1996).

the state.[28] Therefore, as far as measuring autonomy using funding sources, civil society groups in democracies actually have a closer relationship to the state than do those in new democracies.

In light of these debates, I use the conventional definition of civil society as social groups with voluntary memberships but use the term "operational autonomy" in place of the dichotomous term "autonomy." Operational autonomy is simply an organization's freedom to formulate and pursue a self-determined agenda without undue external pressure.[29] This definition incorporates a focus on group goals and allows a continuum of autonomy, which more accurately describes civil society experience. Although the conventional definition of civil society is limited, the term itself is useful for analytical purposes because it identifies a sphere of civic activity and allows for comparisons over time and across states. Focusing on a sphere of activity helps distinguish between the types of groups, in that each sphere operates under a different logic. A political or market logic dictates competition over achieving private goods, whereas a civic logic dictates action to secure public services or policies for a perceived common good. Thus, maintaining the conventional term of civil society but focusing more on operational autonomy allows scholars to research this relationship in a less dichotomous fashion to observe gradual changes in group autonomy.

CHANGING STATE–CIVIL SOCIETY RELATIONSHIPS: POLICY LEARNING UNDER AUTHORITARIANISM

Many China scholars argue that the relationship between the local state and civil society is still corporatism, meaning that groups do not have autonomy from the state but instead function as a subordinate appendage to the bureaucracy using shared financial

[28] The Johns Hopkins Comparative Nonprofit Sector Project, 1995: http://ccss.jhu.edu/.

[29] Shaoguang Wang, "Money and Autonomy: Patterns of Civil Society Finance and Their Implications," *Studies in Comparative International Development* 40, no. 4, 2006: 3–29.

and human resources.[30] However, since the mid-2000s, several scholars have identified variation in the level of autonomy from the state.[31] If, as I find, the relationship shifts from predominantly corporatism in the 1990s to CA in the 2000s, what accounts for this change? In order to explain it, I draw on the social learning–policy transfer literature, which focuses on policy transfer and lesson drawing as processes whereby knowledge about policies, administrative arrangements, or institutions is used across time or space in the development of policies, administrative arrangements, and institutions elsewhere.[32] Simply put, local officials learned about the benefits and dangers of civil society through direct and vicarious (observation) experiences and as a result acted to change the existing relationships to maximize the benefits while minimizing the dangers. This change occurred informally through an increasing number of public–private partnerships and formally through regulatory change.

As Richard Rose points out, a policy maker is not a theorist but a social engineer seeking knowledge instrumentally.[33] Policy makers do not have the time or the knowledge to be maximizers, continuously seeking an ideal policy, and instead act as "satisficers."[34] This means that when the policy routine is disrupted because policy makers can no longer operate on the "assumption that what was satisfactory before is still satisfactory," they seek to change existing policy just enough to dispel this dissatisfaction by using policy ideas that are easily accessible.[35] Dissatisfaction

[30] Kenneth W. Foster, "Embedded within State Agencies: Business Associations in Yantai," *The China Journal*, no. 47, January 2002: 41–65.

[31] Yiyi Lu, "The Autonomy of Chinese NGOs: A New Perspective," *China: An International Journal* 5, no. 2, 2007: 173–203; Shaogang Wang, "Money and Autonomy: Patterns of Civil Society Finance and Their Implications," *Studies in Comparative International Development* 40, 2006: 3–29.

[32] Diane Stone, "Learning Lessons, Policy Transfer and the International Diffusion of Policy Ideas," *Centre for the Study of Globalisation and Regionalisation*, 2000: 2.

[33] Richard Rose, "What Is Lesson-Drawing?" *Journal of Public Policy* 11, no. 1, 1991: 5.

[34] Herbert A. Simon, "Rational Decision Making in Business Organizations," *American Economic Review* 69, no. 4, 1979: 493–513.

[35] Rose, "What Is Lesson-Drawing?" 11.

with a policy originates in a number of ways but is basically a disconnect between the policy's intended and actual outcomes. This disconnect can be caused by uncertainty in the minds of policy makers over goals or results, changes in the policy environment itself, or the simple accretion of unintended consequences. For example, Mark Blyth finds that delegitimation of existing economic institutions created uncertainty in the minds of policy makers during a period of crisis in the United States that motivated a shift from Keynesian policies to monetarist ones.[36]

In China, I find that this dissatisfaction or sense of policy failure stems from local governments' changing responsibility over the provision of public goods and services. Beginning in the 1980s, the central government decentralized fiscal policy to local government by transferring to local governments primary responsibility for the provision of public goods, such as education, health care, infrastructure, and social security programs such as unemployment insurance. However, local governments do not possess the necessary fiscal autonomy to meet these unfunded mandates. The central government restricts the ability to tax local populations and to secure bonds or loans through fiscal budget laws, so local governments cannot issue debt and run fiscal deficits. Nevertheless, with the demands on local governments increasing while fiscal transfers from the central government remain low, most provinces operate a budget deficit, tax illegally, or borrow using special financial vehicles to fund social programs through extra-budgetary revenue.[37] The experience of decentralization in China has led to the creation of unfunded mandates and high levels of local debt.[38] In fact, Victor Shih estimates that local

[36] Mark Blyth, *Great Transformations: Economic Ideas and Institutional Change in the Twentieth Century* (Cambridge, UK: Cambridge University Press, 2002).

[37] David D. Li, "Large Domestic Non-Intermediated Investments and Government Liabilities – Challenges Facing China's Financial Sector Reform," World Bank Working Paper, 2006: accessed on March 2008. Christine Wong, "Budget Reform in China," *OECD Journal on Budgeting*, 2007: 33–56.

[38] Mark W. Frazier, *Socialist Insecurity: Pensions and the Politics of Uneven Development in China* (Ithaca, NY: Cornell University Press, 2010); Hongbin Cai and Daniel Treisman, "State Corroding Federalism," *Journal of Public Economics*, October 2002.

governments were at least 10.7 trillion yuan ($1.68 trillion) in debt by the end of 2009, almost a quarter of which was backed by land.[39] At this level, the size of local debt is roughly one-third of China's 2009 GDP and 70 percent of its foreign-exchange reserves. In addition to high (and illegal) debt levels, local officials increasingly viewed this model of service delivery as a failure in that it did not deliver the desired development outcomes, leading to regional disparities in public services.[40]

Policy failure was important to local officials not only because of the inability to provide necessary services but also because promotion depended on public goods provision. The Target Management Responsibility System (*gangwei mubiao guanli zerenzhi* 岗位目标管理责任制) prioritizes economic targets such as public goods provision to evaluate cadre performance and determine promotions and raises.[41] Officials' dissatisfaction with the service delivery system and competition for promotion created the motivation or "space" for innovation and local policy change, at the level of both formal regulations and informal interactions.

As the policy learning literature highlights, two possible causal mechanisms for behavioral change exist, namely a shift in interests and a process of rational learning.[42] According to the interest-based argument, a change in local officials' interests forces a change in behavior toward civil society organizations. For

[39] Victor Shih, "China's 8,000 Credit Risks," *Asian Wall Street Journal*, February 8, 2010.

[40] Loraine West and Christine Wong, "Fiscal Decentralization and Growing Regional Disparities in Rural China: Some Evidence in the Provision of Social Services," *Oxford Review of Economic Policy* 11, 1995: 70–84.

[41] Susan Whiting, *Power and Wealth in Rural China: The Political Economy of Institutional Change* (Cambridge, UK: Cambridge University Press, 2001); Pierre Landry, "The Political Management of Mayors in Post-Deng China," *The Copenhagen Journal of Asian Studies* 17, 2003.

[42] Peter Hall, "Policy Paradigms, Social Learning, and the State: The Case of Economic Policy Making in Britain," *Comparative Politics* 25, no. 3, 1993; David Dolowitz and David Marsh, "Who Learns What from Whom? A Review of the Policy Transfer Literature," *Political Studies* 44, 1996: 343–357; Frank Dobbin, Beth Simmons, and Geoffrey Garrett, "The Global Diffusion of Public Policies: Social Construction, Coercion, Competition, or Learning?" *Annual Review of Sociology* 33, 2007: 449–472.

example, in China, the changing political economy of decreasing local government capacity to provide the public goods and services necessary for promotion creates new interests on the part of local officials. This argument predicts that poorer provinces should have more collaborative relationships with civil society, so that group resources can be used to help local cadres win promotion. However, I find that this predicted relationship only holds in two of the four cases examined in the following chapters. Thus, the interest-based argument helps establish the political economy in which policy decisions are made but does not determine the decision itself. Officials face many policy options in poor provinces, so why choose to collaborate with civil society organizations instead of applying to the central government for more revenue transfers, for example?

Instead, I argue that a process of rational learning motivates this shift in officials' relationships with civil society. As Peter Hall explains, learning occurs when individuals assimilate new information, including that based on past experience, and apply it to subsequent actions.[43] Therefore, policy learning is a deliberate attempt on the part of government officials to adjust the goals or techniques of policy in response to past experience and new information, and policy changes as the result of such a process. The failure of existing service delivery policies to provide public goods, which to a large extent determine promotions for local officials, motivates officials to search for new policies, but why did they choose to encourage the formation of a more independent civil society? In this section, I examine the causal mechanisms behind this change, namely policy learning through initial experience with an emerging civil society and by observing similar state-society models in other provinces and countries. I contend that a process of rational learning caused a shift in officials' relationships with civil society groups from a corporatist to a consultative authoritarianism one.

Learning occurs when new evidence changes beliefs either directly from one's own experiences or vicariously from the

[43] Hall, "Policy Paradigms, Social Learning, and the State," 278.

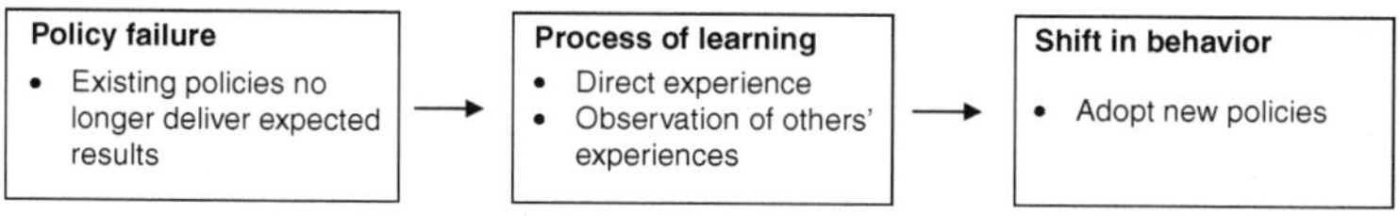

FIGURE I.1. Rational Learning Process

experiences of others. As information accumulates, some beliefs are discarded and others reinforced, but the more consistent the evidence, the more likely policy makers will converge on a narrow range of interpretations.[44] Thus, the emphasis in learning theories is on cognition and the redefinition of interests on the basis of new knowledge that affects the fundamental beliefs and ideas behind policy approaches.[45] As illustrated in Figure I.1, this new information comes from policy makers' experiences or from observation of policy experiments elsewhere.

First, policy makers learn about solutions to policy failures through observing the experience of other policy makers struggling with a similar situation.[46] As these policy makers are satisficers without enough time or resources to independently evaluate all possible policy experiments occurring around the world, they often use cognitive shortcuts in which some sources of learning are more important than others, such as similar countries or highly successful outcomes. For example, research on how countries formulate and implement national pension privatization programs shows a process of social learning from regional neighbors.[47] In this case, policy makers view policy experiments in neighboring countries as more likely to also work in their country because of similar attributes. As the diffusion of neoliberalism illustrates, outcomes that are viewed as highly successful also serve as prominent sources of learning, regardless of perceived "fit" of the origin

[44] Dobbin et al., "The Global Diffusion of Public Policies," 460.
[45] Hall, "Policy Paradigms, Social Learning, and the State."
[46] Barbara Levitt and James G. March, "Organizational Learning," *Annual Review of Sociology* 14, 1988: 319–340.
[47] Sarah Brooks, "Interdependent and Domestic Foundations of Policy Change: The Diffusion of Pension Privatization around the World," *International Studies Quarterly* 49, no. 2, 2005: 273–294.

country.[48] Observations of other policy experiments therefore serve as a source of learning.

Second, policy makers' direct experience plays a key role in this learning process. As Richard Rose notes, in policy-making circles, experience has a unique status as a justification of effectiveness reflecting concerns with feasibility.[49] Policy makers use past and present experiences to inform ideas of policy change in response to the failure of existing policies – what has worked in the past and what is currently viewed as effective.[50] A number of actors are important in this learning process, as either those learning or those providing lessons, including central and local government officials, technical staff at government agencies, civil society groups and INGOs, and intergovernmental organizations.

As I find in China, civil society plays an important role in this learning process through direct interaction with local officials on projects as well as providing information about models or policies used in other places. For example, INGOs, one of the main actors in the policy learning process, influence global public policy through the ability to spread ideas and information on an international level.[51] Many disciplines study how information is transmitted and find that this primarily happens in networks. For example, scholars studying epistemic communities – knowledge-based networks of individuals with policy-relevant knowledge based on common professional beliefs and common policy concerns operating at state, national, and international levels – argue that the intensity of interaction over shared concerns allows for

48 Beth A. Simmons, Frank Dobbin, and Geoffrey Garrett, "Introduction: The International Diffusion of Liberalism," *International Organization* 60, 2006: 781–810.

49 Rose, "What Is Lesson-Drawing?"

50 Hall, "Policy Paradigms, Social Learning, and the State"; George E. Peterson, *Decentralization in Latin America: Learning through Experience* (Washington DC: World Bank, 1997).

51 Dolowitz and Marsh, "Who Learns What from Whom? 11; Norton Wheeler, *The Role of American NGOs in China's Modernization: Invited Influence* (Abingdon, Oxon; New York: Routledge, 2013).

lesson drawing.[52] Much of this scholarship has focused on the spread of environmental policies through transnational networks of scientists, NGOs, activists, and domestic policy makers.

Even though non-state actors, such as international and domestic civil societies, cannot bring about policy change without governments instituting new policies, they can transmit information through networks of technical specialists and officials. Diane Stone contends that whereas policy transfer primarily involves bureaucrats and politicians, non-state actors may provide a "soft" transfer of broad policy ideas influencing public opinion and policy agendas, with officials providing a "hard" transfer of policy practices and instruments involving formal decision making.[53] These non-state policy entrepreneurs help transfer the intellectual foundation supporting policies, such as the rhetoric, language, and scholarly discourse necessary to give substance and legitimacy to policies.[54] Specifically, policy entrepreneurs participate in learning by policy makers through acting as resources for expert and technical information, advocating policy ideas and transmitting information about others' experiences, spreading ideas and information through bureaucratic and advocacy networks across borders, and identifying problems and tying them to best practices. Civil society groups identify problems and link them to policy solutions by "judging, evaluating, synthesising and weeding out 'useful' or 'valid' research and analysis from among the cacophonic welter of information pressed upon public bodies by NGOs, corporations, lobbyists and others."[55] This information-politics role, facilitated by the linkage of many domestic civil society groups into transnational advocacy coalitions, creates an important channel for these groups to

[52] Peter Haas and Ernst Haas, "Learning to Learn: Improving International Governance," *Global Governance* 1, no. 3, 1995: 255–285; Ernst B. Haas, *When Knowledge Is Power: Three Models of Change in International Organizations* (Berkeley: University of California Press, 1991).

[53] Stone, "Learning Lessons"; Diane Stone, "Non-Governmental Policy Transfer: The Strategies of Independent Policy Institutes," *Governance* 13, no. 1, 2000: 45–70.

[54] Dolowitz and Marsh, "Who Learns What from Whom?" 345.

[55] Stone, "Learning Lessons," 22.

participate in public policy, especially in an authoritarian state that does not have many channels for public participation.[56]

As explained in more detail in the following chapter, I find that the failure of service delivery policies and competition for promotion motivated local officials in China to search for new policies, including partnering with civil society, to bridge the resource gap and develop innovative policies. As a senior official in the Ministry of Civil Affairs explained, "The government cannot totally manage health, culture, social welfare and education. In the future China will have a big society and a small government. Social organizations will play a big role."[57] According to interviewed local officials, pressure to provide public goods motivated initial collaborations with civil society because officials could access international funding and resources to further promotion goals and increase welfare in the local community, and if the collaboration appeared to lead to unrest, they could simply shut down the whole project.[58] These partnerships, or direct learning experiences, were also facilitated by an increase in international funding sources for civil society.

Beginning in the early 1990s, international funding agencies and INGOs began to work in China, often explicitly excluding local governments and funding grassroots groups.[59] The World Bank and other international funding agencies, such as the Ford Foundation, wanted to fund development through more bottom-up initiatives.[60] This international environment created

[56] Keck and Sikkink, *Activists beyond Borders*.

[57] Jude Howell, "Prospects for NGOs in China," *Development in Practice* 5, February 1995: 10.

[58] More than 100 author interviews conducted with academics, officials, and civil society leaders in Beijing, Yunnan, Jiangsu, and Sichuan provinces between 2006 and 2010.

[59] Jessica Mathews, "Power Shift: The Rise of Global Civil Society," *Foreign Affairs* 76, January/February 1997; Lester Salamon and Helmut K. Anheier, *The Emerging Not-For-Profit Sector: An Overview* (Manchester, UK; New York: Manchester University Press, 1996).

[60] Bishwapriya Sanyal, "Cooperative Autonomy: The Dialectic of State-NGOs Relationship in Developing Countries," *International Institute for Labour Studies* 100, 1994: 1–72.

rising capacity among domestic groups to help bridge the resource gap and solve welfare provision problems through access to international funding and innovative service models. As one group member explained, "my organization's role is service delivery – providing services that the government cannot provide. While government investment in health is increasing, the majority goes to the cities with 80 percent of the funding serving 20 percent of the population."[61] To take advantage of this new funding stream, local officials partnered with existing groups or supported the creation of new groups. In fact, as one official explained, partnering with these groups opened up a new line of finance with little risk unlike common extra-budgetary channels such as increasing fees and taxes or selling land, both of which create social protest.[62] These partnerships allowed local officials to directly experience the benefits of a fairly autonomous civil society and over time helped change the local state–civil society relationship from corporatism to CA.

In my analysis of policy learning in China, I find that both domestic and international civil society groups play a role by (1) transmitting information and policy preferences through the experiences of partnering officials and (2) sharing best practices observed in other provinces/countries through epistemic communities. These two main mechanisms of personal experience and vicarious experience (observation) create a process of learning that ultimately changes officials' original ideas of the appropriate relationship between an authoritarian state and independent civil society from a corporatist to the more independent one in the CA model. As I discuss in greater detail in the following four chapters, I find that different relationships between the local state and civil society develop in the 1990s in the four provinces selected for this analysis – Beijing, Yunnan, Sichuan, and Jiangsu – ranging from traditional corporatism to a new model of consultative

[61] Author interview with founder of health care association, Simao, Yunnan, February 8, 2007.

[62] Author interview with retired health bureau cadre (卫生局), Yunnan, May 6, 2007.

authoritarianism. These varying relationships reflect divergent ideas on the part of local officials engaged in learning about the appropriate role of these emergent groups in modern Chinese society. During this period, officials' learning is based on the following four primary observations and experiences: (1) the observed success of Western state-society models in mitigating social unrest (2) the observed role of civil society overthrowing authoritarian regimes in the color revolutions (3) positive direct experiences with some development groups, and (4) negative direct experiences with some environmental and human rights organizations. The observation of the role played by civil society in promoting social stability and welfare in Western states and positive experiences with many international and grassroots development groups led local officials to adapt regulations to encourage the formation and activity of civil society. However, the observation of civil society mobilizing citizens in the color revolutions and experiences with environmental and human rights groups using similar mobilization tactics encouraged local officials to develop an expanded toolbox of control tactics. These two competing lessons motivated local officials to construct a new state–civil society model that sought to maximize the benefits of civil society while mitigating the dangers.

Consultative authoritarianism first developed in Yunnan and then Beijing because of the early presence of civil society groups, and it then spread to other provinces such as Jiangsu and Sichuan as officials there observed the success of this model. In the two cases in which a consultative authoritarianism relationship first developed, local officials in Yunnan and Beijing partnered with civil society groups to deliver public goods as a strategy to meet unfunded mandates imposed by the central government. However, in Jiangsu and Sichuan, local officials initially either incorporated or repressed groups in response to initial negative experiences with existing groups and observations of similar experiences in the color revolutions and only later moved toward a CA model after observing its success and having more positive experiences with local groups. An important facet of the learning process is that it is not unidirectional.

Both lessons that support civil society and those that do not exist, and policy makers must base new policies on both sources of learning, leading to variation across provinces initially. However, civil society groups possess agency in this learning process by helping government officials meet goals, thus providing positive direct experiences, or by sharing examples of successful public-private partnerships from other places. For example, through collaboration with civil society groups after the Sichuan earthquake in 2008, local officials learned more about the beneficial role that these groups might play in mobilizing resources and helping the local state more effectively meet goals that ultimately changed the existing relationship.[63] Despite the initial divergence in relationships with an emerging civil society in the 1990s, I find growing convergence on a consultative authoritarianism model of local state–civil society relations across these four provinces and the rest of the country since the mid-2000s. This new CA model simultaneously allowed for the rise of an autonomous civil society and increasing use of nuanced tools of state control over society.

METHODOLOGY AND FINDINGS

The liberal theory of state–civil society relationships predicts state incorporation of groups and suppression of those that cannot be incorporated in authoritarian regimes. However, I contend that there is more variation in these relationships in China, and that the dominant type of relationship shifts from corporatism in the 1990s to consultative authoritarianism in the 2000s. China is an important case for this analysis simply because it is the hardest case. The Chinese leadership has not politically liberalized toward a hybrid regime as many authoritarian regimes have, but it continues to suppress most political participation by society. For example, in 2009, Chinese courts sentenced a professor at Beijing

[63] Jessica C. Teets, "Post-Earthquake Relief and Reconstruction Efforts: The Emergence of Civil Society in China?" *The China Quarterly* 198, June 2009: 330–347.

Normal University, Liu Xiaobo, to 10 years in prison for attempted subversion for his participation in the Charter 08 movement, which was calling for greater freedom of expression, protection of human rights, and political participation, for which he later won a Nobel Peace Prize. If we see changing relationships with civil society in China, which should adhere most closely to the oppositional relationship depicted by liberal theory, then this provides strong evidence of policy learning. Interestingly, this might indicate the possibility of a gradual process of political reform, at least with regard to public participation in policy making, without a democratic revolution.

To analyze changing local state–civil society relationships, the dependent variable, I utilize the characteristic that distinguishes consultative authoritarianism from corporatism – operational autonomy. As the consultative authoritarianism model posits an operationally autonomous civil society interacting with the government as a regulator and project partner versus a direct supervisor, I use the following three regulatory outcomes to indicate the presence of a consultative authoritarianism model: changes in registration requirements, sources of funding, and the development of a system of positive and negative incentives to guide group actions. These changes demonstrate the shift from corporatism to a consultative authoritarianism model by showing the emergence of an indirect versus direct relationship with the state. As I discuss in the following four chapters, I find that the four provinces all change regulations to relax registration requirements, create grant competitions to fund independent group projects, and develop an incentive structure to influence group activity at different points throughout the 2000s.

In the interests of clarity and methodological rigor, it is also necessary to define which state–civil society relationships are not examples of consultative authoritarianism. Corporatism, or those relationships in which civil society groups do not have operational autonomy, is not a CA model. If groups following all relevant national laws are unable to hire and fire, unable to secure different sources of funding including international sources, and unable to design and run projects without constant supervision from local officials, they are not operating within CA model. If the government represses all groups indiscriminately and does not allow for the formation of autonomous civil society organizations, this also is not a CA model.

To support my argument of policy learning as the explanatory variable causing this changing local state–civil society relationships in China, I use a process-tracing methodology in four municipal/provincial cases – Beijing, Jiangsu, Sichuan, and Yunnan. As Alexander George and Andrew Bennett argue, a comparative case study methodology is particularly effective for exploring aspects of complex causality, such as policy learning.[64] I selected these four cases using the two independent, or explanatory, variables outlined in the policy learning literature: measures indicating shifting officials' interests and opportunities for learning. First, these four cases vary in levels of local government revenue, which serves as a proxy for the interest-based explanation of changing behavior on the part of local officials. This argument would predict that officials' relationships with civil society vary as a result of the need for resources to provide social welfare, and thus wealthy provinces such as Beijing and Jiangsu should retain the corporatism model of the 1990s, and poor provinces such as Yunnan and Sichuan should develop the new consultative authoritarianism model. As seen in Figure I.2, Yunnan is the poorest province in this comparison, followed by Sichuan to its north. Beijing is the wealthiest, followed by Jiangsu province to its south. Regarding debt, Sichuan and Yunnan are most indebted, followed by Jiangsu and then Beijing. If the interest-based argument is correct, Yunnan and Sichuan should adopt the CA model, not Jiangsu and Beijing.

However, I find that this prediction only holds for Jiangsu and Yunnan, but not for Beijing and Sichuan. Clearly, the ability of groups to assist in service delivery is important in motivating a learning process but not in determining relationship outcomes.

Second, all of these cases have high numbers of registered civil society groups as a proxy measure for learning opportunities.

[64] Alexander George and Andrew Bennett, *Case Studies and Theory Development in the Social Sciences* (Cambridge, MA: MIT Press, 2005), p. 10.

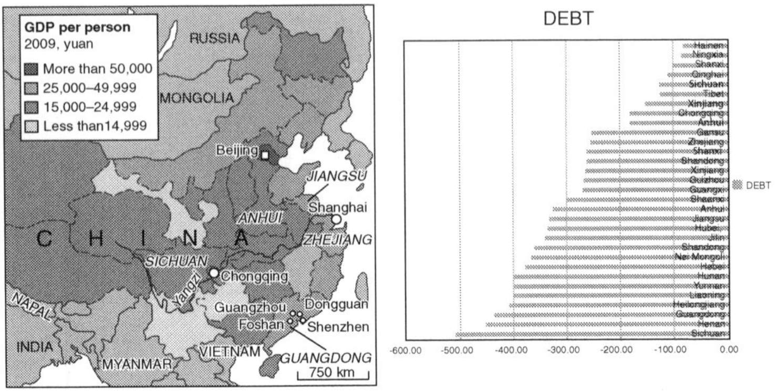

FIGURE 1.2. Provincial Income and Debt Levels in China

Selecting cases with more registered groups was vital to this analysis as provinces without active groups would present little opportunity for officials to learn through personal experience. By examining change over time in these four cases, I demonstrate the causal influence of learning on local state–civil society relationships. However, learning is a difficult thing to observe in that it occurs over (sometimes) a long period of time and is complex, often depending on many factors to result in a lesson learned. To present evidence of learning, I trace officials' self-professed accounts of changing ideas and subsequent policy shifts throughout the 1990s and 2000s through more than 150 interviews. I conducted these interviews in all four provinces between 2006 and 2011 and focused on local government officials, grassroots group leaders, and INGO project managers. Although I did not narrow my analysis to a specific issue area, such as the environment, I attempted to create reliability tests by triangulating my interviews. For example, when interviewing a local government official in the Poverty Alleviation Bureau about his experiences with civil society in his province, I also interviewed the domestic and international poverty alleviation groups to corroborate his account of the relationship. Additionally, I supported my interview evidence with published accounts of policy changes and discussions with Chinese colleagues also conducting research on civil society in China to provide confirmation of officials' interview statements.[65]

In these interviews, I asked questions about this process of learning and the key mechanisms of experience and observation. These questions focused on direct experiences local officials had with civil society groups as well as any observations they had made about relationships with these groups in other provinces or countries. As illustrated in Figures I.3 and I.4 comparing the four cases, I found that Yunnan and Beijing adopted the CA model first, followed by Sichuan and Jiangsu. Figures I.3 and I.4 map each province's position first in the 1990s and then again in the 2000s to illustrate changes in relative positions on the two characteristics of the CA model – increasing numbers of autonomous groups and state controls.[66]

Figure I.3 shows how Yunnan officials allowed for fairly unfettered growth of civil society, whereas Jiangsu most tightly tried to control the emergence of these groups. However, Figure I.4 shows growing convergence by the 2000s on this model of consultative authoritarianism, in that all four of the provinces moved closer to one another in allowing the emergence of more operationally autonomous groups and adopting a set of indirect controls over these groups. This convergence means that whereas Jiangsu has moved away from its corporatist framework, Yunnan has adopted more restrictions on groups to meet in the middle at the CA model, which allows for autonomous civil society but requires more indirect state controls.

This comparative case study methodology enables an analysis of the causes of this observed relationship change in the four

65 Discussions with colleagues at Beijing University's Civil Society Research Center (北大公民社会研究中心), Renmin University's Research Center on Nonprofit Organizations (中国人民大学非营利组织研究所), and Tsinghua University's NGO Research Center (清华非政府管理（NGO）研究所) took place several times between 2006 and 2011.

66 Note that "autonomy" is measured as operational autonomy and identified through interviews with others in the civil society community as well as the author's assessment, and state controls are measured both through formal regulations on registration and funding and informal interactions such as "having tea."

Legend of Change

Province	Groups	Controls
Beijing	⇧	⇩
Yunnan	⇩	⇧
Sichuan	⇧	⇩
Jiangsu	⇧	⇩

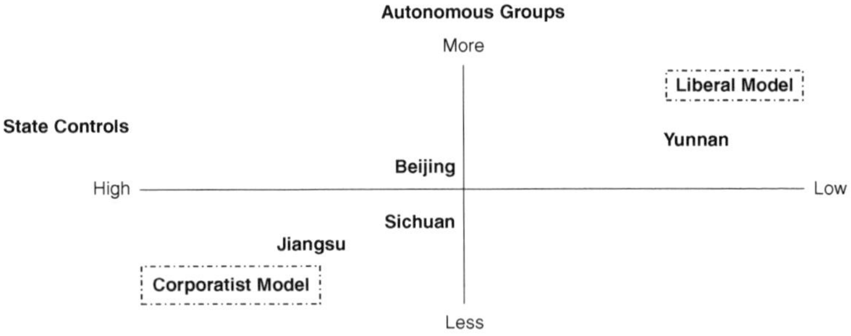

FIGURE 1.3. Local State–Civil Society Relationship Models in the 1990s

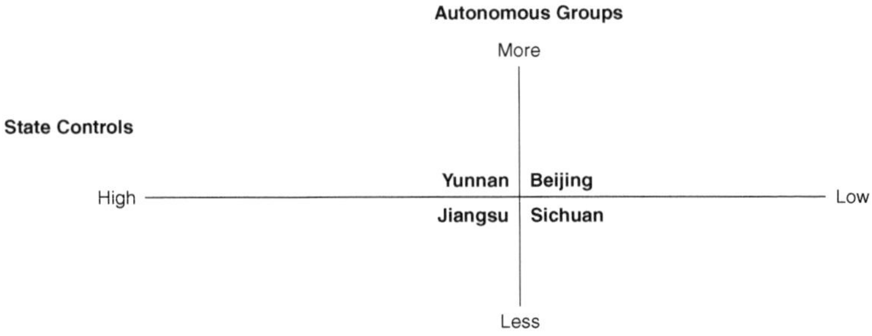

FIGURE 1.4. Local State–Civil Society Relationship Models in the 2000s

selected provinces; however, how generalizable are these findings to the rest of China? The cases used in this analysis include two poorer Western provinces and two richer Eastern provinces/ municipalities, which would account for regional or revenue-driven bias. Beijing is also the capital city, which might increase the number of civil society organizations seeking to advocate policy change to the central leadership; however, social stability pressures might also increase the riskiness of partnering with these groups for local officials. In line with this logic, we should expect that Beijing would be a hard case for observing relationship change, and the fact that I find Beijing adopting a CA model strengthens the reliability of my overall findings. Although variation in local state–civil society relationships across provinces still exists, most other provinces shifted to a consultative authoritarianism model by the late 2000s. In fact, several provinces and municipalities have made regulatory changes similar to those in the four cases in this analysis, such as Chongqing, Shenzhen, Guangdong, and Shanghai; at the national level, the Ministry of Civil Affairs is drafting new policies regulating the registration and activities of civil society expected to be issued by the end of 2014. This evidence of changing relationships supports the contention that this new CA model is beginning to replace the former corporatist one across China.

In the rest of this book, I first analyze the policy failures in social service delivery and influx of civil society in China that initiated learning by local officials. Next, I trace local officials' learning process in the two provinces that first developed this CA model, Yunnan and Beijing, in Chapter 2. In Chapter 3, I conduct the same analysis for Sichuan and Jiangsu and in Chapter 4 examine the important role played by civil society in officials' learning process, focusing on group strategies rather than those of local officials used to help create the CA model. Finally, I conclude with an examination of how this CA model has begun to diffuse to other authoritarian states in a process of authoritarian learning or policy diffusion. A similar learning process as found in China is occurring in other authoritarian regimes and creating a new hybrid state–civil society model.

In fact, scholars who study international policy diffusion find that the occurrences of policy transfer have increased.[67] Public policy now takes place in a globalized world system with rapid

[67] Dolowitz and Marsh, "Who Learns What from Whom?"

information flows, as well as in national political systems. Thus, if policy makers are searching for policy solutions, they are increasingly able to look for new policy solutions abroad. As Dolowitz and Marsh argue, this is much easier because of the growth in all forms of communication, politicians and civil servants from different countries meet more frequently, and international policy entrepreneurs "sell" policies around the world.[68]

One of the largest international policy diffusions has been the worldwide spread of economic and political liberalism in the late twentieth century. Simmons, Dobbin, and Garrett contend that free market–oriented economic reforms such as macroeconomic stabilization, liberalization of foreign economic policies, privatization, and deregulation took root in many parts of the world at the same time as a "third wave" of democratization and liberal constitutionalism.[69] What accounts for this liberal policy diffusion consisting of capitalism and democracy? International policy diffusion scholars argue that national policy choices are interdependent, meaning that governments adopt new policies not in isolation but in response to what counterparts in other countries are doing.[70] I examine this process of policy transfer across authoritarian regimes during the late 2000s and find that a wave of "illiberalization" is also occurring to mirror the wave of liberalization that the previously mentioned authors discuss.

Authoritarian states encounter a similar circumstance as Chinese officials whereby civil society is seen as beneficial in some ways and dangerous in others. As President Putin warned President Hu at a 2005 Shanghai Cooperation Organization meeting, "If you don't get a grip on them [NGOs], you too will have a color revolution!"[71] As leaders of nations such as Venezuela and Russia meet in person

[68] Ibid.
[69] Simmons et al., "Introduction."
[70] Colin Bennett, "What Is Policy Convergence and What Causes It?" *British Journal of Political Science* 21, 1992: 215–233; David Strang and Chang Kil Lee, "The International Diffusion of Public-Sector Downsizing: Network Emulation and Theory-Driven Learning." *International Organization* 60, no. 4, 2006: 883–909.
[71] David Shambaugh, *China's Communist Party: Atrophy and Adaptation* (Berkeley: University of California Press, 2008).

and observe events in one another's countries, they learn about ways of interacting with civil society. For example, Hugo Chávez encouraged the growth of government-funded civil society organizations through "Bolivarian Circles" to advocate for the welfare of the poor and disenfranchised in the 1990s.[72] Chávez's administration incorporated new civil society actors into a corporatist system; however, the existing grassroots groups maintained a relatively autonomous relationship with state agencies as a strategy to access resources in a system without many resources outside of the state bureaucracy. Although these groups are viewed as beneficial for development, the government is attempting to change regulations to restrict funding, especially foreign sources of funding, to suspect civil society groups in response to the idea of a potential color revolution in Venezuela. Venezuela also exhibits a hybrid civil society, with both government-organized and grassroots groups simultaneously operating, and a mix of negative and positive incentives to encourage (or force) groups to follow government signals.

In this way, the consultative authoritarianism model has diffused into other nondemocracies where domestic experiences have supported these lessons. Even though this learning might be partial or poorly implemented, I find evidence of policy sharing between China and many other nondemocracies. This consultative authoritarianism model is viewed as a way to achieve better governance under conditions of authoritarianism, rather than needing to democratize as advocated by Western nations and IGOs such as the World Bank, and thus it has significant implications for understanding the role of civil society inside of authoritarian regimes.

THE SIGNIFICANCE OF THIS RESEARCH: BETTER GOVERNANCE UNDER AUTHORITARIANISM

Support for the liberal oppositional model of state–civil society relations is most clearly illustrated through the practice of some

[72] María Pilar Garcia-Guadilla, "Civil Society: Institutionalization, Fragmentation, Autonomy," in *Venezuelan Politics in the Chávez Era*, Steve Ellner, ed. (Boulder, CO: Lynne Rienner Publishers, 2003), p. 190.

states and agencies of providing international aid to associations operating in authoritarian or hybrid regimes for the promotion of democracy. Since the end of the Cold War, democracy promotion has been an explicit doctrine of U.S. foreign policy, with funding for democracy programs increasing by more than 500 percent between 1990 and 2003.[73] According to this model, an autonomous civil society confronts the authoritarian state and causes democratization through overthrow of the existing regime. For example, in the 2004 Orange Revolution in Ukraine, civil society groups helped mobilize and coordinate protests against the state, ultimately bringing the democratic opposition candidate Viktor Yushchenko to power.[74]

However, although the democratic potential of the global associational revolution provokes much excitement in policy and academic circles, the outcomes to which these groups contribute are often unclear and contradictory.[75] Although civil society may play a facilitating role in democratization, many empirical studies find little support for a determining role.[76] For example, several analysts note that the color revolution in Ukraine was led by political parties and a spontaneous public outpouring of support rather than a coordinated campaign by existing civil society groups, attributing more of a contributing role to these groups.[77] Moreover, research on the consolidation of new democracies finds that civil society can also help facilitate a reverse wave of

[73] Steven E. Finkel, Aníbal Pérez-Liñán, and Mitchell A. Seligson, "The Effects of U.S. Foreign Assistance on Democracy Building, 1990–2003," *World Politics* 59, 2007: 404–440.

[74] Serhiy Kudelia, "Revolutionary Bargain: The Unmaking of Ukraine's Autocracy through Pacting," *Journal of Communist Studies and Transition Politics* 23, 2007: 77–100.

[75] J.A. Booth and P.B. Richard, "Civil Society, Political Capital, and Democratization in Central America," *Journal of Politics* 60, 1998: 780–800; Stephen Knack, "Does Foreign Aid Promote Democracy?" *International Studies Quarterly*, 48, 2004: 251–266.

[76] Jason Brownlee, *Authoritarianism in an Age of Democratization* (Cambridge, UK: Cambridge University Press, 2007).

[77] Taras Kuzio, "The Opposition's Road to Success," *Journal of Democracy* 16, 2005: 117–130.

democratization, as seen in some countries in Latin America.[78] Thus, civil society contributes to a variety of potential outcomes, sometimes confronting and sometimes collaborating with an authoritarian state. In short, much more variation exists in the relationship between state and associations than allowed for in current liberal civil society theories.

Whereas some of the euphoria over the democratic potential of civil society is justified, as seen in the fall of communism in countries such as Poland, basing foreign policy and academic theory on an oppositional model of civil society and the authoritarian state is dangerous. The primary danger, in addition to simple inaccuracy, is that as these groups fail to live up to their democratic potential or policy makers and funding agencies question their legitimacy as independent civil society actors and either stop funding vital projects or attempt to dictate projects from abroad, which obviates the benefits of local civil society participation. Second, as I argue throughout this book, this idea of civil society held by funding agencies, such as USAID, generates distrust between nondemocratic states and associations, leading to the creation of an oppositional relationship that might not have been present before. In this way, advocating a liberal view of state–civil society relationships in authoritarian states creates a self-fulfilling prophesy that might destroy the chance of other potential relationship models, such as the CA model.

In fact, this hybrid CA model that developed in China in the mid-2000s illustrates the variation in authoritarian state–civil society relationships, especially in response to officials' experience with these groups over time. This new model resulted from learning by policy makers from both personal experiences with civil society groups emerging in China in the 1990s, such as Greenpeace, and by observing international experiences with civil society, such as the color revolutions and the Western regulatory-state model.

[78] Samuel Huntington, *Political Order in Changing Societies* (New Haven, CT: Yale University Press, 1968); Carew Boulding, "NGOs and Political Participation in Weak Democracies: Sub-national Evidence on Protest and Voter Turnout from Bolivia," *Journal of Politics*, 72, no. 2 2010: 456–468.

Through this process, local officials learned that civil society could offer many benefits in service delivery, development, and policy innovation; however, these groups also presented a danger to authoritarian regimes because of their ability to mobilize citizens and transmit information independent of the state.[79] As officials learned about civil society, they developed a new model seeking to maximize the benefits while minimizing the dangers represented by these groups. The development of this new model of consultative authoritarianism transforms how scholars understand both the role of civil society and institutional change in authoritarian regimes. First, CA fundamentally changes the nature of policy making in China by expanding the definition of who is a policy maker to include non-state actors such as civil society. In China, as in most authoritarian regimes, policy making is a nontransparent and insular process. Allowing the participation of civil society organizations alters the process of policy making to create more transparency and social feedback. These changes create mechanisms for durable authoritarianism through a flow of information heretofore restricted by the institutional structure of authoritarian institutions. Second, the causal role of learning in catalyzing institutional change in state-society relations highlights a vital role for civil society in authoritarian regimes. As I find, these groups facilitate a learning process both within and across regimes.

In the following chapters, I examine the creation of the CA model in China. Conventional models of authoritarian state–civil society relations are often understood as either repression or incorporation; this model instead depicts a more pluralistic and nuanced relationship, whereby selected groups possess channels for limited participation in the policy process. By increasing transparency and pluralism in the policy making process, civil society improves governance and contributes

[79] Ivan Krastev, "Democracy's 'Doubles,'" *Journal of Democracy* 17, April 2006: 52–62; Larry Diamond, "Authoritarian Learning: Lessons from the Colored Revolutions," *The Brown Journal of World Affairs* 12, Summer/Fall 2005.

to improved welfare outcomes in China. This has important implications for the world's poor, many of whom live under authoritarian rule. However, the diffusion of this model across China is not a democratizing trend but rather a method for achieving better governance under the conditions of authoritarian rule.

CHAPTER 1

Policy Learning in China: Constructing Consultative Authoritarianism

The political economy in which local officials make policy decisions has changed significantly in China since the beginning of the reform era in 1979. As I elaborate on in this chapter, the decentralization of public goods provision to local governments without the same degree of fiscal decentralization created unfunded mandates and difficulty meeting development indicators necessary for promotion. Additionally, the ways in which cadres were promoted changed to a more competitive, target-based system, which encouraged policy innovation. Simultaneously, the international community encouraged a global associational revolution through channeling funding to both domestic civil society groups and INGOs, and increasing the flows of information and policy advocacy across borders through transnational networks. This changing political economy motivated local officials to engage in innovation through learning about new ways to deliver improved public goods and services.

During this search for new policies, most provincial leaders experimented with multiple options throughout the 1990s, such as using extra-budgetary sources of revenue such as land sales and illegal fees, forcing state-owned enterprises to contribute to public services, or issuing IOUs for services like pensions. By the mid-1990s, INGOs began to enter China and assisted the formation of a domestic civil society through capacity-building programs and subcontracting parts of existing programs. This new phenomenon of emerging civil society precipitated a learning process on the part of local officials through direct experiences with these new groups and their activities. Through interaction with primarily service delivery projects throughout the mid-1990s to mid-2000s, local officials began to view civil society groups as possible partners to assist in meeting development goals. As I discuss in more detail later in this chapter, these groups, both domestic and international, played a key role in this learning process by actively partnering with local officials. Practical experiences with these groups led many local officials to gradually shift their understanding of state-society relations from the corporatist view of civil society as an appendage to state agencies to a more collaborative and independent one, whereby these groups introduce innovative models and supply funding from abroad through transnational networks.

Additionally, the observation (vicarious experience) of other countries' experiences with civil society played an important role in this learning process. As discussed in the introduction, policy makers are satisficers without the time or means to evaluate all possible policy solutions and often use easily accessible models and practices from others as cognitive shortcuts in policy learning. Recent research has shown that these models are often selected from two types of sources: successful and similar cases.[1] In the case of civil society, two dominant examples of both successful and similar cases informed officials' learning about the appropriate local state–civil society relationship, namely the Western regulatory state model and the color revolutions in post-Soviet republics. In the case of the former, advanced industrial countries such as Germany and the United States serve as successful examples of the ability to encourage a civil society that does not challenge state authority but instead works to facilitate better outcomes, such as poverty alleviation, needs assessments and policy advocacy for vulnerable populations, and mitigation of

[1] Frank Dobbin, Beth Simmons, and Geoffrey Garrett, "The Global Diffusion of Public Policies: Social Construction, Coercion, Competition, or Learning?" *Annual Review of Sociology* 33, 2007: 449–472.

social anger and unrest. The regulatory state model is based on governing institutions playing a regulatory rather than producer role, and in China implementing this model required a series of administrative reforms to shrink government responsibility and enlarge the space for both private firms and civil society groups. Local officials viewed the state-society relationship in this model as a "small state–big society," encouraging state collaboration with both private firms and civil society groups as a way to meet state goals.

Positive experiences with civil society development projects and observing the Western regulatory state model helped construct the first defining characteristic of this new consultative authoritarianism (CA) model – the increase in group autonomy – that I contend emerges by the mid-2000s. During this time period, autonomous groups formed mostly at the community level and many government-organized groups (GONGOs) previously incorporated into state agencies began to gain more operational autonomy. However, local officials also observed groups mobilizing the public to challenge state authority in the color revolutions that swept the post-Soviet republics in the early 2000s and had several negative experiences with the influx of civil society, such as environmental groups that blocked development projects or human rights groups that exposed abuse of power at the local level. These contradictory observations and experiences with different types of groups led to variation in officials' ideas about the appropriate relationship between state and society and helped construct the second main characteristic of the CA model: a sophisticated system of positive and negative incentives that are intended to indirectly control these groups, rather than through the direct mechanisms used in corporatism.

As I discussed in the Introduction, this term "consultative authoritarianism" is my adaptation of Li Junru's term "consultative democracy (*xieshang minzhu* 协商民主)."[2] Li argues that this observed increase in consultation indicates a process of

[2] Recently, several other scholars have been using this term as well, although in different ways: see Joseph Fewsmith, *The Logic and Limits of Political Reform in*

democratization in China. However, I argue that growing consultation does not indicate a process of democratization but rather the creation of a new model that encourages autonomous civil society groups to participate in policy but also seeks to guide that participation through a system of indirect positive and negative incentives. Kang Xiaoguang and Han Heng also contend that this system of incentives, what they call "differentiated controls," indicates changing state–civil society relations whereby the government uses different tools to control varying types of groups.[3] Groups that are deemed "safe," such as those formed by government cadres or primarily interested in service delivery, are treated differently from those that deal with issues such as human rights advocacy. However, whereas Kang and Han's account centers on government control, my argument illustrates how groups themselves influence the construction of this model through interactions with local officials as civil society first emerges in China. As I examine in Chapter 4, many group leaders also learned from initial interactions in the mid-1990s to develop effective strategies to create the positive learning experience that led to more collaborative relationships with the local state. More collaborative relationships with local officials allow these groups to participate in public policy in ways not allowed by formal authoritarian institutions.

As I explain in Chapter 2, this new CA model first developed in Yunnan and Beijing as the result of policy learning on the part of local officials as they attempted to balance the ability of civil society to both assist in the provision of social services and challenge state authority. In Chapter 3, I explore how as officials

China (New York: Cambridge University Press, 2013); Baogang He and Stig Thøgersen, "Giving the People a Voice? Experiments with Consultative Authoritarian Institutions in China," *Journal of Contemporary China* 19, 2010: 675–692; Oscar Almén, "Only the Party Manages Cadres: Limits of Local People's Congress Supervision and Reform in China," *Journal of Contemporary China* 22, 2013: 237–254.

3 Kang Xiaoguang and Han Heng (康晓光与韩恒), "分类控制：当前中国大陆国家与社会关系研究 (Differentiated Control: Current State and Society Relationship Research in Mainland China)," 社会学研究 *(Sociology Research Journal)* 6, 2005, available at http://www.chinareform.net/2010/0116/8243.html

in Sichuan and Jiangsu observed the successful use of these policy experiments with a more independent civil society, this lesson diffuses to these and other provinces and finally to the central government, as seen in changing regulations for civil society adopted beginning in 2008, such as relaxed registration requirements allowing for more independent grassroots groups to form.

THE POLITICAL ECONOMY OF LEARNING: OFFICIALS' CHANGING RESPONSIBILITIES

Most historians note that prior to the founding of the People's Republic of China (PRC) in 1949, Confucius was the main influence on ideas of the proper state-society relationship, with the primary goal of creating a hierarchal society and government. In contemporary China, the Confucian approach to government and society persists in the idea of an ordered, hierarchal society that is structured in many ways like a family. The relationship therefore between an official and citizen is one of parental authority (*fumuguan* 父母官), whereby parents (governments) were responsible for the future development of children (citizens) and their livelihood.[4] As Yu Keping describes, "In China's traditional political culture, through political behaviors superiors set an important example for the inferiors. Such Chinese idioms as 'the inferiors imitate the superiors', 'setting a good example with good conduct', 'being a paragon of virtue and learning' and 'playing an exemplary role' express the meaning."[5] According to this model, government officials were not accountable for their decisions to citizens but were responsible for providing a good example of morality.

Many of these beliefs were incorporated into Mao Zedong's practice of communism, whereby officials served as the vanguard of the people to inspire them through good examples to achieve national goals.[6] Accountability was still only an "upward"

[4] Yu Keping, "The Emerging of China's Civil Society and Its Significance to Governance," *Focus Asien* 8, April 11, 2001.

[5] Ibid., 17.

[6] Maurice Meisner, *Mao's China and After: A History of the People's Republic* (New York: Free Press, 1999).

concept, with officials answering for their decisions to the party, and mass participation in politics widely distrusted by the government. This view of political participation stemmed from the instances of mass political participation in Chinese dynastic history that usually signaled the collapse of a ruling dynasty. Although many scholars view early Communist history as a time of unprecedented participation, this was through regime-sponsored mass mobilization not voluntary participation.[7] Thus, both governance and political participation were seen as elite-level activities that flowed down to a mass public. Although the status of different classes and some social practices were altered under Mao's leadership, these traditional views of the proper relationship between state and society as a hierarchy persisted.

As part of a newly established single-party state, PRC state officials sought to consolidate power over society and local officials. This was done by creating a Leninist system of corporatism for all social groups and by increasing central tax revenue and consolidating political control via local party branches and promotion decisions. The preceding government, the Guomindang (KMT), was unable to collect more than 7 percent of GNP in taxes each year; however, the CCP expanded this amount by four to five times and rapidly created a modern economy.[8] State fiscal development stalled during the famine of the Great Leap Forward and the chaos of the Cultural Revolution, but it accelerated once more under Deng Xiaoping's economic reform and opening strategy (*gaige kaifang* 改革开放) in the early 1980s. Encountering declining central revenue during the first stage of economic reform, the CCP implemented comprehensive tax and fiscal reforms in 1993 and 1994, which replaced the fiscal-contracting system with a modern tax-assignment system. The implementation of these tax and fiscal reforms under the auspices of a centralized tax administration raised the central government's share of budgetary

7 Elizabeth J. Perry, "Moving the Masses: Emotion Work in the Chinese Revolution," *Mobilization: An International Quarterly* 7, Summer 2002: 111–128.

8 Shaoguang Wang and Angang Hu, *The Chinese Economy in Crisis: State Capacity and Tax Reform* (Armonk, NY: M.E. Sharpe, 2001).

revenue relative to that of the provinces and increased total government budgetary revenue as a percentage of GDP from 10.7 percent in 1995 to 17.1 percent by 2001.[9]

Although a large component of economic reform involved institutional streamlining, including the decentralization of fiscal and welfare functions to local governments, the central government retained ultimate control over finances and promotions to ensure hierarchal control over all cadres. Beginning in the 1980s, the central state increasingly decentralized fiscal policy to local government under the slogan of "cooking in separate kitchens" (*fenzao chifan* 分灶吃饭).[10] Decentralization gave local government limited political devolution with more significant administrative and economic devolution and was intended to increase the ability of local government to regulate local markets and provide public services to society. Decentralization theoretically increases the provision of public goods because local governments better know the needs of citizens and can provide these services more cost effectively, and it creates more responsive institutions by bringing government decision makers in closer proximity to the affected constituency.[11] However, despite the ability of local governments to more effectively identify needs, they often do not have the ability to meet these needs because of a mismatch between responsibilities and funds allocated by the central government. In response, many local governments overspend assuming the central government will supply more funds (soft budget constraints). The experience of decentralization in China unintentionally led to the creation of unfunded mandates and high levels of local debt.[12] Throughout

[9] Dali Yang, "State Capacity on the Rebound," *Journal of Democracy* 14, no.1, January 2003: 43–50.

[10] Yingyi Qian and Barry Weingast, "China's Transition to Markets: Market-Preserving Federalism, Chinese Style," *Journal of Economic Policy Reform* 1, 1996: 149–185,

[11] Pranab Bardhan and Dilip Mookherjee, eds., *Decentralization and Local Governance in Developing Countries* (Cambridge, MA: MIT Press, 2006).

[12] Christine P. W. Wong, "Central–Local Relations in an Era of Fiscal Decline: The Paradox of Fiscal Decentralization in Post-Mao China," *The China Quarterly* 128, 1991: 691–715; Hongbin Cai and Daniel Treisman, "State Corroding Federalism," *Journal of Public Economics*, 88, nos. 3–4, March 2004: 819–843.

the 1980s, the central government transferred to local governments primary responsibility for the provision of public goods, such as education, health care, infrastructure, and social security programs like unemployment insurance. Consequently, the Chinese fiscal system is highly decentralized with the central government accounting for only 30 percent of total budgetary expenditures, and the remaining 70 percent distributed among four subnational levels.[13] In comparison, subnational governments account on average for only 14 percent of total budgetary expenditures in developing countries, and 32 percent in developed countries. As Christine Wong notes, this model of decentralization is even more notable because China is one of the only countries in the world to assign responsibility for providing vital social services such as social security, basic education, health care, and public safety to local governments.[14] Rural provinces also face the challenge of eliminating poverty for about 70 percent of the estimated 80 million citizens living below the poverty line.[15]

Local governments do not possess much fiscal autonomy to meet these unfunded mandates because the central government restricts the ability to tax local populations and to secure bonds or loans.[16] According to China's fiscal budget law, local governments cannot issue debt and should not run fiscal deficits; in reality, with the demands on local governments increasing while fiscal transfers from the central government remain low, most provinces operate a budget deficit or borrow using special

[13] Albert Park, Scott Rozelle, Christine Wong, and Changqing Ren, "Distributional Consequences of Reforming Local Public Finance in China," *The China Quarterly* 147, 1996: 751–778.

[14] Ibid.

[15] These poverty estimates are based on Chinese calculations and not those of the World Bank, which are much higher.

[16] David D. Li, "Large Domestic Non-Intermediated Investments and Government Liabilities –Challenges Facing China's Financial Sector Reform," World Bank Working Paper, 2006: http://siteresources.worldbank.org/INDIAEXTN/Resources/events/359987-1149066764594/WorldBankIFI-DavidLi-060404.pdf

financial vehicles to fund social programs.[17] This gap between responsibilities and funding motivated local government to search for new strategies to deliver social welfare. As I explain more fully later, officials began to view emerging civil society as potential partners in securing international funding and innovative models to bridge the resource gap and solve welfare provision problems.

In addition to unfunded mandates motivating the search for new policy ideas, local officials faced increasing promotion competitiveness as the number of open positions at higher levels declined because of continued government streamlining and stricter quality standards. In the 1980s, the central government began a series of civil service reforms to replace the loyalty-based cadre system with one based on performance. After a number of revisions, the current civil service system uses a Target Management Responsibility System (*gangwei mubiao guanli zerenzhi* 岗位目标管理责任制) that prioritizes performance-based targets. Although there is debate over which performance criteria actually result in promotion, the two most important goals are economic development and social order.[18] Leading cadres ranked as excellent under the Responsibility System receive bonuses, pay raises, medals, honorary titles, and merit records.[19] Although promotion is not officially considered a reward under this system, officials who receive excellent evaluations for two or more years in a row are normally promoted: "In short, today almost all Chinese local officials have been structured into a highly personalized, individualized incentive scheme."[20] In an increasingly competitive

[17] Christine Wong, "Budget Reform in China," *OECD Journal on Budgeting*, 2007: 33–56.

[18] Susan Whiting, *Power and Wealth in Rural China: The Political Economy of Institutional Change* (Cambridge, UK: Cambridge University Press, 2001); see Landry for the view that these goals do not result in promotion in Pierre Landry, "The Political Management of Mayors in Post-Deng China," *The Copenhagen Journal of Asian Studies* 17, 2003.

[19] Maria Edin, "State Capacity and Local Agent Control in China: CCP Cadre Management from a Township Perspective," *The China Quarterly* 173, 2003.

[20] Han Tian, ed., *Lingdao ganbu kaocha kaohe shiyong quanshu (Practical Comprehensive Handbook of Reviewing and Evaluating Leading Cadres).*

promotion system coupled with reduced local capacity, local officials must consistently attain performance goals in order to gain raises or promotions.[21]

Thus by the 1990s, the political economy in which local officials operated encouraged the search for innovative policies to solve governance problems created by rapid economic growth and increasing economic and social complexity, namely the failure to provide necessary public goods and services. As the economy expanded along with these governance problems, the lack of effective channels for relaying the concerns and views of new socioeconomic groups to the state meant that the Chinese Communist Party became increasingly out of touch with the changing needs of society and unable to negotiate and balance an increasingly diverse range of interests.[22]

Local governments still used a slightly updated version of the corporatist state-society model that existed under the Leninist institutions established under Mao to deal with societal demands, including the traditional mass organizations for labor and women. As part of this adaptive corporatism, officials also created GONGOs that served as a social extension of state agencies and incorporated independent grassroots groups and INGOs into state agencies through the dual registration system. As I analyze in this chapter, this adapted corporatist approach slowly changed as a result of local officials learning about new state-society models through observing other models and direct experience with an emerging civil society in China. However, although governance challenges initiated reforms to create a more limited government (*youxian zhengfu* 有限政府) based on the regulatory Western model, creating space for intermediary social organizations to

(Beijing: China Personnel Press, 1999), p. 131, as cited in Shu-Yun Ma and Wai-Yin Chan, "The Provision of Public Goods by a Local Entrepreneurial State: The Case of Preservation of the Nanyue Relics in China," *The Journal of Development Studies*, 40, no. 1, October 2003, 119–141.

[21] David Shambaugh, *China's Communist Party: Atrophy and Adaptation.* (Berkeley: University of California Press, 2009).

[22] Jude Howell, "Getting to the Roots: Governance Pathologies and Future Prospects," in *Governance in China*, Jude Howell, ed. (Lanham, MD: Rowman & Littlefield, 2004), p. 231.

assist the government with social welfare, the lesson drawn by CCP leaders was not to initiate democratization as these Western exemplars did, but to learn how to achieve better governance under the existing authoritarian political system.

LEARNING THROUGH OBSERVATION: RISE OF THE REGULATORY STATE MODEL

As the wave of neoliberalism swept over most of the world in the early 1990s, China also drew lessons from this model that seemed so successful in the United States and the United Kingdom in providing economic growth. Although other development models existed, many relied on neoliberal principles. For example, the East Asian model that developed in Japan combined a neoliberal focus on the use of market mechanisms and expansion of a private sphere with a developmental-state focus on using state institutions to create national champions and compete effectively in international markets.[23] Beth Simmons, Frank Dobbin, and Geoffrey Garrett contend that the worldwide spread of economic and political liberalism was the defining feature of the late twentieth century, consisting of free market–oriented economic reforms such as macroeconomic stabilization, liberalization of foreign economic policies, privatization, and deregulation.[24] This economic liberalism, often called "neoliberalism," refers to policies that reduce government constraints on economic behavior to promote "marketization," which enhance the space available for private firms and citizen organizations to play important roles in both market and political spheres.

[23] Joseph Stiglitz, "Some Lessons from the East Asian Miracle," *The World Bank Research Observer*, 11, no. 2, August 1996: 151–177; Bruce Cumings, "The Origins and Development of the Northeast Asian Political Economy: Industrial Sectors, Product Cycles, and Political Consequences," *International Organization* 38, Winter 1984: 1–40; and Dilip Das, "The Invisible Hand versus the Visible Hand: The Korean Case," *Seoul Journal of Economics* 5, 1992.

[24] Beth A. Simmons, Frank Dobbin, Geoffrey Garrett, "Introduction: The International Diffusion of Liberalism," *International Organization* 60, no. 4, 2006: 781–810.

Many party leaders believed that this process of economic reform required restructuring state institutions designed to *produce* market goods to those designed to *regulate* a combination of state-owned and private firms producing those goods. This caused a shift from the state-society relations existing under the Maoist mobilization system to more of an arms-length regulatory relationship, which motivated reforms to develop regulatory institutions and policies, build a professional and technocratic civil servant corps, decentralize fiscal and public welfare functions to local governments, and expand the private sector composed of both firms and civil society organizations. Although several senior party members, including the former head of central market planning Chen Yun, contested this concept of a regulatory state and advocated more efficiency in the existing economic structure, this idea was consolidated and achieved clear policy dominance following Deng Xiaoping's southern tour in 1992.[25] Party leaders altered the original Western model to meet the existing Chinese context of an economy based on state-owned enterprises by using a dual-track strategy to reform the state-owned sector while encouraging the growth of a private sector.[26] State officials pursued a strategy of institutional reform and the small state–big society initiative to transition state institutions to this adapted regulatory state model.[27]

Based on this model, neoliberal proponents instituted institutional reforms to streamline government agencies to create efficient institutions capable of regulating an increasingly complex market economy and society. Party leadership planned to transition these state institutions from producers to regulators by

[25] Suisheng Zhao, "Deng Xiaoping's Southern Tour: Elite Politics in Post-Tiananmen China," *Asian Survey*,. 33, no. 8, 1993: 739–756.

[26] Barry Naughton, *The Chinese Economy: Transitions and Growth* (Cambridge: The MIT Press, 2007); Jessica C. Teets and Orion A. Lewis, "A China Model? – Understanding the Evolution of a 'Socialist Market Economy,'" 2009, http://www.glasshouseforum.org/

[27] X. Ru, ed., *Xiao zhengfu da shehui de lilun yu shiqian [Theory and Practice of Small Government and Big Society]*, Beijing: Social Sciences Collections Publishing House, 1998.

reducing both responsibilities and size through streamlining government, divesting government of its businesses, strengthening the fiscal and regulatory capacity of economic governance, disciplining bureaucrats through public management reforms, curbing corruption, and creating more transparency. In fact, one round of government restructuring in 1998 reduced the number of central government ministries from 40 to 29; trimmed total ministry staff size by nearly half; downsized party organizations; and cut the staffing size of 21 mass organizations including the All China Federation of Trade Unions, the Chinese Communist Youth League, and the All China Women's Federation by 25 percent.[28] In addition to this streamlining, officials intended that civil servant administration reforms would create a more professional public administration capable of regulating the newly developing private sector. These public management reforms promoted professionalization, reduced hiring discretion, and increased transparency and public service ethic in the civil service. The goal, as former Personnel Minister Song Defu states, is that "government civil servants should acquire the mentality of serving taxpayers."[29] Public management reforms, especially criteria such as age limits and college degrees, encouraged hiring younger, better educated government employees to build a technocratic public administration capable of regulating a diversified market economy and emergent civil society.

As part of this institutional restructuring, the central government initiated the small state–big society reforms in the late 1980s (*xiao zhengfu, da shehui* 小政府, 大社会), designed to achieve a substantial downsizing of the party-state apparatus accompanied by the rise of an autonomous sphere of associational life.[30] These small state–big society reforms were also part of the neoliberal reforms as seen in the United Kingdom under Margaret Thatcher

[28] Dali Yang, *Remaking the Chinese Leviathan* (Stanford, CA: Stanford University Press, 2004), p. 37.

[29] Cited in Yang, *Remaking the Chinese Leviathan*, p. 172.

[30] Richard Baum, "The Limits of Consultative Leninism," *Asia Program* 131, Woodrow Wilson International Center, June 2006: 13–20.

and the United States under Ronald Regan. In fact, Xibai Xu notes that China's reform path was heavily influenced by neoliberal scholars, such as Milton Friedman who traveled to China three times throughout the 1980s and early 1990s to advise the top leadership on monetary reform.[31] As the government decided to withdraw from society as a producer, it focused on a smaller number of functions, such as the provision of public goods, infrastructure development, security, and regulating both market and society, which created more space for civil society organizations, ranging from neighborhood committees to industrial associations and professional organizations.[32] Groups were encouraged to undertake former government responsibilities at local levels, especially village and street levels, as these institutions were dismantled. In this way, the neoliberal regulatory state model helped create an emerging legitimate space for these groups.

Lessons drawn from observing the Western regulatory state model initiated institutional changes that significantly impacted state–civil society relationships by the mid-1990s.[33] These reforms both intentionally and unintentionally created space for civil society activity in areas formerly controlled by the local state by changing the institutional roles of both state and society. This more collaborative role of an autonomous civil society was supported by the small state–big society model found in the advanced industrial economies of both the United States and Germany. In fact, study groups were sent to the United States to investigate the relationship between state and civil

[31] Xibai Xu, "Neoliberalism and Governance in China," unpublished working paper, 2011: http://dosen.narotama.ac.id/wp-content/uploads/2012/03/Neoliberalism-and-Governance-in-China.pdf

[32] Shenjing He and Fulong Wu, "Property-Led Redevelopment in Post-Reform China: A Case Study of Xintiandi Redevelopment Project," *Journal of Urban Affairs* 27, no. 1, 2005: 1–23.

[33] Dali Yang, "Economic Transformation and Its Political Discontents in China: Authoritarianism, Unequal Growth, and the Dilemmas of Political Development," *Annual Review of Political Science* 9, 2006: 143–164; Youyu Xu, "The Debates between Liberalism and the New Left in China since the 1990s," *Contemporary Chinese Thought* 34, 2003: 6–17.

society.[34] In these countries, the state maintains a collaborative relationship with civil society whereby groups provide public goods, mediate social unrest, and promote good governance.

LEARNING THROUGH EXPERIENCE: CIVIL SOCIETY DEVELOPMENT IN CHINA

Civil society organizations not based on kinship or lineages are fairly new in China (*gongminshehui* 公民社会 or *shiminshehui* 市民社会).[35] An associational revolution began to occur in China in the mid-1990s, with the number of civil society groups and participation rates in these groups increasing dramatically. The Ministry of Civil Affairs reports that registered groups increased from fewer than 5,000 in 1988 to more than 400,000 in 2009, with unregistered groups greatly exceeding this number (Figure 1.1).

In 1995, Beijing hosted the United Nation's International Women's Forum, and officials witnessed a dramatic influx of domestic and international NGOs to Huairou, a town outside of

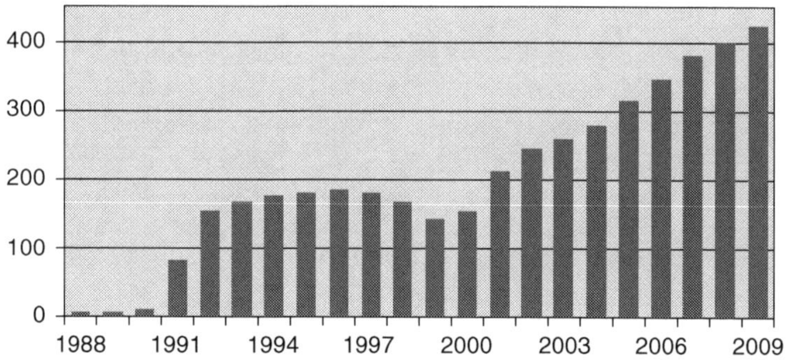

FIGURE 1.1. Registered Groups in China (in thousands)

[34] David M. Lampton interview, cited in Norton Wheeler, *The Role of American NGOs in China's Modernization: Invited Influence* (New York: Routledge, 2013., 37.

[35] For a discussion of the history of social organizations in China, see William T. Rowe, "The Problem of 'Civil Society' in Late Imperial China," *Modern China* 19, April 1993: 139–157.

Beijing. As Elizabeth Knup from the National Committee on United States–China Relations recounted,

> The NGOs . . . were used to having access, and they were totally furious that they were really far away. But two things happened. One was a lot of Chinese NGOs, nascent NGOs, or individuals that had that inclination were kind of empowered by all these other NGOs; they hung out with them in Huairou, and they learned from them. . . And, secondly, the Chinese government learned that, in fact, NGOs aren't all bad . . . Not all NGOs are confrontational like Greenpeace. In fact, they provide things that they government can't provide in society. So, from that period forward, China slowly began to be more accepting of NGOs in general.[36]

Chinese branches of INGOs proliferated during this time period, reaching approximately 150 by 2000. For example, The Nature Conservancy alone opened three offices in Western China and Beijing, in addition to multiple project offices.

The scope of civil society also expanded to encompass social organizations, business and industry associations, charities, foundations, and nonprofits. These groups, broadly called nongovernmental or nonprofit organizations (*minjianzuzhi* 民间组织, *shehuituanti* 社会团体, *feizhengfuzuzhi* 非政府组织, and *feiyinglizuzhi* 非营利组织), formed to deliver services and advocate for vulnerable populations in society. Based on a survey of Chinese civil society in 2008, researchers found that more than 43 percent of groups were involved in social services, 40 percent in industry or university activities, 35 percent in cultural or art-based activities, 25 percent in legal aid and policy advocacy, and 21 percent in poverty alleviation.[37] These groups ranged from small grassroots organizations with two or three employees to large groups with more than twenty employees, such as the Center for Biodiversity

[36] Elizabeth Knup interview, July 28, 2005, cited in Wheeler, *The Role of American NGOs in China's Modernization*, 36.

[37] 熊伟 (Xiong Wei) and 秦梦 (Qin Meng), "论中国NGO本土能力的困境和出路 ('An Analysis of Chinese NGO's Weak Capacity and Solution to This Predicament')," 中国思想网 *(Chinese Thought Network)*, June 17, 2008: note that multiple categories were allowed to be selected: accessed at http://www.jianghuaisw.com/bbs/viewthread.php?tid=5635

and Indigenous Knowledge in Yunnan or Friends of the Earth in Beijing.[38] Even though the numbers of groups and participants are increasing, most organizations still have low capacity in domestic funding, staffing, and geographic reach.[39] In fact, most large groups and branch offices of INGOs receive the majority of their funding in the form of international grants and transfers from INGOs and international foundations.

At the beginning of the associational revolution, officials attempted to incorporate groups into the existing corporatist system by forming GONGOs and using the dual registration system to restrict funding and legal status to certain grassroots groups.[40] For example, without securing legal status as a non-profit and being added to a list of charities and foundations allowed to raise funds domestically, many groups depend on membership dues and local government grants that restrict the potential size and capacity of these groups. Although membership dues increasingly constitute a larger portion of overall group funding, small memberships mean that this source alone cannot support most groups.[41] The mass organizations (and other government-sponsored groups) are most likely to secure funding from the government, although grassroots groups sometimes secure limited funding from their supervising units.[42] However, since the mid-1990s, even mass organizations such as the Women's Federation must seek increased member funding because of declining state funding.[43] Many groups illegally

[38] Anthony Spires, Lin Tao, and Kin-man Chan, "Societal Support for China's Grassroots NGOs: Evidence from Yunnan, Guangdong, and Beijing." Forthcoming in *The China Journal*.

[39] Ibid.

[40] Qiusha Ma, "The Governance of NGOs in China since 1978: How Much Autonomy?" *Nonprofit and Voluntary Sector Quarterly* 3, September 2002: 305–328.

[41] 熊伟 (Xiong Wei) and 秦梦 (Qin Meng), ("An Analysis of Chinese NGO's Weak Capacity and Solution to This Predicament.")

[42] Author interview with member of indigenous knowledge NGO, Lijiang, Yunnan, April 5, 2007.

[43] Author interview with Women's Federation members, Simao, Yunnan March 9, 2007.

fundraise inside of China but raise only small amounts of money because of the need for low exposure of the fundraising events or activities.[44]

In addition to power over fundraising, the adapted corporatist system also controlled legal status. The Ministry of Civil Affairs regulates all civil society groups through a three-step process known as the "dual management system" (*shuangchong guanli tizhi* 双重管理体制): groups register with the local Civil Affairs bureau, secure a government agency as a sponsor (主管单位 *zhuguan danwei*), and undergo an annual review.[45] Although many groups choose not to register and either act informally or register as a for-profit enterprise, the ones that do register must place themselves under the professional management of a state organ with responsibilities in its area of work, in addition to being registered and reviewed annually by Civil Affairs departments. The professional management agency (or mother-in-law) holds a wide range of responsibilities, including supervising the organizations' ideological work; financial and personnel management; research activities; contacts with foreign organizations; and the reception and use of donations from overseas, which is the primary funding source for larger groups.[46] The intention motivating the dual management system was to incorporate these new groups into existing corporatist structures. However, this system is so expensive and difficult for most groups to navigate that many simply register as a for-profit organization and pay taxes or operate informally without any legal status resulting in great variation in the legal status of these associations.

The restrictive registration process and the explosion of civil society activity initiated a debate in the 1990s over the

[44] Author interview with foreign volunteer for health-related NGO, Kunming, Yunnan, June 6, 2007.

[45] Supervisory agencies are often called "mother-in-laws" to denote their perceived role of monitoring and controlling groups while employing rhetoric of "guiding groups" for their own good. This is an important but tricky relationship to navigate, with asymmetric power and information.

[46] "Guanyu chongxin queren shehui tuanti yewu zhuguan danwei de tongzhi" ("Circular on Reconfirming the Professional Management Units of Social Organizations"), Ministry of Civil Affairs, 2000.

relationship of civil society groups with the state: was this an autonomous civil society or merely a new corporatist framework?[47] Many of the scholars involved in these debates critiqued the use of liberal civil society theories imported from the West as inappropriate to Chinese culture and history, and those who argued that this concept should be used across cases found that an autonomous civil society simply did not exist in China.[48] For example, X. L. Ding found that civil society groups are incorporated into the state through registration procedures (*guakao danwei* 挂靠单位) and share responsibilities and staff with these government agencies.[49] Thus, in the 1990s, most scholars concluded that these groups were not autonomous from the state and comprised a corporatist structure called "state-led civil society."[50] However, a few scholars suggested that these groups possessed limited autonomy and that the close relationship between state and civil society suggested an alternative to traditional models – a civil society with Chinese characteristics.[51]

As discussed in the Introduction, this focus on autonomy from the state derives from one of the most commonly used liberal definitions of civil society, which defines civil society as composed of autonomous, voluntary associations acting in the public

47 Timothy Brook and B. Michael Frolic, "The Ambiguous Challenge of Civil Society," in *Civil Society in China*, Timothy Brook and B. Michael Frolic, eds. (New York: M.E. Sharpe, 1997); Heath Chamberlain, "On the Search for Civil Society in China," *Modern China* 19, April 1993: 199–215; Gordon White, Jude Howell, and Xiaoyuan Shang, *In Search of Civil Society*. (Oxford, UK: Clarendon Press, 1996).

48 Philip Huang, "'Public Sphere'/'Civil Society' in China?: The Third Realm Between State and Society," *Modern China* 19, April 1993: 216–240; Francis Fukuyama, "Social Capital and the Global Economy: A Redrawn Map of the World," *Foreign Affairs*, September/October 1995: accessed at http://www.foreignaffairs.com/articles/51402/francis-fukuyama/social-capital-and-the-global-economy-a-redrawn-map-of-the-world

49 X.L. Ding, "Institutional Amphibiousness and the Transition from Communism: The Case of China," *British Journal of Political Science* 24, July 1994: 293–318.

50 B. Michael Frolic, "State-Led Civil Society," in *Civil Society in China*, Brook and Frolic, eds.

51 Heath Chamberlain, "Civil Society with Chinese Characteristics?" *The China Journal* 39, 1998: 69–81.

sphere.[52] Relying on this dichotomous understanding of autonomy, civil society must be either completely autonomous similar to the liberal model or completely co-opted by the state similar to the corporatism model. This use of autonomy as a defining characteristic of civil society engenders the problem of how to understand autonomy from the state, such as, is this dichotomous or a continuum of state-society relationships? If not dichotomous, how much autonomy is necessary for the component groups – nonprofits, nongovernmental organizations, social clubs, and associations – to act as these theories predict for a civil society?

Autonomy from the state is defined as separation and often measured through funding and other resources, such as shared employees and office space. In this aspect, the experience of civil society groups in China challenges this conventional understanding by illustrating that autonomy from the state is not a static dichotomous relationship. Different groups in Chinese civil society have varying relationships with the state over time, ranging from complete autonomy matching an ideal Western grassroots model to complete co-option matching a state corporatism model. Wang Ming, the head of Tsinghua University's NGO Research Center, argues,

> Due to funding sources and relationship with the government two models of NGOs exist: one from above to below and one from below to above. The first one usually serves as a branch of the government, sharing its functions, people and funding. However, recently these groups have had conflict between serving as the government's assistant and the interests of the social groups they serve. The other type of NGO has more autonomy, but less money and less access points (mostly informal) to government.[53]

Currently, grassroots groups rely on international funding for the bulk of group resources, along with donations and dues from the local community. Moreover, as Wang Ming observed in the preceding quotation, as GONGOs received less from government budget allocations and relied more on membership dues

[52] Jürgen Habermas, *The Structural Transformation of the Public Sphere: An Inquiry into a Category of Bourgeois Society* (Cambridge, UK: Polity, 1989), p. 54.

[53] 王名(Wang Ming), "China's NGO and Civil Society Development," *Caijing (Finance and Economy Magazine)*, 2002: 350–352.

throughout the late 1990s, they became more aggressive in advocating for the interests of their members and lobbying government departments for policy action.[54] This illustrates even more variation in funding sources and government relationships. In addition to the empirical variation in groups' relationship with the government, this theoretical reliance on a dichotomous category of autonomy also does not reflect reality and distracts scholars from understanding the development of civil society. For example, Lester Saloman finds that most Western governments fund NGOs at high levels – Western European NGOs receive 56 percent of their funding from the state.[55] Thus, even in Western countries, civil society is less autonomous from the state than our theories prescribe.

As Gordon White, Jude Howell, and Xiaoyuan Shang argue, "in brief, the extent to which a specific social organization embodies the defining qualities of 'civil society' – autonomy, separation and voluntariness – is a question of degree rather than either/or."[56] Therefore, autonomy should be understood as part of a continuum of state-society relationships, with some groups closer to the state than others at different times. In a developing state context, groups might not have access to multiple funding sources outside of the state. These findings in China illustrate the need for a more empirical approach to understanding state–civil society relationships, especially how interaction between the two over time changes initial relationships.

Liberal theories contend that autonomy from the state is vital to forming an independent civil society that plays an oppositional role to the state and fosters democracy. If not autonomous, civil society cannot generate the democratic will-formation necessary for

[54] Scott Kennedy, *The Business of Lobbying in China*. (Cambridge, MA: Harvard University Press, 2005); Andrew Walder, "Factory and Manager in an Era of Reform," *The China Quarterly* 118, June 1989: 242–264.

[55] Lester M. Salamon, S. Wojciech Sokolowski, and Associates, *Global Civil Society: Dimensions of the Nonprofit Sector*, vol. 2 (Bloomfield, CT: Kumarian Press, 2004); Shaoguang Wang, "Money and Autonomy: Patterns of Civil Society Finance and Their Implications," *Studies in Comparative International Development* 40 (Winter 2006): 3–29.

[56] White et al., *In Search of Civil Society*.

legitimizing or opposing state action. In fact, in Eastern and Central Europe, many scholars credit an autonomous civil society with opposing and ultimately toppling communist governments in the early 1990s.[57] However, it is unclear that autonomy from the state is necessary for democratic will-formation, based on the experience of civil society in Western states. Saloman finds that NGOs in the United States receive more than half of their funding from government and other public sources; however, many scholars use these groups as prototypical examples of groups contesting the state and forming a democratic will.[58] This suggests that full autonomy might not be necessary for associations to play an oppositional role, simply relative autonomy.[59]

These examples illustrate that future civil society scholars need a better understanding of how much and what kinds of autonomy groups need to play a variety of civil society roles – democratic will-formation, contesting or opposing the state, revolution, policy advocacy, or service delivery. Depending on the goals of civil society groups, the desired relationship with the state might differ. In fact, as I explore in Chapter 4, many groups aspiring to change policy use a more collaborative relationship with the local state to secure access to a policy-making process closed to citizen participation. Therefore, as an alternative to using autonomy in a dichotomous fashion to define civil society, I argue that the relationship between civil society and the state should be part of the research question allowing us to better analyze the nature and consequences of this dynamic interaction.

[57] Vladimir Tismaneanu, *Reinventing Politics: Eastern Europe from Stalin to Havel* (New York: Free Press, 1992); Larry Diamond, "Rethinking Civil Society: Toward Democratic Consolidation," *Journal of Democracy* 5, no. 3, July 1994: 4–17.

[58] Benjamin Barber, *Strong Democracy* (Berkeley: University of California Press, 1984).

[59] Gary Rodan, "Theorizing the Political Opposition in East and Southeast Asia," in *Political Opposition in Industrializing Asia*, Gary Rodan, ed. (London: Routledge, 1996); Lars Jorgensen, "What Are NGOs Doing in Civil Society?" in *NGOs, Civil Society and the State: Building Democracy in Transitional Societies*, Andrew Clayton, ed. (Oxford, UK: The International Non-Governmental Organisation Training and Research Centre, 1996: 38.

THE ASSOCIATIONAL REVOLUTION AND LOCAL CADRE LEARNING

The associational revolution in China beginning in the early 1990s created opportunities for officials to interact with civil society groups, both INGOs and grassroots groups. As I explain in the following three chapters, these experiences taught local officials that civil society groups are good partners for development projects but also represent a potential challenge to state authority. Variation in experiences with civil society influenced local officials to maintain different relationships with groups depending on issue area or interpersonal trust with the group leader and by the mid-2000s developed into what I am calling a consultative authoritarianism model. This CA model represents a hybrid between liberal and corporatist state-society models. Local officials sought to balance the observed benefits of civil society groups in development with the potential danger of social mobilization by encouraging the formation of autonomous groups while developing a system of positive and negative incentives to guide group activities in desired directions.

As described earlier, unfunded mandates for public goods provision created incentives for local officials to partner with civil society groups to solve social problems at the local state level. Through a process of learning from experience and observation, local officials began partnering with civil society as a strategy to bridge the resource gap, allowing them to meet development promotion goals.[60] Civil society organizations help local officials meet economic and social promotion goals through running pilot programs to deliver public goods, generating research and policies for the legislative use of local officials, and acquiring international funding and resources to use for public-private projects. Thus, the

[60] Kiril Tochkov, "Interregional Transfers and the Smoothing of Provincial Expenditure in China," *China Economic Review* 18, 2007: 54–65; Dali Yang, "Rationalizing the Chinese State: The Political Economy of Government Reform," in *Remaking the Chinese State: Strategies, Society, and Security*, Chao Chien-min and Bruce J. Dickson, eds. (London: Routledge, 2001).

potential of groups to bridge the resource gap and secure community participation encourages local officials to view these groups as assisting in achieving established promotion goals. Moreover, the legacy of decentralized experimentation in China further encourages local government officials to partner with civil society groups in search of new models of development in order to be noticed and promoted out of the large pool of local officials. This policy-making methodology entails a decentralized policy process that is initiated from individual "experimental points" (*shidian* 试点) and driven by local initiatives with the formal or informal backing of higher-level policy makers.[61] If judged to be conducive to current priorities, "model experiences" (*dianxing jingyan* 典型经验) extracted from the initial experiments are disseminated through media coverage, conferences, visitation programs, and appeals for emulation to more regions and eventually integrated into national policies.[62]

The case of the adoption of a national thin-plastic bag ban in 2008 represents a paradigmatic example of this process of official learning about the benefits of cooperating with civil society groups. In 1997, the Old Town of Lijiang in Yunnan province was designated a UNESCO World Heritage site in response to rapidly increasing tourism to this area; foreign arrivals increased more than 70 percent annually from 1985 to 1996.[63] The central and provincial governments recognized tourism as the most lucrative form of development in this mountainous area, and early realization of the importance of environmental quality to sustainable tourism led to an awareness of the problem of environmental degradation including waste from tourists. As the head of the local Environmental Protection Bureau (EPB) Zhang Wei explained,

[61] Sebastian Heilmann and Elizabeth Perry, eds., *Mao's Invisible Hand: The Political Foundations of Adaptive Governance in China* (Cambridge MA: Harvard University Press, 2011).

[62] Sebastian Heilmann, "From Local Experiments to National Policy: The Origins of China's Distinctive Policy Process," *The China Journal* 59 (January 2008): 1–30.

[63] "Tourism Development in Lijiang County, Yunnan," *Food and Agriculture Organization of the United Nations*, 1997, available at http://www.fao.org/forestry/37243/en/

Lijiang had a serious problem with plastic bag waste as a result of increased tourism.[64]

In the early 2000s, an INGO in Lijiang hired a retired cadre as its director who used his connections at the local EPB to initiate a number of pilot programs in partnership with the local government – ecotourism, alternative energy, and conservation.[65] The home office of the INGO supplied funding, and the local government contributed other resources for these cooperative projects, such as staffing and regulatory waivers, but did not supply direct funding. One of the cooperative projects between the group and local government involved a campaign to decrease the use of thin plastic bags piloted first in Zhongdian in 2001, another tourist destination in Yunnan, and expanded to Lijiang in 2003. The INGO first presented a research report to the local government and EPB outlining the costs of making and disposing of plastic bags and then suggested a policy of reducing bag use through applying a tax paid by consumers on each bag. When consumers purchased an item, they could also buy a plastic bag for one yuan, which would create an incentive to either bring reusable bags or reuse previously purchased plastic bags. The INGO then partnered with a local grassroots group to publicize this new policy to relevant local communities once it was implemented and to distribute reusable cloth bags to merchants.

In the wake of a number of environmental crises such as deforestation, the local government championed this policy upward to the provincial and ministry levels to demonstrate local innovation in dealing with environmental problems caused by development. In late 2007, Shenzhen followed this model and publicized draft regulations to ban thin plastic bags. As a result of the successful pilot projects, the Ministry of Environmental Protection (MEP) advocated the adoption of this policy throughout China, resulting in the national thin-plastic bag ban in

64 Ke Xuedong, "Lijiang's War on 'White Pollution,'" *China Dialogue*, February 28, 2008: available at https://www.chinadialogue.net/article/show/single/en/1755-Lijiang-s-war-on-white-pollution-

65 Interview with two staff members of INGO, Kunming, Yunnan, May 10, 2007.

June 2008. More than 1 million reusable cloth bags were sold on various Chinese merchandising websites, and many local environmental groups, such as Shanghai Roots & Shoots, promoted and gave away cloth bags in schools.[66] This case illustrates how officials' direct experience with an emerging civil society in the late 1990s initiated a learning process that taught officials that these groups could help meet development goals through the application of international models using international resources. As staff members of the environmental INGO explained, the group "does not ask for government funds but instead invests international money into Chinese projects, so the local government welcomes our assistance."[67]

This collaborative relationship is effective in meeting goals the local EPB and the INGO hold in common and motivates continued cooperation. For example, the local EPB later requested the group's assistance in drafting local environmental laws that the bureau did not have the technical capacity to complete without requesting that scientists be sent from either the provincial capital or Beijing.[68] When asked why this INGO has influence in local policy, one staff member argued that it is because of the "trust between the group and the local government – trust earned through cooperation."[69] She also stated that this cooperation is possible mostly because of the ability of the INGO to access international money and expertise to help complete the government's projects, and its ability to help local cadres promote their reputation primarily by taking credit for the successful pilot projects run by the INGO.[70] As a result of the realization of mutual benefits and increasing trust between local officials and groups through these collaborative projects, a positive learning

[66] David Biello, "China Sacks Plastic Bags: Ban Could Save 37 Million Barrels of Oil and Alleviate 'White Pollution,'" *Scientific American*, May 23, 2008.

[67] Interview with two staff members of INGO, head office, Kunming, Yunnan, May 10, 2007.

[68] Series of interview with staff member of INGO, project office, Lijiang, Yunnan, first date: March 7, 2007.

[69] Ibid., April 2, 2007.

[70] Ibid.

experience encouraged local officials to consider future interactions with civil society organizations.[71]

The process of experimental policy making allows local officials to develop models to resolve difficult governance problems, which if successfully diffused into national policy elevates their status and aids in promotion. Many local officials mentioned this as a reason to partner with civil society groups; not only do groups offer international best practices in poverty alleviation, community participation, and environmental conservation, they also offer financial and technical resources to help implement these ideas.[72] As local officials learned through direct interaction, groups provide the government with community networks, specialized knowledge (training, new models, technology), and also run pilots for the government to test new policy ideas.[73] To further encourage decentralized policy experimentation, both the central and provincial governments create "innovation awards" to encourage policy innovation at lower levels that can then be tested and disseminated by provincial leaders.[74] For example, in one province with such an innovation in governance award, the district leader agreed to partner with a community-participation group in order to develop a new model for integrating economic migrants and their children into new urban communities. This experimentation with reforming the household registration system (*hukou* 户口) enabled the county head to win the governance award with its cash award and recognition from the mayor.[75] Recognition of social innovation by supervisors helps secure promotion to the next level of government, as illustrated by the famous example of Zhao Ziyang pioneering the use of the Household Responsibility System for privatizing farmland before

[71] Author interview with head of domestic environmental group, Lijiang, Yunnan, March 20, 2007, and with local EPB official, Lijiang, Yunnan, April 1, 2007.

[72] Author interview with local official, Chengdu, Sichuan, July 10, 2008.

[73] Author interview with Health Bureau cadre, Kunming, Yunnan, June 6, 2007.

[74] For example, the Innovations and Excellence in Chinese Local Governance Program: Keping Yu, *Innovations and Excellence in Local Chinese Governance* (Beijing: Social Science Literature Press, 2002).

[75] Author interview with staff member of community participation NGO, Beijing, June 1, 2008.

being promoted to premier in 1980 and general secretary of the Communist Party in 1987.[76]

However, as the example of Zhao Ziyang who endured house arrest for 15 years after the 1989 Tiananmen protests also illustrates, the idea of civil society groups assisting local government in solving development issues is balanced with social stability concerns. The Target Management Responsibility System prioritizes both economic development and social order. Concerns with social stability, or perceived anti-state activities, permeate the party leadership and all levels of government and are broadly defined as social unrest that might threaten economic development and the party's political hegemony.[77] Both the social stability path used successfully by Jiang Zemin during the 1989 protests and the governance innovation path used by Zhao Ziyang have proven to be successful, so the selection of one promotion strategy over the other might depend on the types of learning experiences or lessons drawn as illustrated in the four provincial case studies.

In fact, many local officials' initial experiences with civil society also demonstrated that these groups threaten local government development goals and social stability. For example, Greenpeace-China accused a multinational logging company, Asia Pulp & Paper (APP), of illegally destroying natural forests in Yunnan in 2004. APP had signed an agreement with the Simao local government in Yunnan, and the local government claimed that the project raised the living standard of local people by creating jobs, generating tax revenues, and building roads and other infrastructure in the area.[78] After the local government's defense of APP's practices, Greenpeace-China coordinated a series of protests and succeeded in winning media coverage of the controversy

[76] David Zweig, *Freeing China's Farmers: Rural Restructuring in the Reform Era* (Armonk, NY: M.E. Sharpe, 1997).

[77] Thomas Heberer and Gunter Schubert, "Political Reform and Regime Legitimacy in Contemporary China," *Asien* 99, April 2006: 9–28.

[78] Gang Guo, "Environmental Security and the Lancang Mekong River Basin: Conflicting Interests of Stakeholders in China," *Foundation for Environmental Security and Sustainability*, June 2007: available at http://www.fess-global.org/publications/issuebriefs/ES_and_the_Lancang-Mekong_River_Basin.pdf

and a boycott of APP paper products by the Zhejiang Province Hotels Association's 417 member hotels. Other environmental NGOs, such as the Global Village of Beijing, started to get involved in the protests.[79]

In January 2005, the State Forestry Bureau asked the Yunnan Province Forestry Bureau to conduct a thorough investigation. However, not only did the bureau find that APP's practices did not adversely affect the environment, the local government through its Yunnan Provincial Development Investment Corporation signed an agreement to expand APP's forest access. Greenpeace-China then helped coordinate mobilization among grassroots environmental groups, scientists, and journalists to pressure the central government into intervening. Protests organized by this coalition took place in six major Chinese cities, including Beijing and Guangzhou, during May and June 2005, with protesters demonstrating in front of shopping centers asking customers to not purchase the company's products.[80]

As a result of the public pressure, on February 7, 2007, a spokesperson for the State Forestry Bureau announced that the bureau had instructed the Yunnan Provincial Government to stop the purchase because the agreement was against state policies on the transfer of state-owned forest. Wang Zhuxiong, deputy director of the bureau's Forest Resources Management Department, confirmed that "We believe both APP and the [Simao] local government are responsible for the violation."[81] This experience, although celebrated by many in the environmental community in China as a success, highlighted the role civil society can play in challenging state authority and inhibiting local officials from meeting development goals. The local Simao and provincial

79 Rui Xia, "Illegal Logging Goes on in Yunnan," *Asia Times*, August 9, 2005: available at http://www.atimes.com/atimes/China/GH09Ad02.html

80 Ibid.

81 "Guojia linyeju zecheng tingzhi yinni jinguang jituan binggou guoyou senlin [State Forestry Bureau demands end to purchase of state-owned forest by Indonesian APP Corporation]," *Xinhua News Agency*, 2007, available at http://news.xinhuanet.com/politics/2007-02/07/content_5711370.htm

government subsequently banned Greenpeace-China's further activity in the province.

As these examples illustrate, local government officials recognize an important role for civil society, especially in public service delivery and advocacy for vulnerable populations; however, the question is how to balance the need for strengthening civil society with the need for social order that groups might challenge.[82] These contradictory experiences with groups are evidenced by fluctuations in government relationships with civil society throughout the 1990s and resulted in the development of the CA model by the mid-2000s as an attempt to maximize the benefits of these groups while minimizing the dangers.

LEARNING THROUGH OBSERVATION: THE COLOR REVOLUTIONS IN THE 2000S

The fears of civil society mobilizing people to challenge state authority were further strengthened by the wave of color revolutions in the early 2000s. In contradistinction to the neoliberal model in the 1990s of regulatory states collaborating with civil society to solve problems, the color revolution model provided examples of civil society mobilizing protests and helping overthrow the government. The color revolution model originated from the Bulldozer Revolution in Serbia in 2000, where the United States spent $41 million on a democracy-building campaign in the months prior to the presidential election, including U.S.-funded consultants running tracking polls, training thousands of opposition activists, and helping organize a parallel vote count.[83] The Serbian model was characterized by collaboration between international democracy promoters and domestic opposition groups to overthrow the existing regime and was

[82] Jonathan Schwartz and Shawn Shieh, eds., *State and Society Responses to Social Welfare Needs in China: Serving the People* (London: Routledge, 2009).

[83] Michael Dobbs, "U.S. Advice Guided Milosevic Opposition: Political Consultants Helped Yugoslav Opposition Topple Authoritarian Leader," *Washington Post*, December 11, 2000: available at http://www.highbeam.com/doc/1P2-565855.html

transmitted by Serbian activists and democracy-promotion groups to other post-Soviet republics such as Georgia for a Rose Revolution in 2003, Ukraine for an Orange Revolution in 2004, and Kyrgyzstan for a Tulip Revolution in 2005. Chinese analysts note that this color revolution template contains efforts to infiltrate from both outside and within the designated state, using foreign aid, special Western democracy-promotion programs, Western media, the instigation of what the Chinese referred to as "street politics" (*jiedao zhengzhi* 街道政治), and youth mobilization.[84] In China, civil society groups were identified as a chief transmission mechanism: "NGOs are an instrument that the Western states like to use. They are a 'Trojan horse' planted by the Western intelligence agencies."[85]

Given rising social unrest in China, local officials were afraid that civil society would use these grievances to mobilize opposition to the party. Statistics illustrate growing mass incidents of demonstrations, protests, and riots throughout the 2000s – totaling 87,000 in 2006, an increase of 6.6 percent from 2005.[86] Since 2008, officials express rising concern about protests in the minority areas of both Tibet and Xinjiang in Western China, as well as the possibility that rising income gaps and unemployment among the rural population and recent college graduates might trigger increasing unrest.[87] The idea of civil society presenting a potential threat to social order and the party's political hegemony has been strengthened by the observed lessons of the color revolutions in the post-Soviet republics.

In response to the color revolutions, in 2005, President Hu Jintao was reported to have issued a report at an internal CCP

84 Jeanne L. Wilson, "Colour Revolutions: The View from Moscow and Beijing," *Journal of Communist Studies and Transition Politics* '25, June 2009: 369–395.

85 Pan Rulong and Dai Zhengqin, "'Yanse Gemin' yu Guoji Fei Zhengfu Zuzhi [Color Revolutions and NGOs]," *Dianzi Keji Taxue Xuebao Shekeban* 7, 2005: 78.

86 Murray Scot Tanner, "China Rethinks Unrest," *The Washington Quarterly* 27, Summer 2004: 137–156.

87 Colin Mackerras, "Xinjiang at the Turn of the Century: The Causes of Separatism," *Central Asian Survey*, 20, no. 3, 2001: 289–303; Peter Ford, "China's Ant Tribe: Millions of Unemployed College Grads," *The Christian Science Monitor*, December 21, 2009.

conference that called for "vigilance" against U.S. efforts to launch a color revolution in China and directed researchers to examine the circumstances surrounding the color revolutions.[88] The lesson for a government desiring to retain power is repression or revolution, which establishes a confrontational relationship between state and civil society. In the wake of the Tulip Revolution in Kyrgyzstan in March 2005, Chinese authorities ordered a comprehensive review of all registered civil society groups receiving foreign funding. As I explore in the following chapters, the color revolutions provided an observation, or vicarious experience, of civil society as a threat to authoritarian governments and played a significant role in changing state–civil society relationships throughout the 2000s.

BETTER GOVERNANCE UNDER AUTHORITARIANISM: THE CONSULTATIVE AUTHORITARIANISM MODEL

As illustrated in this chapter, governance challenges arising in the 1980s and 1990s during the process of economic and institutional reforms motivated local officials to search for new ways to meet development goals required for promotion. Positive experiences working with civil society groups that provided access to international funding and innovations to solve these problems taught officials that civil society could play a beneficial role. Furthermore, observation of the regulatory state model in countries such as Germany and the United States supported this lesson of civil society as a collaborator in achieving good governance. However, many local officials' experiences with civil society also demonstrated that these groups might challenge state authority and social stability. The observed color revolutions model in the post-Soviet republics supported this lesson drawn from negative experiences. These contradictory lessons encouraged local officials to create a new state-society model to balance two potential

[88] Frank Ching, "No Changing Colors in China," *The Japan Times*, November 2, 2005: available at http://www.japantimes.co.jp/opinion/2005/11/02/commentary/no-changing-colors-in-china/#.UnlZ3Pmko_4

roles for civil society – good governance and authoritarian challenge. The resulting model is a hybrid between liberal and corporatist state-society relationship models that encourages the development of a relatively autonomous civil society and simultaneously establishes a system of positive and negative incentives to control group activities.

This model is characterized by two main elements: a pluralistic civil society participating in policy formation and implementation, and the use of multiple indirect tools of state control. Whereas the goals of this consultative authoritarianism are the same as far as the desire to control social activity, the social pluralism and differentiated state controls present in this model distinguish it from the corporatist model. The first distinctive characteristic is the existence of officially tolerated group autonomy. Unlike the corporatist model described by Jean Oi, groups no longer serve as appendages to the state but possess independent staff, resources, and projects.[89] In fact, Jude Howell finds that most groups receive little government funding, and the majority of groups were started voluntarily from the grass roots, although some groups also involved officials in activities to informally access resources and contacts, enhance the prestige of the organization, and gain political protection for activities.[90] Although groups are required to register with the Ministry of Civil Affairs and a supervisory agency, these regulations have not substantially limited the expansion of civil society in China to date. Attempts to restrict the space and range of organizational activity through registration have turned into a "facade of monopoly," rather than a true monopoly on power.[91] For the most part, these groups establish independent projects and strategies, and any cooperation with local government is the result of

[89] Jean Oi, "Fiscal Reform and the Economic Foundations of Local State Corporatism in China," *World Politics* 45, 1992: 99–126; Anita Chan and Jonathan Unger, "China, Corporatism, and the East Asian Model," *The Australian Journal of Chinese Affairs*, 33, 1995: 29–53.

[90] Jude Howell, "New Directions in Civil Society: Organizing around Marginalized Interests," in *Governance in China*, Howell, ed., p. 157.

[91] Ibid., p. 158.

mutual recognition of comparative advantage: "We [the Yunnan Reproductive Health Association] need a government network, like the Women's Federation, for this makes our work convenient. It helps us to organize a focus group discussion or visit households. So there is a cooperative relationship."[92] Local government often collaborates with unregistered groups, and as Shaoguang Wang finds, these groups also possess operational autonomy.[93]

Additionally, more pluralism is offered in this model than under corporatism, with multiple groups competing inside of one policy space or region. Under the corporatist model, the state recognizes only one organization, such as the Women's Federation, as the sole representative of the interests of the individuals or businesses comprising that organization's constituency. Only through this channel may incorporated organizations participate in the policy-making process. This former model of corporatism limits the number of actors participating in the policy process and thus controls the actions of the members. In fact, the regulations governing civil society state that the Ministry of Civil Affairs (MoCA) may deny registration if a social organization is already active in the same administrative area in the same *(xiang tong)* or similar *(xiang si)* area of work. According to Professor Ge Yunsong, official documents describe this provision as aiming to avoid a situation in which there might be too many organizations "developing without planning" and possibly causing "malicious competition" among organizations.[94] Under this corporatism framework, the state incorporates societal groups into the state structure as a way to mediate social interests without challenging state authority. As Philippe Schmitter defines,

[92] Cited in ibid., p. 159; author interview with Federation staff, Yunnan, June 4, 2007.

[93] Wang, "Money and Autonomy."

[94] Karla Simon and Hang Gao, "Opening the Space: New Developments for China's Community Organizations," *Columbus School of Law* Legal Studies Series, Accepted Paper No. 2010–25, 2010: available at http://papers.ssrn.com/sol3/papers.cfm?abstract_id=1581687

> Corporatism can be defined as a system of interest representation in which the constituent units are organized into a limited number of singular, compulsory, noncompetitive, hierarchically ordered and functionally differentiated categories, recognized or licensed (if not created) by the state and granted a deliberate representational monopoly within their respective categories in exchange for observing certain controls on their selection of leaders and articulation of demands and supports.[95]

However, since the early 2000s, multiple groups representing the same constituency in a region proliferated, and some groups such as environmental NGOs increasingly link members across the country through online forums and resources.[96] These groups and practices proliferated to such as extent that the director of one group engaged in linking civil society actors across regions argues that now the official federations view grassroots groups as policy and resource competitors.[97] These groups also participate in the whole process of policy making, including policy formation, and no longer just in policy implementation as seen with the former corporatist model.[98]

The second distinctive characteristic of this new model is the type of control mechanisms used by the state. These mechanisms are called "differentiated controls" by Kang Xiaoguang, who finds that the state increasingly uses more sophisticated and indirect methods to create positive and negative incentives, encouraging groups to work toward meeting state goals.[99] The example of a group called

[95] Philippe C. Schmitter, "Still the Century of Corporatism?" *The Review of Politics* 36, January 1974: 94.

[96] Peter Ho, "Greening without Conflict? Environmentalism, NGOs and Civil Society in China," *Development and Change* 32, no. 5, 2001: 893–921.

[97] Author interview, director of civil society group, Beijing, July 26, 2007.

[98] Andrew Mertha, "'Fragmented Authoritarianism 2.0': Political Pluralization in the Chinese Policy Process," *The China Quarterly* 200, 2009: 995.

[99] 韩恒,康晓光(Han Heng and Kang Xiaoguang),"分类控制：当前中国大陆国家与社会关系研究[Differentiated Control: Current State and Society Relationship Research in Mainland China]," 社会学研究[Sociology Research Journal] 6, 2005: http://www.chinareform.net/2010/0116/8243.html; and author interview with Kang Xiaoguang, Beijing, July 7, 2010.

One Kilogram More (*DuoBeiYiGongJin* 多背一公斤) illustrates the positive incentives used under the consultative authoritarianism framework.[100] The founder of this grassroots group set up an online network on the QQ platform to coordinate between needy rural schools and potential urban donors. Since 2004, thousands of urban citizens have participated in One Kilogram's network by carrying a kilogram of books or other school supplies in their luggage to distribute to children in the impoverished rural areas they visit, and at the same time to share information on the website about the condition of rural schools.

This group helps the local government in Beijing and two other provinces address problems with income inequality between rural and urban areas, including gaps between rural and urban education. According to the group's founder, "By combining travel with doing good, we hope to change the reality of the imbalance of education between rural and urban areas in China. Although enrollment in higher education is increasing, the proportion continuing their studies in rural areas is far lower, and education standards much poorer."[101] Since the network started in 2004, some 10,000 One Kilogram "volun-tourists" have collected detailed data on more than 600 rural schools, distributed books and stationery benefiting at least 1 million people, and developed new websites representing almost all major Chinese cities.

One Kilogram initially supported its activities by offering corporate social responsibility consulting to businesses; however, the Beijing municipal government recently supported this network as a way to encourage a charity approach to help rural schools by using three main positive incentives – social incubators, government grants, and new registration laws. The Beijing municipal government funds an incubator program run privately by Chao Lu, who in 2006 established the Non-Profit Incubator (NPI), which trained One Kilogram staff members in professional project management, auditing and accounting skills, and grant

[100] Author interview, head of a capacity-building group working with One Kilogram, Beijing, June 30,2010.

[101] One Kilogram website: http://1kg.blogbus.com/

writing.[102] Additionally, the municipal government eased registration regulations for selected groups that now only require registration with the local Bureau of Civil Affairs and no longer require a supervisory agency and also initiated a grants program in 2010 of 300 million yuan (US$44 million) to fund groups proposing social innovation projects. The grants and incubation experience allowed One Kilogram to expand into physical offices in Beijing and Guangzhou. These positive incentives guide groups toward areas in which the local state would like to see the groups working, such as social innovation to solve welfare provision problems.

However, this model also uses negative incentives as evidenced in the example of the INGO Oxfam. Oxfam successfully partnered with many local governments to undertake poverty alleviation programs; however, when it attempted to link college student volunteers with migrant workers in Beijing – two sensitive populations given high unemployment rates – the Ministry of Education instructed all Beijing universities to stop collaborating with Oxfam.[103] Oxfam was allowed to continue operating its poverty alleviation programs including those with migrant populations, but indirect control mechanisms such as cutting off the supply of student volunteers were used to guide the group back onto a more service-oriented path and away from anything potentially disruptive of social order. Oxfam closed down this program because of a lack of student volunteers, which illustrates the more nuanced and indirect tools of state control that local officials use to balance the strategic ideas of meeting development goals and maintaining social order. Unlike the former model of corporatism, autonomous civil society groups are expanding in size, scope, and significance; however, government control over these groups while still present is increasingly nuanced.

Since 2009, many local governments in municipalities such as Beijing, Shanghai, Chengdu, and Shenzhen have been experimenting with reforming the registration process so that groups

[102] Author interview, Fudan University professor, Shanghai, July 5, 2010.
[103] Author interview, Renmin University professor, Beijing, July 7, 2010.

register directly with local Civil Affairs Bureaus.[104] The new direct registration policies dismantling the supervisory agency system break the last link between the local state and independent civil society existing under the former adaptive corporatism model.

These same municipalities also initiated rounds of government contracts to provide domestic funding for independent civil society groups.[105] Local governments increasingly contract out the provision of social services to nonprofit organizations, creating a new channel of funding.[106] Initially fundraising was also strictly controlled, with only government-organized charities such as the China Red Cross Society allowed to fundraise domestically. These restrictions meant that most organizations have low capacity in domestic funding, staffing, and geographic reach.[107] Smaller grassroots groups argue that only larger groups, groups that cover certain popular issues, or branches of INGOs secure international grants and transfers.[108] Despite primarily funding larger groups, the impact of past international funding on the capacity and development of groups in China cannot be overstated. For example, the Ford Foundation initiated a capacity-building project in Yunnan in the mid-1980s that sent a number of volunteers to training sessions and further education both inside and outside of China. When these

[104] Karla Simon, "The Regulation of Civil Society Organizations in China," *International Journal of Civil Society Law* 9, 2011: 55–84.

[105] Shaojie Huang, "Govt Plans to Spend on Civil Societies: Plan to Financially Assist NGOs Involves Exerting More Influence," *Huanqiu Shibao [Global Times]*, July 13, 2010.

[106] Jessica C. Teets, "Reforming Service Delivery in China: The Emergence of a Social Innovation Model," *Journal of Chinese Political Science*, 17, no. 1, 2012: 15–32; Yijia Jing and E.S. Savas, "Managing Collaborative Service Delivery: Comparing China and the United States," *Public Administration Review* 69, no. s1, 2009: S101–S107.

[107] Anthony Spires, Lin Tao, and Kin-man Chan, "Societal Support for China's Grassroots NGOs: Evidence from Yunnan, Guangdong, and Beijing," Forthcoming in *The China Journal*; Spires, Anthony J., Lin Tao, and Kin-man Chan, "Societal Support for China's Grassroots NGOs: Evidence from Yunnan, Guangdong, and Beijing." Forthcoming (Jan. 2014) in *The China Journal*, no. 71.

[108] Author interview with member of indigenous knowledge NPO, Lijiang, Yunnan, April 5, 2007.

volunteers returned, the majority established grassroots groups and received funding and additional capacity-building training from the Ford Foundation.[109] These organizations and the newer groups in which they helped build capacity comprise most of the civil society community in Yunnan.[110] INGOs and the transnational networks they create enable grassroots groups in China to access networks of human resources, financial resources, and best practices (or intellectual resources), which greatly expand capacity and allow these groups to offer significant benefits to local officials in order to create learning opportunities and ultimately change the relationship.

However, as international funding declines, the ability to fundraise domestically is vital to the continued expansion of civil society.[111] Since late 2010, the national regulations relaxed to allow registered public foundations such as the film and martial arts celebrity Jet Li's One Foundation to conduct fundraising on the mainland.[112] Additionally, in certain areas, like Beijing, groups partner with public foundations to share "special funds" that the foundations raise for specific partner groups as a way to navigate around fundraising restrictions.[113] For example, the China Social Welfare Education Foundation, a GONGO, allows groups with a "similar philosophy and direction as the Foundation" to register under them (*guakao* – hang under) and use a newly established special fund for fundraising through the supervisory agency. The supervisory agency currently has 24

109 Author interview with staff member of environmental INGO, Kunming, Yunnan, May 10, 2007.

110 "The Stars of Asia – Opinion Shapers," *Business Week*, June 9, 2003: available at http://www.businessweek.com/magazine/content/03_23/b3836627.htm

111 Wang Hui, "New Trends in Philanthropy and Civil Society in China: International Donors and NGOs Need to Establish an Equal Partnership," *China Development Brief*, no. 45, Spring 2010: available at http://www.chinadevelopmentbrief.cn/?p=270

112 Karla Simon, "Regulation of Civil Society in China," *International Journal of Civil Society Law* 9, 2011: 55–84.

113 Wang Hui, "Grassroots NGOs Use Special Accounts to Raise Funds," *China Development Brief*, no. 48, Winter 2010: available at http://www.chinadevelopmentbrief.cn/?p=209

special funds and many registered groups, such as the Beijing China Dolls Care Association that received 100,000 renminbi (RMB) at the end of 2009.[114]

In addition to regulatory changes in registration and funding, the government is also creating new channels for institutionalized public participation in policy making.[115] At town hall meeting and through public comment periods, local officials often invite civil society groups to provide information to citizens and policy makers.[116] It has also been increasingly common for groups to directly consult with all levels of government in writing draft legislation. The government, through the *People's Daily* website, has been operating an "E-government Square" since May 2009, allowing Internet users to interact with National Peoples Congress (NPC) representatives and other government officials: "Guo Xia, a project officer with Society of Entrepreneurs & Ecology (SEE), recalls that the public and local NGOs started submitting proposals to the NPC via representatives some years ago – but these were mostly just calls for something to be done. In 2010 this practice became more common, and 2012 saw an increase in both the number and quality of submissions."[117] The e-government site had more than 14,000 comments submitted in two years, ranging from pollution concerns to laws protecting stray animals.

Although provincial variation still exists, there is increasing evidence of a national convergence on this model as seen in the use of the Beijing model of "social management" to develop new national regulations for civil society. As the Minister of Civil

[114] Wang Hui [王辉], "Grassroots NGOs Borrow from Special Funds to Secure Funding [草根 NGO 借道专项基金筹募资源]," *The China Development Brief [中国发展简报2010冬季刊]*, Winter Issue, 2010: available at http://www.chinadevelopmentbrief.org.cn/qikanarticleview.php?id=1138

[115] Baogang He, "Civic Engagement Through Participatory Budgeting in China: Three Different Logics at Work," *Public Administration and Development* 31, 2011: 122–133.

[116] Genia Kostka and Arthur Mol, "Implementation and Participation in China's Local Environmental Politics: Challenges and Innovations," *Journal of Environmental Policy & Planning* 15, 2013: 3–16.

[117] Zhang Chun, "Civil Society's Changing Role in the Chinese Political System," *Dialogue*, 18 March 2013: available at http://www.chinadialogue.net

Affairs announced in 2011, "The ministry will take Beijing's experiences as reference and promote them, but the steps will not be as wide-ranging as Beijing's."[118] Thus, this consultative authoritarianism model might be adopted nationally and serve to promote the growth of operationally autonomous groups and further indirect social controls. As Yu Keping argues:

> The Party and the government have already begun the transition from focusing on control in dealing with social organizations to focusing on nurturing and encouragement. In the current 12th Five-Year Plan, "strengthening the building of social organizations" is raised for the first time in a prominent position [as a priority]. This is a substantial transformation. And along with the major shift, there has been a clear improvement in the supplying of resources to civil society. Government financial aid, subcontracting of services and social welfare spending have begun to increase.[119]

These changes in the local state–civil society relationships since 2008 illustrate the emerging convergence on this model of consultative authoritarianism, which encourages the growth of autonomous civil society at the same time as it develops new, indirect tools of social management.[120] The next chapter examines the initial construction of this model in Beijing and Yunnan.

118 Zou Le, "NGO Registration Rules to Be Relaxed Nationwide: Civil Affairs Minister," *Global Times*, May 25, 2011.

119 Keping Yu, "Moving toward Shared Governance by the Government and the Public," *Southern Metropolis Daily*, May 8, 2011: available at http://cmp.hku.hk/2011/05/12/12198/

120 周本顺 [Zhou Benshun], "Social Management of Innovation with Chinese Characteristics [走中国特色社会管理创新之路]," *Qiushi Magazine [求是杂志]* 10, 2011.

CHAPTER 2

Let Many Civil Societies Bloom: Building Consultative Authoritarianism in Beijing and Yunnan

Consultative authoritarianism developed first in Yunnan and Beijing in response to an earlier influx of civil society, first in the form of INGOs and then grassroots groups in the early 1990s. This influx initiated a learning process for local officials who were struggling with the policy failure of public goods and services decentralization. Although initially lacking direct experience with civil society, local officials observed other countries' experiences with development and social unrest. Both of these sources of learning contributed to the construction of CA in Yunnan and Beijing by the mid-2000s.

As illustrated in Figure 2.1, Yunnan was a poor, mountainous province in the 1990s, with a great deal of ecological and ethnic diversity. The province's poverty and ecological diversity attracted a number of INGOs, including The Nature Conservancy and Oxfam. The local government welcomed these groups initially as a source of foreign investment, much in the same way as foreign firms along China's east coast. These INGOs funded the development of many grassroots organizations, and Yunnan became known as having one of the most welcoming environments for groups.

Beijing, on the other hand, attracted INGOs because of its status as the capital of China. In the 1990s, many INGOs established headquarters in Beijing and field offices in other provinces, and grassroots groups dealing with national issues, such as

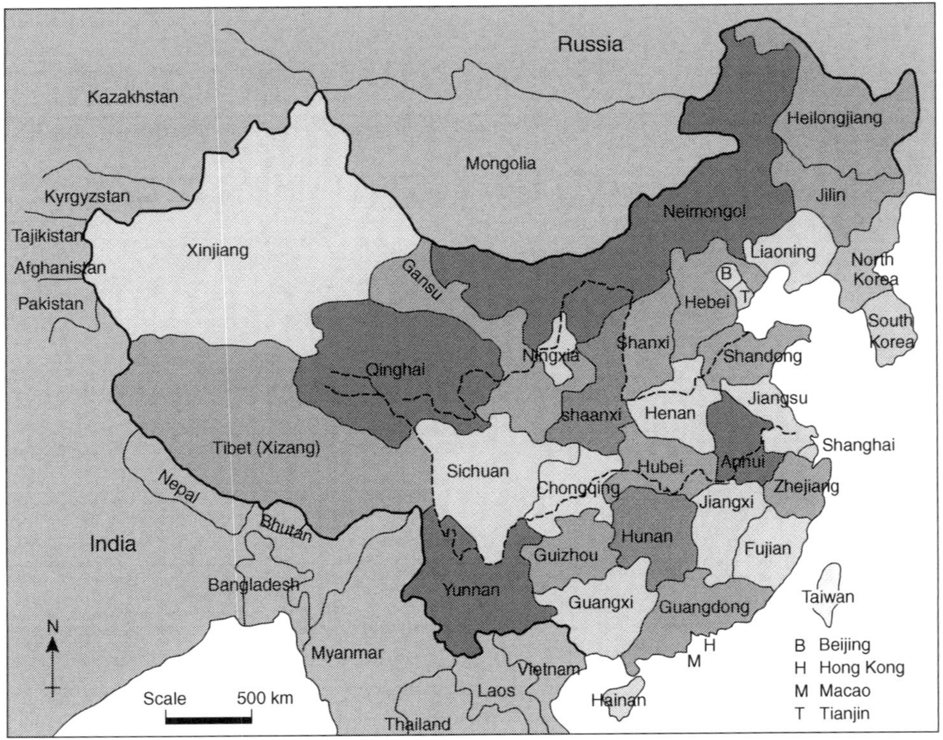

FIGURE 2.1 Provincial Map of China

Friends of Nature, also formed at this time. This influx of groups was met initially with wary acceptance on the part of local officials, as they sought to incorporate these groups into existing corporatist arrangements. Although allowing the formation of these groups, local officials sought to tightly control group activities and development through corporatism and also often heavy-handed means.

This associational revolution created opportunities for learning through direct interaction and experience, as officials in both Yunnan and Beijing experimented with solutions to address the policy failures created by decentralization. Beijing officials observed the neoliberal model promoted by the central government and directly experienced several successful partnerships with civil society pioneering new models of service delivery, leading to an increase in the number of autonomous groups. Beijing soon rivaled Yunnan in the number of active INGOs and grassroots groups. However, Beijing officials also observed the role of civil society in mobilizing citizens in the color revolutions, and this lesson led to the development of indirect tools of control versus the direct ones used previously. In a culmination of this learning process, the local Beijing government adopted regulations allowing more autonomous groups and created more indirect tools resulting in the ideal-type model of CA.

Yunnan initially allowed for the unchecked proliferation of civil society as a way of addressing the policy failures of decentralized service provision. Direct experience with these groups over a decade taught local officials that these groups play a largely positive role in development, poverty alleviation, and health outcomes. This lesson encouraged local officials to allow for the formation of increasing numbers of civil society groups. However, negative experiences with environmental groups and observing civil society overthrowing authoritarian regimes during the color revolutions also generated lessons for local officials about the dangers presented by these groups. In response, officials developed a set of new tools with which to control these more autonomous groups. For example, Yunnan established a new set of regulations governing INGO registration and financing of grassroots groups in 2009.

As Beijing increasingly allowed the formation of autonomous groups, Yunnan developed more sophisticated tools of state control, converging on the consultative authoritarianism model. In this chapter, I first trace the development of this CA model in Beijing, and then a similar process in Yunnan. Although this CA model first developed in Beijing and Yunnan, it soon diffused to other provinces as I examine in the next chapter.

LEARNING IN BEIJING: BUILDING CONSULTATIVE AUTHORITARIANISM[1]

Beijing (北京) is a city-province in northern China bordering Hebei and Tianjin provinces, and it is divided into 16 urban and suburban districts with two rural counties. Beijing is unique in that it serves as both a provincial and national capital; however, the local government in Beijing is organized in a similar fashion to that in other provinces with a four-level municipal government and local party authority held by the Beijing Party Secretary (北京市委书记). Beijing also houses national governmental and political institutions, including the National People's Congress. This dual role influences local politics in that officials are more exposed to national and international ideas in ways not experienced by cadres in the other three cases. In this way, Beijing local officials serve as both a mirror and microcosm of political trends occurring both nationally and regionally.

Beijing is one of the most developed cities in China with 26 *Fortune* Global 500 companies, the third highest in the world behind Tokyo and Paris. In 2012 Beijing's GDP per capita was 85,287 yuan (US$14,000) and nominal GDP was 1.8 trillion yuan (US$2.9 billion), representing a 9 percent increase from the previous year. The rapid development and urbanization in Beijing create a multitude of problems, such as strained social welfare provision and a large migrant population without access to basic

[1] Portions of the Beijing case also appear in the following article: Jessica C. Teets, "Let Many Civil Societies Bloom: The Rise of Consultative Authoritarianism in China," *The China Quarterly* January 2013: 1–20.

social services. China uses a household registration system that enables citizens of each locality to receive social services, such as education and health care, now provided by that local government after the collapse of the work-unit model of social services developed under Mao. The registered population of Beijing consists of those holding a permanent residence permit (*hukou* 户口) or a temporary residence permit. As of February 2010, the combined population of permanent and nonpermanent residents exceeded 22 million, with the latter category numbering 8 million to 9 million.[2] This large population places pressure on Beijing's local government to provide social welfare services such as compulsory education, health care, unemployment benefits, and pensions and eldercare services.

Eldercare services represent a large and growing portion of local budget expenditures; for example, in 2004, 10 percent of the population in Beijing was age 14 or younger, 79 percent between 15 and 64, and 11 percent were age 65 or older. The predicted population change by 2040 is approximately eight years, meaning that Beijing's population of more than 22 million residents will include a surge in senior citizens that will "break the back of China's state pension system."[3] Whereas eldercare is traditionally provided by the family, China's one-child policy limits the size of families so that a greater proportion of resources must be provided by the local state. In addition to the difficulty in developing new affordable models to provide these services to residents, a large number of migrant workers (*min gong* 民工) live in Beijing without official residence permits of either kind, which limits access to social services for the migrants and their children. In response to the need for new and innovative social welfare models, as well as Beijing's status as national capital, many domestic and international civil society groups opened offices in Beijing in the 1990s. The majority of groups active in

[2] "Beijing's Population Exceeds 22 Million," *China Daily*, February 26, 2010: available at http://www.chinadaily.com.cn/china/2010-02/26/content_9511839.htm

[3] Nicholas Eberstadt, "Power and Population in Asia," *Hoover Institute Policy Review* 123, 2010.

local issues focus on social welfare issues such as migrant education and eldercare.

By the 1990s, many of the consequences of public service and goods decentralization were visible in Beijing, as local officials struggled to meet the needs of a growing migrant population and provide the goods and services expected by urban workers after the dismantling of the danwei (work-unit) system, such as pensions and health care. At this time, many INGOs and grassroots groups began to form in Beijing seeking to address these problems. Initially, local officials attempted to incorporate these new organizations using the existing corporatist system by registering groups under the supervision of government agencies responsible for group activities and finances. This system hindered the formation of autonomous groups and used direct tools to control groups, such as repressing activities or sources of funding disapproved of by the supervisory agency. However, many groups bypassed the corporatist system. Larger groups often registered as for-profits and smaller ones operated without any legal status. Through observing the state–civil society relationships of advanced industrial states and gaining direct experience with these new groups, local officials slowly began to learn the governance benefits offered by an autonomous civil society.

Conversely, through observing the color revolutions in the early 2000s and having negative direct experiences with civil society, local officials also learned the dangers of these groups in their ability to mobilize citizens to challenge the state. In response, local officials developed a hybrid model of state–civil society relationships that encouraged autonomous civil society while developing new indirect tools of state control to guide groups in directions deemed beneficial by local officials. The CA model encourages pluralism as an autonomous civil society advocates policies and delivers services with local government partners; however, this model also creates control mechanisms through a toolbox of indirect positive and negative incentives. Next, I trace the process of learning though observation and experiences resulting in the development of the CA model in Beijing, as indicated through regulatory changes allowing for direct registration and new sources of funding.

LEARNING THROUGH OBSERVATION: IMITATING THE REGULATORY STATE MODEL

Local state officials in Beijing in many ways mirrored the national debate over developing a regulatory state in the early 1990s. This regulatory-state idea consists of transitioning governing institutions from a producer to more of a regulatory function, similar to the advanced industrial models of Germany, the UK, or the United States. Many party leaders, including Deng Xiaoping and Jiang Zemin, believed that economic reform required restructuring state institutions designed to produce market goods to those designed to regulate a combination of state-owned and private firms producing market goods. This idea of a regulatory state dominated local policy in Beijing, as well as nationally during the first 20 years of economic reform, and initiated reforms consisting of developing regulatory institutions and policies, building a professional and technocratic civil servant corps, decentralizing fiscal and public welfare functions to lower levels of government, and expanding the private sector composed of both firms and civil society organizations.

According to this model of a regulatory state, as the state withdraws from its former responsibilities, civil society develops to mediate problems associated with development and globalization, which benefits the local government as well as broader society. For example, Jude Howell argues that as the work-unit system of welfare disintegrated, social intermediaries became necessary to provide health and other welfare services and absorb the unemployed workers.[4] As a senior official in the Ministry of Civil Affairs succinctly explained, "The government cannot totally manage health, culture, social welfare and education. In the future China will have a big society and a small government. Social organizations will play a big role."[5] As pointed out by a professor

[4] Jude Howell, "New Directions in Civil Society: Organizing around Marginalized Interests," in *Governance in China*, Jude Howell, ed. (Lanham MD: Rowman & Littlefield, 2004), p. 144.

[5] Cited in Jude Howell, "Prospects for NGOs in China," *Development in Practice* 5, February 1995: 10.

at Peking University's Civil Society Research Center, this rhetoric of small state–big society legitimized the participation of civil society groups in aspects of public policy in a ways that were not possible earlier.[6]

The regulatory state model supports a collaborative but autonomous role for civil society, whereby groups provide public goods, mediate social unrest, and promote good governance, and the state provides a supportive legal and fiscal structure. For example, in addition to tax-exempt status, the U.S. government contributes approximately 56 percent of civil society groups' funding through a mixture of grants and contracts, and the German government supplies 65 percent.[7] The United States and Germany, as developed capitalist states, represent examples of China's potential future that policy makers use to discuss how the state, society, and economy might evolve over time. Throughout the 1990s, policy makers debated how to advance economic reform while maintaining social stability, and they used the regulatory-state model as a template for state-society reforms.[8] In response, the Chinese Communist Party undertook several rounds of government downsizing and decreased funding to mass organizations to encourage more space for the growth of social organizations to take over former government responsibilities, such as promoting self-governing trade and industry associations.[9] The Beijing municipal government allowed for a great deal of civil society activity and local innovation, ranging from charities to community-participation organizations to trade associations. These groups increasingly partnered with local government, often without official legal status.

6 Author interviews with professor at Peking University, Beijing, December 2006–January 2007.

7 Lester M. Salamon, *The Emerging Nonprofit Sector: An Overview*, (Manchester, UK: Manchester University Press, 1996).

8 Yang Cao and Victor G. Nee, "Comment: Controversies and Evidence in the Market Transition Debate," *American Journal of Sociology* 105, 2000: 1175–1189.

9 周师, "国内学术界关于私营企业主: 政治参与研究综述," 甘肃理论学刊 *Gansu Theory Research* 1, 2006: available at http://d.wanfangdata.com.cn/Periodical_gsllxk200601005.aspx

However, whereas this collaborative state-society model might be the ultimate goal, the method of transition and process of reform are fraught with opportunities for social unrest and state challenge. Therefore, the desire to control, but not completely halt, the process of civil society development drives the relationship between the local state and civil society groups. Throughout the reform era, officials proceeded with economic restructuring by "crossing the river by groping for stepping stones" (*mozhe shitou guo he* 摸着石头过河), which implies that change occurs by moving slowly from one stage to another after recalibrating to adjust for any negative effects. Beijing officials also apply this approach to political reform, especially the development of civil society.[10] This is the fundamental balance of government decision making in Beijing – encouraging the ability of civil society groups to solve social problems without sacrificing political control, often discussed as "social stability."

The observation of the successful state–civil society model used in the regulatory state model in the 1990s encouraged local officials to create a big state–small society by withdrawing the state from some of its former responsibilities and depending on social intermediaries like civil society to take up these responsibilities. Although this model was adapted for local conditions to form a regulatory state with Chinese characteristics, it was influential in local officials' learning process of appropriate state-society models for modern China. Furthermore, the lesson learned from observing the regulatory state model was reinforced by many initial experiences with emerging civil society groups in Beijing.

[10] See Wen Jiabao's and Hu Jintao's speeches about piloting political reform in Shenzhen; summary available at http://www.afpc.org/publication_listings/viewBulletin/1042. Also Hu Shuli, "Wen zongli de si 'yao' zhuzhang tigang jiling, wenhan shenyi, keshi wei zhenggai topokou, er zuizhongyaode shi jinkuai xingdongqilai" [Premier Wen outlines his proposal for the four "musts," which is profound and foresighted, and most important, can be mobilized quickly], Caijing guancha, August 28, 2010: available at http://www.chinaelections.org/printnews.asp?newsid=185772

LEARNING THROUGH EXPERIENCE: SOCIAL SERVICES INNOVATION

The responsibility for the provision of social welfare services, such as education, health care, elder and disabled care, resides with local government as part of a decentralized system of governance in China. With the collapse of the work-unit model of social welfare provision in the 1980s, local government faced pressure to develop a new model to provide these services. Beijing is divided administratively into districts (*qu* 区), supervised by Street Affairs Offices (*jiedao banshichu* 街道办事处) responsible for Residents' Committees (*jumin weiyuanhui* 居民委员会) in communities of approximately 2,000 households. These municipal administrative layers correspond roughly to the rural system of governance – county, township, and village levels.

Most Residents' Committees have six or seven staff appointed by the Street Affairs Office who have developed various service delivery models as part of the "community construction" (社区建设) initiative established by the central government to encourage local government to adapt to the rapid changes in service delivery in urban China – including both the influx of rural economic migrants and the wide service gaps left by the collapse of the work-unit model. Even though Beijing is a wealthy city-province, officials lacked models for service delivery that were not linked to state-owned enterprises, traditional practices of eldercare by families, and stable migration practices governed by the legal residence system (hukou). This difficulty in creating new service delivery models is illustrated by surveys from the Horizon Research Group conducted between 2003 and 2005 that find that the majority of Beijing residents are not satisfied with government service, primarily because of an overly bureaucratic approach to welfare, a "one size fits all" model that does not actually address existing problems.[11] In response to these

[11] Horizon Research Group as cited in Tony Saich, "Citizens' Perceptions of Governance in Rural and Urban China," *Journal of Chinese Political Science* 12, 2007: 1–28.

problems, especially providing social welfare services to vulnerable communities in Beijing such as the elderly and migrants, civil society groups initiated projects providing many of these services. Local officials allowed the proliferation of these projects at the lowest levels of administration to test innovative international models piloted by the groups, and this successful collaboration reinforced the idea of civil society mediating social problems advocated by the regulatory state model.

Shining Stone Community Action (SSCA), one of these grassroots groups, uses a community-participation model to deliver services to the migrant communities in the Beijing suburbs, and it contends that public participation in China's municipal affairs will increase citizen satisfaction as the government involves citizens in the provision of social services as partners of the local government, thereby giving them some influence in selecting types of services.[12] The founder of Shining Stone, Song Qinghua, joined one of China's original NGOs, Global Village of Beijing, in 1997 to encourage recycling. Five years later, Song formed SSCA (灿雨石) and registered initially as a consulting company as a result of difficulty receiving permission to register as a civil society group. The group focuses on developing urban community capacity to sustain participatory governance and has received a number of international grants to operate these projects. For example, Shining Stone initiated training programs for Street Affairs Office staff in Beijing with a grant from the Ford Foundation in 2002. After working in Beijing for seven years, the group finally was allowed to register as a nonprofit in 2009 and currently has seven full-time staff.

Shining Stone partnered with the Qingyuan Street Office to initiate a pilot project for service delivery to the growing migrant population in Beijing in 2007. This office supervises 28 neighborhoods with a total of 110,000 registered residents and 20,000 migrant workers. Each neighborhood has its own Residents' Committee responsible for household registration; public safety; enforcement of the one-child policy; and services for the elderly,

[12] Shining Stone Community Action website, http://www.ssca.org.cn/

disabled, and unemployed. SSCA worked with the Residents' Committees to train government officials and residents in participative methods and project management skills.[13] Next, using these skills, the participants jointly identified needed services and designed a pilot program to create participatory mechanisms to solve future problems cooperatively. The Qingyuan Street Office funded promising projects suggested by participants, such as a training center for migrants employed as domestic helpers and a cultural association, run by the participating residents and members of the Residents' Committees. These SSCA-proposed projects assist the Residents' Committees in meeting the social innovation requirement outlined by the municipal government of each committee implementing at least one such civic project by 2010. Many of the projects implemented with Shining Stone assistance address service delivery problems with either elderly or migrant residents, such as library and kindergarten programs for migrant children, community dinners where pensioners can buy a meal for less than one yuan, and training courses for migrants in urban skills such as learning how to use ATM machines.

In the past, urban and community development was strictly controlled by the local government without the participation of community members. However, in response to the collapse of the former model of welfare delivery, municipal officials recognize they must satisfy the needs of residents to prevent unrest but are uncertain how to adopt new models of service delivery without being overwhelmed by dissatisfaction as soon as they open channels for participation.[14] Additionally, both local officials and residents lack practical experience with policy participation. Shining Stone's pilot programs in Beijing help local officials manage the transition from former service delivery models to a new participatory model based on practices in advanced industrial states without generating a flood of social unrest and public

[13] Joern Geisselmann and Christine Warmer, "Public Participation in China's Municipal Affairs," *D+C Development and Cooperation Tribune*, July 2009: 294–296.

[14] Author interview with Ministry of Civil Affairs official, Beijing, January 16, 2007.

grievances.[15] Through its extensive training programs, SSCA promotes a new understanding of the roles of both state and civil society actors. According to this model of service delivery, local officials no longer provide all necessary services or use a "one-size" plan; instead, they fund and supervise projects proposed and run cooperatively by residents and committees. This collaboration allows both committees and community leaders to help the local state mediate between various interests and does not treat participation as "mass mobilization" in the way that previous models depending on public participation did. In this way, Shining Stone's pilot program in Qingyuan created positive collaborative experiences for local officials and a model for other communities to follow, both of which reinforce the idea of civil society partnering with the state to mediate social problems.

In addition to creating a stable path to transition to new social welfare models, Shining Stone's projects in Beijing improve local governance, which also positively reinforces the idea of collaborating with civil society. For example, as the Horizon surveys found, many residents view the Residents' Committees and Street Offices as intervening in their private affairs and acting in an arbitrary manner with little concern for their needs. The committees often do not investigate diverse needs across communities and use the same programs in communities with different needs, leading to noncooperation and occasional outbreaks of protest on the part of displeased residents. As SSCA's founder notes, uniform welfare provision presupposes that every neighborhood has identical needs, yet this is simply incorrect.[16] For example, she finds that in contrast to poorer areas, families in richer neighborhoods have their own books at home so library use is negligible; thus, government funding would be better spent meeting needs identified by the residents themselves rather than providing a community library in every community.

[15] Author interview with Beijing municipal representative, Beijing, June 22, 2010.

[16] Nick Young and Tina Qian, "Listening to the Community Is the Main Ingredient in Chinese NGO Recipe for City Governments," *China Development Brief*, March 2, 2006.

Services identified and provided by residents after deliberation with committees and Street Affairs Offices offer better local governance because residents stress quality and efficiency as they are directly affected by welfare provision and understand the local context and needs. As Song finds,

> The other day the staff in one neighborhood were discussing how, when they have to announce a new decision or policy, if they just put up posters (*tongzhi* 通知) to communicate this, people always criticize and complain. But if they hold a meeting to explain and discuss changes with the community, people usually see the point and are supportive, and there is less conflict.[17]

In addition to satisfied citizens, local officials gain recognition from supervisors through innovation awards that many provincial governments award to encourage policy innovation at lower levels that can then be tested and disseminated by provincial leaders. For example, in Beijing, one district official who partnered with Shining Stone in order to develop a new model for integrating migrant families into their new communities won an innovation in governance award with its cash reward and recognition from the municipal government.[18] This type of experience reinforces officials' idea of civil society partnering with the local state to mediate development problems, such as urbanization.

Shining Stone's successful collaboration with Street Affairs Offices and Residents' Committees in Beijing created a learning opportunity for local officials to see that civil society groups assist the state in mitigating social problems through innovation difficult for the state to achieve without public participation. Song argues that collaboration has changed officials' ideas of service delivery and more broadly of the role of civil society from the early 1990s: "Some people at the very top understand the need for this, but local government is more generally populated by bureaucrats operating on remote control. Many Chinese officials have their own idea of citizen participation: "We decide, you participate."[19]

17 Ibid.
18 Author interview with staff member of Shining Stone, Beijing, June 1,2008.
19 Young and Qian, "Listening to the Community Is the Main Ingredient.".

However, after the first pilot projects in selected communities in Beijing in 2002, Shining Stone's model of service delivery spread first across Beijing and then to other provinces. Throughout 2003, the group trained cadres and community workers across 26 urban communities in Beijing and 22 in Wuhan with funding support from the Ford Foundation, and then it trained local officials in Tianjin, Nanjing, and Shanghai with funding from the Ministry of Civil Affairs. In late 2006, Shining Stone secured funding from Oxfam Hong Kong to support a program to help migrant communities develop a plan for future development in Chengdu, Nanchang, and Ningbo. In this way, the participatory model of service coordination advocated by Shining Stone improved community welfare provision in Beijing and created a new model of service delivery that then diffused to other provinces.

The rapid growth of civil society in Beijing created many opportunities for this type of learning experience and reinforced the lesson of the regulatory state model that an autonomous civil society should be encouraged.

LEARNING THROUGH OBSERVATION: THE COLOR REVOLUTIONS

Illustrated by the Shining Stone case, collaboration with civil society helps local officials solve development issues and improve governance; however, officials must balance these benefits with social stability concerns. The Target Management Responsibility System prioritizes both economic development and social order goals for officials. Concerns with social stability, defined as social unrest that might threaten economic development and the party's political hegemony, permeate the party leadership and all levels of government in Beijing.[20] Statistics illustrate growing mass incidents of demonstrations, protests, and riots throughout the 2000s – totaling 87,000 in 2006, which was an increase of 6.6

[20] Author interview with faculty member of Central Party School, Beijing, June 30, 2007.

percent from 2005.[21] Since then, the number of protests in China doubled between 2006 and 2010, rising to 180,000 reported "mass incidents."[22] Since 2008, central government officials have shown rising concern about protests in the minority areas of Tibet and Xinjiang in Western China, and local officials in Beijing worry about the possibility that rising income gaps and unemployment among the migrant population and recent college graduates might trigger increasing unrest.[23] The ability of civil society organizations to mobilize citizen action against the state is well understood in Beijing in the wake of the color revolutions in the post-Soviet republics in the early 2000s, and local officials must balance the benefits of partnership with concerns for social mobilization and instability.

Observing the role played by civil society groups in the color revolutions, local officials learned, or were reminded of, how civil society can mobilize citizens to challenge the state. This lesson reinforces the need for more state control over group activity. As Dehong Yin notes, a constant concern of the Chinese government is that NGOs supported by governments of Western countries may subvert the rule of the Chinese Communist Party through "peaceful transformation," which encourages officials to pay particular attention to groups with funding from overseas foundations or foreign NGOs to prevent a color revolution in China.[24] As unemployment persists in both migrant and recent graduate populations in Beijing, local officials fear the ability of civil society groups to mobilize and link these populations as seen in the youth movements during the color revolutions.

[21] Murray Scot Tanner, "China Rethinks Unrest," *The Washington Quarterly* 27 (Summer 2004): 137–156.

[22] Alan Taylor, "Rising Protests in China," *The Atlantic*, February 17, 2012: available at http://www.theatlantic.com/infocus/2012/02/rising-protests-in-china/100247/

[23] Peter Ford, "China's Ant Tribe: Millions of Unemployed College Grads," *The Christian Science Monitor*, December 21, 2009; Jeremy Goldkorn, "*Legal Daily* Report on Mass Incidents in China in 2012," *Danwei*, January 6, 2013: available at http://www.danwei.com/a-report-on-mass-incidents-in-china-in-2012/

[24] Deyong Yin, "China's Attitude toward Foreign NGOs," *Washington University Global Studies Law Review* 8, 2009.

Thus, observing the color revolutions generated lessons that undermined the idea of civil society as a partner advocated by both the regulatory state model and successful collaboration experiences, such as with Shining Stone. As one staff member of a Beijing group notes, "After the color revolutions government officials have frequently visited our office and invited me to have tea to discuss the goals and strategies of the group."[25] She contends that the color revolutions led local officials to attempt to learn about all unregistered groups' "intentions and organizational structure."[26] Groups that were seen as attempting to organize broad segments of society were subject to harassment as described earlier, and in some cases were temporarily shut down. This was the experience of the China Development Brief (CDB), a group that serves as an information platform and capacity-building tool for China's growing nonprofit and philanthropic sectors, throughout 2007. This organization was temporarily closed using a prohibition on conducting surveys after staff organized a party to celebrate its twelfth anniversary, which managed to easily attract many founders of Chinese NGOs, researchers, staff from international development agencies, and journalists to one location. This rapid mobilization was seen as threatening to local Beijing officials. As Nick Young, the founder of CDB explained, "In the past two years, prompted by concerns about 'color revolutions' elsewhere, security agents had been keeping a close watch on China's civil society. It seems that a sweep of potential troublemakers was deemed overdue."[27] However, CDB reopened shortly after Nick Young left and currently has more than 47,000 subscribers to its online newsletter and 5,000 to its print issues.[28]

In addition to the lessons drawn from observations of the color revolution, the global financial crisis helped discredit the regulatory

[25] Author interview with staff member of domestic NGO, Beijing, February 1, 2007.

[26] Ibid.

[27] Nick Young, "Why China Cracked Down on My Nonprofit," *Christian Science Monitor*, December 4, 2007.

[28] See the CDB website at http://www.chinadevelopmentbrief.cn

state model now seen as a failure rather than a successful model. During the global financial crisis, Beijing's local economy was not as tied to exports as was that of the coastal cities in the south; thus, it felt less of a manufacturing impact but instead suffered the decline of the construction sector and hiring freezes by multinational corporations that disproportionately affected migrants and recent college graduates. After central and local officials implemented a stimulus package, Beijing experienced a surge in consumer sales and a slow resurgence in building as evidenced by a 10 percent increase in local GDP in 2009. This perceived success of the state-led model over the regulatory state model increased the prominence of ideas that imagined a larger, more active state role than under the regulatory-state idea, now delegitimized by the decline in the U.S. economy during the economic crisis. A group of scholars and policy makers advocating "New Left (*xin zuopai* 新左派)" ideas of an active state challenged the hegemony of the 1990s regulatory-state idea.[29] Although policy shifts toward the New Left were already underway before the global economic crisis, the crisis accelerated this trend. The perceived failure of the U.S.-style capitalist model has greatly undermined neoliberal reformers in China who would like to see a more complete dismantling of the state-owned sector and rise of non-state actors such as civil society.[30]

New Left ideology is characterized by an emphasis on state power to redress the problems of injustice and other negative effects of privatization, marketization, and globalization. Following the Marxist tradition, New Left theorists believe that the capitalist mode of production is grounded in exploitation, and that a civil society developed under capitalism is simply a vehicle for ensuring the dominance of capitalist interest groups.[31] Thus,

[29] Pankaj Mishra, "China's New Leftist," *The New York Times Magazine*, October 15, 2006.

[30] Zhiyue Bo and Gang Chen, "Global Financial Crisis and the Voice of the New Left in China," *East Asian Institute Background Brief* No. 443, March 26, 2009: available at http://www.eai.nus.edu.sg/BB443.pdf

[31] Wang Hui, "Contemporary Chinese Thought and the Question of Modernity," in *Whither China? Intellectual Politics in Contemporary China*, Xudong Zhang, ed. (Durham NC: Duke University Press, 2001), p. 185.

the New Left advocates the development of new state-controlled mechanisms for participation and distrusts current civil society in China as representing dominant capitalist interests at the expense of social justice. However, New Left ideas differ from Maoist ideology, whereby civil society was incorporated into the state, in promoting instead state guidance of a fairly autonomous civil society similar to the CA model.

The rising influence of the New Left illustrated in the Harmonious Society policies adopted in 2005 represents a process of ideational divergence from the regulatory-state ideas of the 1990s.[32] Policy makers in Beijing after the mid-2000s responded to these contradictory lessons by creating a new state–civil society model that simultaneously allows for the expansion of relatively autonomous groups and the development of nuanced state control mechanisms.

DEVELOPMENT OF CONSULTATIVE AUTHORITARIANISM IN BEIJING

This learning process in Beijing resulted in the development of a new model of state–civil society relationship that merges the advanced industrial state idea of a relatively autonomous civil society collaborating with the state to solve social problems with the New Left idea of state guidance of groups to protect society from narrow interest groups and social instability. This consultative authoritarianism model is characterized by two main aspects – a pluralistic society participating in policy formation and implementation and the use of multiple nuanced tools of state control. As explained at the end of Chapter 1, whereas the goals of this consultative authoritarianism are the same (i.e., control), the social pluralism and differentiated state control present in this model distinguish it from the earlier corporatist model.

For example, the CA model differs significantly from corporatism by allowing the presence of multiple, competing autonomous

[32] He Li, "Debating China's Economic Reform: New Leftists vs. Liberals," *Journal of Chinese Political Science* 15, 2010: 1–23.

groups. These groups no longer serve as appendages to the state but possess independent staff, resources, and projects.[33] Although groups were initially required to register with Civil Affairs and a supervisory agency, as described in the preceding chapter, these regulations have not caused the incorporation of civil society. Despite variation in autonomy, most groups establish independent projects and strategies, and any cooperation with local government results from mutual recognition of comparative advantage. Additionally, local government allows the creation and often collaborates with unregistered groups, as the SSCA example illustrates. These groups compete with one another for resources and policy space and also participate in the whole process of policy making, including policy formation, no longer just in policy implementation as seen with the corporatist model.[34]

The second difference between the CA and corporatist models is the type of control mechanisms used by the state. Instead of using direct methods of control, the state increasingly uses more nuanced and indirect methods to create positive and negative incentives for group behavior.[35] Positive incentives consist of access to funding, the policy process, and legal status, whereas negative incentives consist of police harassment of staff, fines, and uncertain legal status. This model uses new tools to reach former corporatist aims of encouraging groups to work toward meeting state goals, as the earlier examples of One Kilogram More and Oxfam illustrate. The positive incentives Beijing officials used with One Kilogram More and negative incentives used with Oxfam demonstrate how these new indirect tools are used to direct civil society activity. As these examples illustrate, local officials are using more nuanced tools of state control to manage autonomous civil society groups, resulting in the creation of a new model of consultative authoritarianism.

[33] Anita Chan and Jonathan Unger, "China, Corporatism, and the East Asian Model," *The Australian Journal of Chinese Affairs* 33, 1995: 29–53.

[34] Andrew Mertha, "'Fragmented Authoritarianism 2.0': Political Pluralization in the Chinese Policy Process," *The China Quarterly*, 200, 2009: 995.

[35] Author interview with Kang Xiaoguang, Beijing, July 7, 2010.

Observations of successful regulatory states and experiences with groups like SSCA taught Beijing officials the benefits of autonomous civil society participation. However, observations of the color revolutions and experiences with the mobilization capacity of groups like CDB taught official the potential dangers of civil society. This learning process gradually created the CA model in Beijing, where local officials encouraged the expansion of autonomous civil society through regulatory change. Since 2009, the municipal government eased registration regulations for selected groups that now only require registration with the local Bureau of Civil Affairs and no longer require a supervisory agency (直接登记) and initiated a grants program in 2010 of 300 million yuan (US$44 million) to fund groups proposing social innovation projects.[36] This model that the Beijing government calls "Broad Registration, Tight Supervision (宽审批、严监管)" has two main goals – to register all approved groups and directly supervise the development of these groups. Government officials are being encouraged not to operate social organizations on their own, but to let citizens start groups (民间化) to create a grassroots civil society operated by citizens rather than officials.[37] These regulatory changes encourage the formation of independent civil society and tools to guide groups toward activities in which the local state would like to see the groups working, such as social innovation to solve new welfare provision problems.

In Beijing, the evolution from less autonomous groups–direct controls to more autonomous groups–indirect controls occurred through the learning process detailed in this chapter throughout the 1990s and 2000s. Although variation still exists across provinces in the degree of adoption of this new local state–civil society relationship, after 2008, there is increasing evidence of a rough

[36] 陈荞 [Chen Qiao], "民政部：公益慈善类等3类社会组织有望直接登记 [Ministry of Civil Affairs: Sees Potential for Three Types of Social Organizations to Register Directly]," 京华时报*[Beijing Times]*, May 24, 2011.

[37] 温薷 [Wen Ru], "北京公务员等将逐步退出社会组织 [Beijing Officials Will Progressively Withdraw from Civil Society Groups]," 新京报 *[Beijing Times]*, February 27, 2011.

national convergence on this model, as I explore next in Yunnan province.

LEARNING IN YUNNAN: DEVELOPING NEW TOOLS OF STATE CONTROL

Yunnan province (云南) is located in the southwest of China, bordering Myanmar, Laos, and Vietnam. Yunnan is a mountainous area, especially near its northwestern border with Tibet, and is the most diverse province in China ecologically as well as ethnically. Yunnan has 18,000 of the 30,000 species of plants in China, and 25 of the country's 56 ethnic groups, with approximately 38 percent of the population members of minority groups including the Yi, Bai, Hani, Zhuang, Dai, and Miao.[38]

Yunnan's three main economic sectors are natural resources, such as mining and hydroelectric power, tourism, and agriculture, especially cash crops such as tobacco. The province's GDP in 2012 was 1.03 trillion yuan (US$166 billion) with an annual growth rate of 13 percent, compared to 5.41 trillion yuan (US$881 billion) in Jiangsu, one of the wealthiest provinces. The hydroelectricity industry is part of the West-East Electricity Transmission Project, whereby the electricity produced in Yunnan is transported east to Guangdong Province. Tourism is a large component of the economy, with 2.75 million Chinese visiting during the National Holiday alone in 2008. In 2004, tourism revenues amounted to 37 billion yuan (approximately US$5 billion), accounting for 13 percent of GDP, and this has increased over the past few years. By 2012, international tourism revenue rose 30.7 percent from the previous year to 5.5 billion yuan (US$920 million), and domestic tourism revenue increased 24 percent to 70.62 billion yuan (US$11 billion).

The main development challenges facing Yunnan's government are poverty reduction, environmental protection for tourist sites, and HIV/AIDS prevention and treatment. Yunnan is one of

[38] "Global 200 List Priority Ecoregion" WWF (World Wildlife Fund), 1996: available at http://www.biodiversityconservancy.net/indexWhere.htm

China's most underdeveloped provinces with more poverty-stricken counties than other provinces. For example, in 1994, about 7 million people lived below the poverty line, set at less than an annual average income of 300 yuan per capita. This rate has been reduced from 4.05 million in 2000 to 2.86 million by 2008, through a poverty alleviation plan focusing on soil improvement, resource conservation, and infrastructure development. Despite this impressive achievement in poverty reduction, Yunnan still lags behind most other provinces in overall development, with the most impoverished counties in 2012. In addition, Yunnan accounts for the largest number of reported AIDS cases in China, with the exception of Henan province. In 1989, the first indigenous cases were reported in heroin users near the Burmese border.[39] Officials estimate that the province has 80,000 infected people, mostly intravenous drug users who have spread the disease by sharing needles. However, low awareness of the transmission and prevention of the virus is a major contributor to spreading the epidemic from high-risk groups (such as drug users and sex workers) to the general population, often through blood donations at state-owned hospitals.

In response to these problems of poverty, conservation, and disease, many domestic and international civil society groups formed in Yunnan in the 1990s. Yunnan is often cited as one of the top three provinces in regard to civil society activity, although this claim is difficult to verify because many domestic groups operate informally and international groups register as for-profit enterprises. As a result of Yunnan's development challenges and ecological diversity, the majority of groups initially focused on the environment and poverty alleviation. In the capital city of Kunming, several groups formed to focus on AIDS testing and treatment in response to the growing AIDS epidemic. Although national laws required that these groups register through the dual

[39] Ministry of Health, Joint United Nations Program on HIV/AIDS, and World Health Organization, *Update on the HIV/AIDS Epidemic and Response in China*, 2006: available at http://data.unaids.org/publications/External-Documents/rp_2005chinaestimation_25jan06_en.pdf

management system, local officials struggling with the challenges of poverty, a growing AIDS epidemic, and rapid environmental degradation allowed many groups to exist informally as for-profit enterprises or without any legal status whatsoever. As indicated in the comparative chart in Figure I.4, Yunnan had relatively few controls that local officials used with civil society and because of its ecological and human challenges attracted many INGO and grassroots groups in the 1990s. During this time period, Yunnan was characterized by high levels of group autonomy and low levels of state control, in comparison to the lower levels of group autonomy and higher levels of state control found in Beijing.

Throughout the 1990s, local officials worked with several groups to use international resources to battle these development challenges. Although many of these collaboration experiences taught local officials that civil society offers practical benefits, negative experiences with environmental groups hindering development projects in the 2000s offered the opposite lesson. In response, Yunnan province adopted new, more stringent provincial laws in 2009 enforcing the dual registration system, especially for INGOs. The addition of state controls moved Yunnan toward the Beijing model of consultative authoritarianism.

LEARNING THROUGH EXPERIENCE: TREATING THE AIDS EPIDEMIC

In the 1980s, problems such as AIDS were still seen as the sole responsibility of the government, and local officials viewed with suspicion any nongovernmental participation. However, as a result of required local government streamlining beginning in the late 1980s and accelerating through the 1990s, the size of local government in Yunnan was reduced with a corresponding decrease in capacity.[40] Additionally, many new responsibilities

[40] See Kiril Tochkov, "Interregional Transfers and the Smoothing of Provincial Expenditure in China," *China Economic Review* 18, 2007: 54–65, for a description of lower revenue for localities: "In the second half of the 1990s, the cushioning effect of net transfers fell even further and reached a historic low of 53 percent. This suggests that the reform of 1994, which put an end to the

were devolved from the central government without supplementary funding, creating a problem of unfunded mandates. Yunnan is one of the most indebted provinces, with budget shortfalls of more than 400 million yuan (US$65 million) in 2004, and the National Audit Office ranked the capital city, Kunming, as one of nine most indebted cities with a debt-to-GDP ratio more than 100 percent in 2012. In this environment, local governments needed to provide higher levels of goods and services with fewer staff and decreased budgets. In addition to declining capacity and unfunded mandates, competition for promotion and recognition from higher levels of government further motivated local officials to cooperate with civil society to deliver public services. The legacy of the "experimental points" policy process is that local officials are encouraged with the formal or informal backing of higher-level policy makers to experiment with local policy. If judged to be conducive to current priorities, model experiences extracted from the initial experiments are disseminated to other regions, and these local leaders are typically promoted to higher positions creating an innovation incentive.[41]

This decrease in local state capacity corresponded with an increase in funding sources for civil society groups in the 1990s. These funding sources explicitly excluded local governments but actively sought to fund projects for grassroots groups.[42] The World Bank and other international funding agencies, such as the Ford Foundation, desired to fund development through

system of fiscal contracts and strengthened the fiscal power of the central government, did not reverse the decline in expenditure smoothing." See also Chan Che-Po and Gavin Drewry, "The 1998 State Council Organizational Streamlining: Personnel Reduction and Change of Government Function," *Journal of Contemporary China* 10, no. 29, 2001: 553–572; and Yang Dali, "Rationalizing the Chinese State: The Political Economy of Government Reform," in *Remaking the Chinese State: Strategies, Society, and Security*, Chao Chien-min and Bruce J. Dickson, eds. (London: Routledge, 2001).

41 Sebastian Heilmann, "From Local Experiments to National Policy: The Origins of China's Distinctive Policy Process," *The China Journal* 59, January 2008: 1–30.

42 Jessica Mathews, "Power Shift: The Rise of Global Civil Society," *Foreign Affairs* 76, January/February 1997; Lester Salamon and Helmut K. Anheier, *The Emerging Not-For-Profit Sector: An Overview* (Manchester, UK; New York: Manchester University Press, 1996).

more bottom-up initiatives.[43] Thus, as the local government lost capacity, local groups were gaining capacity through access to international resources from which the local state was excluded. This environment created the motivation for local officials to collaborate with civil society groups in service delivery as well as rising capacity among these groups to undertake expanded projects in the poorest areas. As one group member explained, "my organization's role is service delivery – providing services that the government cannot provide. While government investment in health is increasing, the majority goes to the cities with 80 percent of the funding serving 20 percent of the population."[44] In order to take advantage of this new funding stream, officials in Yunnan partnered with existing groups or supported the creation of new groups throughout the late 1990s and early 2000s, creating opportunities for learning through experience.[45]

One example of local officials learning about civil society through direct experience is from the spread of the AIDS epidemic across Yunnan in the 1990s. Despite a population of more than 44 million, the province employed only 200 health workers trained in AIDS testing and treatment by the end of the 1990s. As local finances and medical expertise could no longer cover testing and treatment, local officials in the Kunming Health Bureau began to collaborate with AIDS groups to gain this expertise and funding. Through this experience, policies regulating AIDS testing and treatment changed to align with Western practices, and the relationship between local officials and these groups strengthened.

Kunming (昆明) is a prefecture located in central Yunnan province composed of Kunming, the capital city of the province, and the surrounding counties and townships. Yunnan neighbors

[43] Bishwapriya Sanyal, "Cooperative Autonomy: The Dialectic of State-NGOs Relationship in Developing Countries," *International Institute for Labour Studies*, 1994: Available at http://www.ilo.org/global/publications/ilo-bookstore/order-online/books/WCMS_PUBL_9290145307_EN/lang–en/index.htm

[44] Author interview with founder of professional health care association, Simao, Yunnan, February 8, 2007.

[45] Kenneth Foster, "Associations in the Embrace of an Authoritarian State: State Domination of Society?" *Studies in Comparative International Development* 35, Winter 2001: 84–109.

the "golden triangle" area spanning the mountains of Myanmar, Laos, and Thailand that is one of Asia's two main opium-producing areas, and combats drug and human trafficking occurring across its borders. The government blames this easy access to drugs for the HIV/AIDS epidemic (*aizibing* 艾滋病) seen primarily in Kunming but also in other border cities in Yunnan. The local health bureau initially dealt with HIV/AIDS through establishing an office to administer all HIV/AIDS programs and providing testing and treatment at state-owned hospitals. Testing and treatment at the hospitals required registration with an identity card, which meant that many people chose not to receive testing or treatment for fear of being arrested. This was a valid concern as local police frequently attempted to meet quotas for arrests by waiting in front of the testing and treatment clinic to arrest suspected drug offenders.[46] Officials viewed AIDS primarily as a law-and-order issue and only secondarily as a health issue, giving the Public Security Bureau policy predominance over this issue. Additionally, many of the state-owned clinics lacked the financial and medical resources necessary for AIDS testing and treatment.

In response, by the late 1990s, many grassroots and INGO health-related groups formed in Kunming. Whereas some of these groups represented sex workers and others drug addicts, all presented their projects as impacting the health of the broader society in Yunnan. Under the pressure of dealing with a growing health epidemic with limited resources, local officials in Kunming's Health Bureau began to discuss possible collaboration with these new groups that could access international funding and models, as many Western countries had already invested many resources in creating testing and treatment models in the 1980s. Using the interpersonal networks of employees and grassroots groups working on AIDS-related issues, several INGOs proposed pilot programs with the Health Bureau in Kunming.[47] For

[46] Author interview with staff member at health-related INGO, Kunming, June 4, 2007.

[47] Author interview with health-related INGO staff members, Kunming, May 30, 2007.

example, the head of one of these grassroots groups, whose founder is a retired Health Bureau official, worked with his former colleagues to convince the Health Bureau to permit a pilot program introducing a new model of HIV/AIDS testing and medical care to treat the growing epidemic with resources to which the local government did not have access.[48] Thus, Yunnan province began one of the first pilot programs of this type in the country, along with Guangxi Autonomous Region, in 1999.

Although local officials considered other options, these were perceived as politically risky. For example, local officials could appeal to the central government for more resources, but then they would have to reveal the extent of the problem and the fact that the local government could not address it. This would likely have resulted in the demotion of provincial officials at a minimum. A second option would have been the strategy of repression of AIDS patients and activists seen in Henan; however, this strategy led to whole villages decimated by AIDS and the creation of an epidemic that might have been prevented.[49] The Yunnan government originally followed this strategy also; however, it viewed the escalating spread of the disease and decided this method was too costly and risky for the long term. Central officials forced Henan officials to increase subsidies to AIDS patients and to change treatment policies to be directly monitored by the Ministry of Health.[50] Local officials chose the strategy of collaboration with civil society based on initial learning experiences and access to trusted partners though interpersonal networks.

One of these pilot programs beginning in the early 2000s and organized by Population Services International (PSI/China), partnered with several small grassroots AIDS groups to combine the

[48] Author interview with head of health-related group, Kunming, May 6, 2007.

[49] For a good overview of how INGO activity has changed local officials' perceptions of civil society, see Vincent Rollet, "The Transnational Origin of a Local Response to HIV/AIDS in Henan Province," *China Perspectives* 1, 2009: 17–28: available at http://chinaperspectives.revues.org/4769

[50] *Xinhua*, "Ten-Fold Subsidy Increase for Henan AIDS Patients," December 17, 2012, available at http://news.xinhuanet.com/english/china/2012-12/17/c_132045931.htm

international resources of the INGO with access to this vulnerable population and government agencies through the grassroots groups.[51] Because of the expense of the medicines and technology, PSI supplied these resources; however, because the clients trusted the members of the grassroots groups, they were willing to receive testing and treatment at the clinics. These two partnered with the local Health Bureau to create clinics separate from the state-owned hospitals that specialized in HIV/AIDS. The Health Bureau secured all necessary permits and also, through the Public Security Bureau, instructed local police to not make arrests at the clinics. In addition to advocating anonymous testing and free treatment at the clinics, these groups also promoted a clean needle and methadone program for drug users. As a result of the success of this pilot, the Health Bureau received funding to expand the program in 2004 by opening more than 1,500 methadone-maintenance treatment clinics for about 300,000 heroin users by 2008 and establishing a National Training Center for methadone-maintenance treatment to provide clinical and technical support.

This successful collaboration taught officials at the local Health Bureau about the benefits of civil society. In fact, upper-level government officials recognized these officials for governance innovation. The spread of AIDS is not only an important challenge facing the Yunnan government, but also many other provinces and the national government. Following the successful Yunnan pilot and foreign study tours, the State Council and Ministry of Health officially advocated needle programs for all provinces.[52] In addition to recognition from supervisors, the local Health Bureau claimed increased treatment numbers while not using any additional government resources, helping officials meet promotion goals. This collaboration experience not only taught

[51] Author interview with PSI staff members, Kunming, May 30, 2007.

[52] Jim Yardley, "Chinese City Emerges as Model in AIDS Fight," *The New York Times*, June 16, 2005: available at http://www.nytimes.com/2005/06/16/international/asia/16aids.html?ex=1179374400&en=92eb25ad0168b6ad&ei=5070

local officials about how civil society might serve as a partner to battle social problems, but also created a model for other civil society groups in Yunnan and across the country.

In addition to the experience of direct project collaboration, the use of trainings, research briefs, and site tours conducted by many AIDS groups convinced the Kunming Health Bureau to approach HIV/AIDS differently than other provinces in China. The groups advocated for anonymous HIV/AIDS testing and care, which create less fear among drug users or sex workers.[53] Also, the groups advocated treating HIV/AIDS as a public health concern rather than a law-and-order issue, moving policy responsibility more firmly under the Health Bureau's exclusive purview. This approach differs dramatically from that in other provinces, such as Anhui and Henan with recently revealed AIDS epidemics. As one staff member noted, "We do not have a mandate for advocacy, but I believe that groups do influence government policy indirectly through pilot projects and informal discussions with government officials. By gaining officials' trust and then offering outside funding and best practices we play a role in influencing thinking and policy."[54] Collaboration allowed these groups to use access to policy makers in the Health Bureau to indirectly advocate for changes in Kunming policy toward HIV/AIDS.[55] As explained in Chapter 4, this information role played by civil society allows groups to participate in local officials' learning process indirectly as well as directly through project partnerships.

Collaboration resulted in improved provision of public goods, recognition and advancement for local officials, and changing local AIDS policy from a criminal focus to a health care focus. By 2012, there were 180 active groups in this policy area, and Yunnan served as the national model for an AIDS Action Plan that

[53] Author interview with domestic AIDS group staff member, Kunming, June 6, 2007.

[54] Author interview with PSI staff member, Kunming, May 30, 2007.

[55] Author interview with staff member in health-related INGO, Kunming, June 4, 2007.

encourages expanding the role of social organizations.[56] This positive experience of collaborating with civil society taught local officials about the governance benefits offered by emerging civil society and motivated the continued expansion of more autonomous civil society in Yunnan. In fact, after the international foundation Global Fund to Fight AIDS, Tuberculosis and Malaria (Global Fund) froze funding to approximately 106 groups in 2011, local officials continued to fund at least half of these projects directly.[57]

LEARNING THROUGH OBSERVATION: THE ECO-ETHNIC TOURISM MODEL

In addition to the direct experiences with emerging civil society analyzed earlier, Yunnan officials were also exposed to the ecotourism model used in Costa Rica, where many local officials traveled in the mid-1990s on study tours to learn about public-private partnerships (PPP) in the tourism industry.[58] This PPP model requires that the government collaborate with private tourism firms and local community groups to create sustainable tourism that benefits the local community. Yunnan, like Costa Rica, is known for its biodiversity and is a popular destination for both domestic and international tourism, comprising a large part of local revenues. Promoting tourism is a vital factor in the evaluation of local officials, which motivated officials to study the ecotourism model in Costa Rica. INGOs, such as The Nature Conservancy (TNC), and the provincial government financed and organized these study tours and then disseminated the model to local officials at all levels of government through study sessions and pilot-site visits. This model depends on preserving the

[56] *The China Action Plan to Prevent and Control AIDS during the 12th Five-Year Plan Period.* State Council, 2010: available at http://www.wpro.who.int/health_services/china_nationalhealthplan.pdf

[57] Author interview with Marta Jagusztyn, consultant on the HIV Sector in Yunnan, December 14, 2012.

[58] Author interview with local official from Tourism Bureau, Lijiang, Yunnan, March 22, 2007.

environment and including local populations to create sustainable tourism. Motivated by lessons drawn from this model, a party secretary and county official collaborated with two ethnic-preservation groups in the Simao prefecture, proposing cultural protection projects to promote eco-ethnic tourism. This model of tourism focuses on both ethnic harmony and sustainable tourism, important targets in cadre evaluations. In these two examples from Simao, civil society indirectly and directly influences the learning process: indirectly through TNC advocacy of international best practices and directly through official collaboration with grassroots groups. In response to learning about this eco-ethnic tourism model used abroad, local officials partnered with two grassroots groups to preserve tourism sites such as temples.

Simao prefecture (思茅), which changed its name in 2007 to Pu'er (普洱), is located in southern Yunnan province and is composed of Simao city and the surrounding counties and townships. It is a middle income and population prefecture in the province concentrating mostly on agriculture, especially the famous Pu'er tea. Although it contains a number of farmers' cooperatives and poverty-alleviation groups, ethnic-preservation groups are the most prevalent civil society organizations. Simao prefecture is one of the most ethnically diverse areas in China with more than 24 minority groups. Whereas consistent governance of minority regions is important for promotion because of social stability concerns about separatist movements, these areas are also becoming more important for developing the local economy as a result of ethnic and ecological tourism.

In many provinces, preservation of cultural and ethnic heritages increases tourism associated with sites on the UNESCO World Heritage List, which aids in economic development and poverty alleviation.[59] For example, 52.4 million tourists traveled to Yunnan in 2002, representing an average increase of 16 percent from 1998. Over this same time period, the total income of the

[59] Ma Shu-Yun and Chan Wai-Yin, "The Provision of Public Goods by a Local Entrepreneurial State: The Case of Preservation of the Nanyue Relics in China," *The Journal of Development Studies* 41, October 2003: 119–141.

province from the tourism industry increased from 13.69 billion yuan to 28.99 billion yuan (US$2.2 billion to $4.7billion), and the proportion between total tourism income and GDP increased from 7.6 percent to 12.8 percent. In addition to providing a large percentage of local state revenue, the number of people directly or indirectly engaged in the tourism industry reached 1.605 million by the early 2000s. In fact, the *Plan for Development of Tourism Industry during the Tenth Five Year Plan Period in Yunnan* emphasizes the creation of cultural and ethnic preservation sites to increase ethnic tourism in Yunnan, especially the Xianggelila area and cities of Dali, Lijiang, and Diqing in what local officials call a "bio-culture" tourism model whereby areas of biological interest such as tropical rainforests are combined with the traditions and customs of the minority nationalities.[60]

In the 1990s, two ethnic groups formed community advocacy organizations in Simao prefecture to protect ethnic culture, religion, music, and traditions. These two organizations, representing the Dai and Wa ethnicities, are informal and unregistered. In the mid-2000s, the Dai group advocated for government funding to rebuild a temple and community center; the Wa group sought government funding to build a traditional housing complex to use as a community center. The village leader (*cunzhang* 村长) at that time headed the Dai group and used his official status to access local decision makers at upper levels of government as well as informal channels of personal networks.[61] He and the local party secretary went to Beijing four times to appeal for protected status for the temple and finally secured it in 2006. This protected status means that the temple receives money from the local, provincial, and national levels of government for preservation and cultural activities, such as traditional music training. By securing a protected cultural status for the temple, the group leader ensured that the continued preservation of the temple is enshrined in local

60 Margaret Byrne Swain, "Developing Ethnic Tourism in Yunnan, China: Shilin Sani," *Tourism Recreation Research* 14, 1998: 33–40.
61 Author interview with head of ethnic Dai group, Simao, February 19, 2007.

policy. In the second case, the leader of the Wa group is a retired village leader and used his personal connections in local bureaucracies to help garner financial support from the county government.[62] He secured more than 300,000 yuan (US$49,255) in funding from the county government to protect ethnic culture through building a community center offering classes and activities. Although current and retired officials run both of these groups, interviews indicated that the motivation for advocacy was responding to the ethnic group's needs and not mandated from the local government.[63]

These two cases raise an important question: why would local officials agree to fund these projects with declining local revenue and increasing public goods responsibilities? Several rounds of interviews with these local officials suggest that based on ecotourism models from abroad, they agreed to preservation projects with these groups to meet promotion goals of economic development through eco-ethnic (bio-cultural) tourism. These projects were also intended to assist with social stability maintenance through good community relationships with ethnic minorities. As the county official noted, funding the community center project supports the local government's minority protection policy and helps promote ethnic tourism in Yunnan.[64] Similarly, as the party secretary contended, he assisted the Dai group for three reasons: to promote ethnic tourism that will help residents through job creation, to help him receive a promotion by reaching development and stability goals, and to promote his status and reputation in the local community (he called this "people's opinion").[65] Although local officials initially collaborated with ethnic-preservation groups to imitate the tourism and development

[62] Author interview with head of ethnic Wa group, Simao, February 15, 2007.

[63] Author interviews, Simao, February–March 2007.

[64] Author interview with county official, Simao, March 9, 2007.

[65] Author interview with a local party secretary in Simao prefecture, February 18, 2007; see Lily Tsai for an in-depth examination of how embeddedness in local communities creates accountability for government officials without democracy: *Accountability without Democracy: Solidary Groups and Public Goods Provision in Rural China* (Cambridge, UK: Cambridge University Press, 2007).

success found in the ecotourism model, successful collaboration experiences reinforced the idea of partnering with civil society to help meet evaluation requirements for economic development and social stability in an ethnically diverse province. As a result of this collaboration, the party secretary was recognized by the vice governor as a "rising official," likely to be quickly promoted.[66]

These two cases emphasize how local officials learned first through observation of this ecotourism model but then through direct experience with grassroots groups in the community. In this instance, similar to the AIDS case, INGOs played a vital role in disseminating information that encouraged more collaboration with civil society. Not only did TNC's study tours and information sessions help provide this information to local officials, but the organization also ran a series of pilot programs in Northern Yunnan that offered opportunities for direct experience.[67] Exposure to this model coupled with the successful experience of partnering with grassroots groups reinforced the lesson of pursuing a more collaborative relationship.

LEARNING THROUGH EXPERIENCE: WATER WARRIORS CONFRONT THE LOCAL STATE

As illustrated by the AIDS and eco-ethnic tourism cases, the majority of local officials' experiences with civil society in Yunnan had positive outcomes that reinforced the idea of the local state maintaining a collaborative relationship with autonomous groups. These experiences were further supported by the PPP model of Costa Rican ecotourism. However, not all experiences with civil society in Yunnan motivated local officials to have a collaborative relationship with these groups. Environmental conservation groups clashed with local officials over development projects and generated lessons about how civil society mobilizes

[66] Author interview with the vice governor of Yunnan province, February 20, 2007.

[67] Series of author interviews with TNC staff, Kunming and Lijiang, 2007–2011; see TNC's nature reserve model for more information about this eco-tourism model, available at http://blog.nature.org/2010/11/in-china-a-new-old-approach/

citizens to challenge state authority. For example, many environmental INGOs and grassroots groups opposed local governments' plans to develop hydroelectric projects on the Nu River.[68] Despite the opposition of a few agencies, the majority of local government agencies desired these projects to increase hydroelectricity output, which is one of the largest sectors in the Yunnan economy.[69] This source of revenue helps the local government increase development in the region and also offsets the revenue lost first to the recentralization of taxes in 1994 and then to the raising of the income tax floor as part of the New Socialist Countryside Policy in 2005.

In 2004, many grassroots groups such as Green Watershed of Yunnan, Wild China, Green Earth Volunteers, Friends of Nature, and China Rivers Network protested the proposal to build 13 dams in Yunnan. Green Watershed, the first Chinese NGO specializing in river management, partnered with an international environmental group to provide rafting trips for journalists and government officials, including from the Ministry of Environmental Protection, so they could discover the natural and ethnic diversity of the river and oppose the proposed dam projects.[70] Yu Xiaogang, the founder of Green Watershed, also organized trips for villagers slated for relocation at one dam site in Yunnan to speak with villagers from other dam sites, whose relocation had been far from successful. Green Watershed's advocacy was not well received by the Yunnan local government, which branded him a "troublemaker" and the group an "extremist organization."[71] However, his actions in concert with those of other groups were more successful with the central government,

[68] Andrew Mertha, *China's Water Warriors: Citizen Action and Policy Change* (Ithaca, NY: Cornell University Press, 2008); Michael Buesgen, "Environmental NGOs' Role in Expanding Social Spaces – Diversification with Chinese Characteristics: A Case Study of ENGOs' Opposition to the Nujiang Dam in China's Yunnan Province," *China Journal of Social Work* 1, 2008: 160–171.

[69] Interview with local government official, Lijiang, Yunnan, April 1, 2007; see Mertha, *China's Water Warriors*, for an excellent overview of the bureaucratic dynamics of hydroelectric politics in Yunnan.

[70] Author interview with founder of environmental INGO, Lijiang, Yunnan, March 28, 2007.

[71] Mertha, "Fragmented Authoritarianism 2.0."

especially the Ministry of Environmental Protection (MEP) and the State Council.

In fact, as a result of these trips and the subsequent media publicity, MEP ordered a halt to 30 large construction projects that failed to meet environmental impact assessment procedures or standards.[72] In addition to MEP's intervention, Premier Wen Jiabao also ordered officials to conduct a major review of the hydropower project on the Nu River: "We should carefully consider and make a scientific decision about major hydroelectric projects like this that have aroused a high level of concern in society, and with which the environmental protection side disagrees."[73] Although this outcome was a policy success for the environmental groups in Yunnan, this experience taught local officials that civil society could threaten promotion prospects by hindering the achievement of development goals and creating mass incidents that are viewed unfavorably by supervisors.[74] These experiences with civil society taught local officials about the need for mechanisms of state control over group activities. For example, although Yu's group was not closed down, he has been prevented as an individual from traveling outside the province to speak with other environmental groups.[75]

THE DEVELOPMENT OF CONSULTATIVE AUTHORITARIANISM IN YUNNAN

With the influx of INGOs and the development of grassroots civil society in the 1990s, Yunnan had many autonomous groups operating across the province and maintained fairly low levels of

[72] Fu Tao, "Respite for Yunnan Anti-Dam NGO as Movement Mourns Loss of Key Activist," *The China Development Brief*, January 20, 2005: available at http://www.chinadevelopmentbrief.com/node/104/print

[73] Jim Yardley, "China's Premier Orders Halt to a Dam Project Threatening a Lost Eden," *The New York Times*, April 9, 2004: available at http://www.nytimes.com/2004/04/09/international/asia/09DAMS.html

[74] Civil Society Workshop, Peking University, Beijing, January 14, 2007.

[75] "2009 Ramon Magsaysay Awardee," available at www.rmaf.org.ph/Awardees/Citation/CitationXiaogangYu.htm

control over these groups. Learning about the benefits offered by civil society in the realm of service delivery through direct experience with these emerging groups encouraged local officials to allow the formation and operation of more INGOs and grass-roots groups. Many of these groups sought to change local policies and develop stronger collaborative relationships through informational activities such as training sessions and study tours.

As a result of this learning process, Yunnan adopted stricter regulations on foreign NGOs and international funding for civil society in 2009.[76] This policy shift aligns Yunnan with the CA model that was developing in Beijing at the same time, which merges encouraging more independent groups with using more indirect tools of control such as regulatory oversight. Currently the local state in Yunnan maintains more collaborative relationships with environmental groups supporting development goals such as ecotourism and more confrontational relationships with those opposing development projects in the name of conservation.[77] Whereas the high number of autonomous groups and low levels of state control characterized the original Yunnan model, learning about the confrontational role civil society might play triggered the adoption of stricter regulations on INGO activity and international funding for civil society.[78] Specifically, officials' fears of civil society groups potentially mobilizing politically sensitive populations, especially in the years preceding national and local leadership transitions in 2013, and lack of information or state control over group

[76] Author interview with staff member of Yunnan environmental INGO, Beijing, June 21, 2010; see also Karla W. Simon, "Recent Developments in Chinese Law Affecting CSOs/NGOs," *International Journal of Civil Society Law*, June 2010: available at http://www.iccsl.org/admin/object/gallery/China_Recent_Develop ments_June_10.pdf

[77] Author interview with staff member of Yunnan International Non-Government Organization Society, Kunming, Yunnan, April 25, 2007; author interview with staff member of environmental INGO, Beijing, June 18, 2010.

[78] Author interview with staff member of Yunnan environmental INGO, Beijing, June 21, 2010; see also Simon, "Recent Developments in Chinese Law Affecting CSOs/NGOs."

activity challenged the original model and pushed Yunnan officials to add controls to converge on the CA model.

The central government passed a new regulation controlling international fundraising by Chinese civil society that was implemented by Yunnan officials in March 2010.[79] This regulation affects the ability of INGOs in Yunnan to fund grassroots groups; however, the more onerous regulation was the new local regulation for INGO supervision in Yunnan (云南省规范境外非政府组织活动暂行规定) passed in 2009 and implemented in January 2010. This regulation requires that all INGO projects and activities be registered at the Civil Affairs Bureau and Foreign Affairs Bureau. Any activities not previously registered and approved are considered illegal. When INGOs or international donors sign memoranda of understanding with domestic groups, they must submit a copy of this contract to the supervisory unit, Civil Affairs Bureau's technical office, and the Foreign Affairs Bureau. INGOs are also responsible for submitting annual (or semiannual) reports to the Civil Affairs Bureau and re-registering every two years. From January to August 2010, thirteen INGOs were investigated and their activities registered, and by December 2010, a total of 140 INGOs registered activities and projects with the Civil Affairs Bureau. Some of the registered INGOs are The Nature Conservancy, Oxfam Hong Kong, Orbis International, CBM Society, China California Heart Watch, MSI Professional Services, Health Unlimited, Humana People to People, International AIDS Alliance, Operation Smile China, SIL, and Sowers Action and Voluntary Service Overseas UK. This policy shift aligns Yunnan more closely with Beijing in allowing for the expansion of autonomous civil society but simultaneously

[79] Notice of the State Administration of Foreign Exchange (SAFE) on "Issues Concerning the Administration of Foreign Exchange Donated to or by Domestic Institutions,"《国家外汇管理局关于境内机构捐赠外汇管理有关问题的通知》No. 63 [2009] of the State Administration of Foreign Exchange (effective 3/1/2010).

adopting a larger toolkit with which to control group development and activities.

As analyzed in this chapter, consultative authoritarianism developed first in Beijing and Yunnan in response to an earlier influx of civil society, initially in the form of INGOs and then grassroots groups in the early 1990s. This influx initiated a learning process for local officials struggling with the policy failure of public goods and services decentralization. Although initially lacking direct experience with civil society, local officials observed other countries' experiences with these groups, including post-Soviet republics, industrialized Western states, and Costa Rica. Both of these sources of learning contributed to the construction of CA by the mid-2000s. In the following chapter, I analyze the development of CA in Jiangsu and Sichuan Provinces, both initially characterized by higher levels of control over a smaller autonomous civil society sector.

CHAPTER 3

Converging on Consultative Authoritarianism: Civil Society Development in Jiangsu and Sichuan

As illustrated in charts I.3 and I.4, Jiangsu and Sichuan did not have as many civil society groups as Beijing and Yunnan in the 1990s and also maintained relatively high levels of control over those groups that did exist, especially compared to Yunnan. However, as a result of direct experiences with emerging civil society, local officials began to learn about the benefits of civil society as well as the limitations of the corporatist methods of control. By the late 2000s, both provinces developed the more autonomous civil society and indirect tools of state control characteristic of the CA model.

In the 1990s, Jiangsu officials used administrative tools such as civil society registration to control groups and repress most activity. Between the mid-1990s and early 2000s, officials' experiences with groups such as the Amity Foundation and the explosion of unregistered community groups taught them about the benefits of groups assisting with meeting development goals and possible challenges to social stability goals. Officials responded to community group proliferation by developing new tools of state control, as existing tools such as the dual management system seemed ineffective. By the mid-2000s, Jiangsu officials expanded administrative control channels to incorporate all unregistered groups into the registration process to prevent groups from threatening stability. However, experiences with groups such as Amity taught officials that civil society offered benefits also, which led to the development of the CA model in Jiangsu later in the decade.

Sichuan officials also attempted group repression throughout the 1990s because of fears of social instability and loss of state authority; however, lower state capacity meant officials were unable to totally repress these groups, and incomplete repression instead generated the very social protests and unrest feared by local officials. As unrest increased, so did officials' fears of social organization and mobilization to challenge state authority. However, collaboration experiences with civil society in the early 2000s on poverty alleviation and after the 2008 Wenquan earthquake taught officials that civil society could assist the state in developing new models of poverty alleviation and mitigating the root causes of social unrest, influencing an increasing willingness to collaborate with groups that are able to supply external funding and new models to address development challenges. In particular, collaboration with poverty alleviation groups served to introduce new ideas about the potential role of civil society in Sichuan and created discrete policy changes.

Collaboration for earthquake relief efforts served as a learning process whereby local government officials discovered how quickly civil society groups could mobilize resources and play a complementary role to government efforts that increased effectiveness and the reach of government resources. However, the local state, including the military, responded very effectively to the earthquake, which reinforced the idea that the state is more effective than social organizations and any resources given to these groups simply wastes that which could be used more competently by the state. In response to these contradictory lessons, local officials balanced fears of competition with civil society and erosion of local state authority with the benefits of collaboration by cautiously partnering with "trusted" groups – those led by former government officials or INGOs with extensive financial resources. This shift aligns Sichuan more closely to the CA model in that officials allow more civil society activity while still attempting to maintain state controls, although the type of controls used has changed to more indirect ones than those used in corporatism.

Although Sichuan and Jiangsu initially shared a more confrontational relationship with civil society than Beijing or Yunnan, as in those cases, I find growing convergence on a new model of state-society relationship in China that emphasizes the simultaneous rise of a relatively autonomous civil society with differentiated state controls.

LEARNING IN JIANGSU: REDESIGNING THE MECHANISMS OF STATE CONTROL

Jiangsu province currently possesses the fifth largest number of registered groups and is one of the wealthiest provinces in China with a GDP of 5.41 trillion yuan (US$881 billion) in 2012. Located along the more developed east coast of the country as illustrated in Figure 2.1, Jiangsu has a fairly strong private sector, although not as strong as its neighboring Zhejiang province with the famous Wenzhou economic development model. By the end of 2007, Jiangsu had about 680,000 private enterprises, an increase from 286,000 in 2002. This acceptance of private enterprise has translated to a more limited degree to the civil society sector.

Jiangsu's civil society sector is characterized by several large government-organized groups (GONGOs) such as the labor federation and charity programs run by the Communist Youth League; large private charities such as the Amity Foundation (a Catholic charity); and a myriad of nonprofits engaged in private education and professional training, such as training centers run by professional accounting associations. Lacking the same development challenges that attract INGOs to Yunnan, charities, professional associations, and private business groups predominantly form in Jiangsu. For example, although Jiangsu has the fifth largest number of registered groups in the country, most of these groups are actually private schools registered as nonprofits. Industry and business associations comprise the majority of other registered organizations. The mid- to large-size environmental, HIV/AIDS, and cultural advocacy groups found in Beijing and Yunnan are missing in Jiangsu. However, Jiangsu has recently witnessed a proliferation of small, unregistered community-based organizations (CBOs) engaged in social services.[1]

When civil society first emerged in the early 1990s, Jiangsu officials attempted to tightly control all social activity outside of state-controlled channels to protect against any possible social unrest. Jiangsu is known as a leadership training ground for the national level, so most officials zealously protect social order as a strategy to win promotion.[2] This is a successful strategy for advancement, based on the rise of both Jiang Zemin in Shanghai during the 1989 Tiananmen protests and Hu Jintao in Tibet to national office. Jiangsu officials controlled civil society groups through local registration procedures (*zhifa jiandu gongzuo* 执法监督工作) based on the dual management system, which requires government agencies to supervise group activities. These registration procedures require four steps: (1) register with the Civil Affairs Bureau (2) secure a supervising government agency (3) undergo an annual inspection that requires the self-reporting of funding, members, and events, followed by a Civil Affairs inspection visit; and (4) register all planned events with the local government office. For example, if an environmental group wants to hold an activity on a college campus, it must register and get approval for the activity from the college administration. Civil society scholars argue that these regulations served to tightly control groups and limit autonomy from the state.[3]

Whereas the dual management regulations apply to all groups in China, provincial governments are responsible for enforcement. As seen in Beijing and Yunnan, these regulations are often waived or ignored. However, in Jiangsu, the Civil Affairs Bureau consistently enforced these regulations. In response to experiences with the influx of CBOs in the early 2000s, the local government realized that these control mechanisms were ineffective and

[1] Author interview with academic expert on state-society relationships, Nanjing, June 11, 2008.

[2] Author interview with staff member of a foundation working in Jiangsu, Beijing, June 22, 2008.

[3] Nick Young, "NGOs and Civil Society in China," in *Berkshire Encyclopedia of China*, Linsun Cheng, ed. (Barrington, MA: Berkshire Publishing, 2009).

adopted new tools, such as using lower levels of government, including street committees and media organizations, to alert the bureau to unregistered group activity.[4] In fact, between 2006 and 2008, the bureau banned more than 150 groups and conducted more than 10 hearings about the activities of groups deemed to threaten social order. However, experiences with groups like Amity also taught officials about the benefits offered by collaborating with these groups. As I explain next, Amity's collaboration with local government on migrant services led to an understanding of the ability of civil society to reach vulnerable communities. These contradictory experiences led to the development of the CA model already under construction in Beijing and Yunnan.

LEARNING THROUGH EXPERIENCE: THE AMITY FOUNDATION

The Amity Foundation, an independent Chinese charity, was established in 1985 in Nanjing, the capital city of Jiangsu province, to fund education and humanitarian programs. Although the Amity Foundation is the largest private charity in Jiangsu, it conducted fewer projects in the headquarters city of Nanjing in the 1990s than in Yunnan, Qinghai, or Guangxi.[5] When Amity first began operating in Nanjing, the government actively attempted to restrict group activities. For example, when Amity proposed a different model of education for students with handicaps to be used in the local schools, the Education Bureau refused to work with the group. Amity responded by establishing its own small schools to focus the curriculum more on life skills and vocational training programs. Amity's experiences in Nanjing throughout the 1990s illustrate the tight controls adopted by local officials that greatly restricted the development of autonomous civil society. In fact, local officials

[4] Author interview with local official from the Civil Affairs Bureau, Nanjing, Jiangsu, June 20, 2008.

[5] Author interview with representative of the Amity Foundation, Nanjing, Jiangsu, June 10, 2008.

viewed Amity as a competitor for state authority when the group opened these schools, effectively competing with public schools operated by the Education Bureau. Based on this experience, one staff member stated that initiating a project without talking to the relevant agency in Nanjing is similar to "going into someone's house and doing your own business in their house without their permission."[6]

However, through more than two decades of experience with Amity, officials appeared to finally recognize the group's contributions to public policy: "In the beginning there was not much government understanding of the group or its goals, but through the last 20 years the Nanjing government's attitude has changed due to working on many projects that the government cares about such as development and improving living conditions."[7] Two projects in which Amity partnered with the local government are a school for migrant children (Henancun School in Nanjing) beginning in 2004 and the Amity-sponsored Migrant Workers Legal Aid Station in Nanjing with support from the Jiangsu Province Department of Justice, the Nanjing City Bureau of Justice, and the Yuhuatai District Bureau of Justice to distribute a "Migrant Workers' Rights Manual" beginning in 2007.[8] These experiences with Amity's processes and outcomes, especially helping the local government meet service delivery goals by providing funding and running pilot projects with vulnerable populations, has led to more understanding on the part of the Nanjing government. In fact, the Nanjing government allowed Amity to start an AIDS education and treatment project for migrants in collaboration with the Health Bureau in 2007; when this program was first proposed in the early 1990s, local officials banned it outright. Although many officials still are suspicious of civil society as a threat to state authority and control, collaboration experiences such as those with Amity taught them that civil society can

[6] Ibid.

[7] Author interview with representative of the Amity Foundation, Nanjing, Jiangsu, June 10, 2008.

[8] For more project descriptions, see http://www.amityfoundation.org

also play a complementary governance role. Amity also currently partners with both the central and local governments to develop policy ideas and strategies to promote the development of an autonomous NGO sector in Nanjing, similar to NPI in Beijing.

LEARNING THROUGH EXPERIENCE: COMMUNITY-BASED ORGANIZATIONS

By the early 2000s, Jiangsu province had a vibrant and expanding informal CBO sector. These small CBOs are mostly clubs dedicated to common interests such as traditional music or to meeting community needs such as legal aid groups. For example, one CBO, Jiangsu Tongtian Workshop, formed in 2002 and by 2009 had almost 20 staff and volunteers and a budget of 25,000 yuan (US$3,727).[9] This small group created an information hotline for the homosexual community in Jiangsu and also conducted outreach, STD prevention education, and HIV testing. Although this group is unregistered, it partnered with the Jiangsu Center for Disease Control to distribute information about HIV/AIDS and initiate an education campaign in 2004 stressing that being homosexual is not equivalent to having AIDS.

As the Nanjing Civil Affairs Bureau's Resident Director Zhang Renping explained,

> According to our records, during these last few years "work unit man" [organized around the danwei] has changed into "social man" [organized around social organizations] and community-based organizations have emerged with powerful growth potential (*shequ minjian zuzhi chengxian qiangjing fazhan shitou* 社区民间组织呈现强劲发展势头). By the end of last year [2006], Nanjing's 852 communities developed over 3,700 community-based organizations.[10]

[9] For more information about this group, see http://www.plosone.org/article/info%3Adoi%2F10.1371%2Fjournal.pone.0069740

[10] 魏巍 and 赵文婧 (Wei Wei and Zhao Wenjing), "城市连线 南京的社区组织要备案 [City Connection: Nanjing's Social Groups Want to Register]," 东方今报, February 6, 2007: available at http://www.meetingec.cn/index_news_show.aspx?ID=6447

By 2008, the Civil Affairs Bureau had registered more than 7,640 new CBOs in Nanjing alone. However, many more CBOs remain unregistered, and therefore outside of the bureaucratic controls established by the Civil Affairs Bureau. In fact, one official at the bureau stated that it was impossible to find these groups unless they draw attention to themselves by becoming too big or holding large events.[11] The Civil Affairs Bureau office in Nanjing employs only around 80 staff members, who cannot supervise thousands of registered groups and many more unregistered ones. In short, the bureau and municipal government simply do not possess the resources to monitor the rapid increase of small community groups.

The experience of this rapid expansion of CBOs in Nanjing in the early 2000s taught local officials that the control mechanisms used in the adapted corporatist model, such as dual registration, were no longer effective at controlling this new type of organization. In response to the failure of existing tools for social control, the Bureau of Civil Affairs and the municipal government increasingly began to rely on the lower-level street and community branches of government to control the expansion of this unregistered CBO sector. Although this technique of social management is from the Maoist era, the tools are modern, such as an intranet for communicating with and receiving up-to-date information from these lower-level offices.

According to an internal Civil Affairs report, the bureau pursues four goals for this social management strategy: (1) increase the agency's research ability regarding group activities (2) increase the sources of information such as the intranet, Bureau of Public Security, and lower-levels of government more embedded in the community (3) use local law professors to train government staff in using administrative techniques to enforce social regulations; and (4) update the bureau's objectives in light of the experiences of the past six years, such as collaborative projects

[11] Author interview with representative of the Civil Affairs Bureau, Nanjing, Jiangsu, June 20, 2008.

with groups and signs of social instability.[12] This last point illustrates how experience with emerging civil society shaped officials' understanding of the civil society's role in local policy making. The lessons learned by officials as a result of the proliferation of CBOs has been that the majority of these groups seem to build strong community networks for the elderly and mediate community problems, both of which local officials find beneficial. However, fears of citizen mobilization still encourage officials to warily watch these groups for signs of instigating social unrest. In response to CBO proliferation, local officials developed new tools of state control, such as using communication networks to gather information on group activities, indicating the development of the CA model in Jiangsu.

BUILDING CONSULTATIVE AUTHORITARIANISM: NEW TOOLS OF CONTROL

Prevalent promotion strategies emphasizing political stability in Jiangsu influenced local officials to initially form a more confrontational relationship with emerging civil society. Throughout the 1990s, high state capacity enabled local officials to control most civil society activity through administrative regulations. This led to the unusual character of Jiangsu's civil society sector – the "missing middle." Jiangsu possesses a number of large government-organized groups and a thriving small community organizations network but lacks medium-size groups with the exception of a few such as the Amity Foundation. However, officials' failure to incorporate CBOs into the corporatist system and collaborative experiences with Amity motivated the creation of more indirect tools of state control and the formation of more autonomous groups.

As the direct tools of corporatism were revealed to be ineffective in managing the rapid development of small CBOs,

[12] Author's translation of a Bureau of Civil Affairs internal document, 2008: "四是实行目标考核。我们连续六年将社会组织执法监督工作列入全市工作的考核目标，对区县的社会组织执法工作进行全面考核，发挥了目标管理的导向和激励作用"(3).

Jiangsu officials developed indirect tools including relying on media, professors, and street-level officials to guide group activities in ways viewed as beneficial and not threatening stability. In Jiangsu, officials' learned that independent civil society groups did offer benefits but still could threaten state control. By the 2000s, officials' positive experiences with civil society groups such as Amity have led to slightly more collaboration. As in Beijing, experiences with civil society since the late 1980s motivated local officials to collaborate more with civil society groups and develop new control mechanisms. For example, local officials expanded tools such as social monitoring but also sought to open registration to informal CBOs with the intention of bringing them under a common control system. In 2009, following the Beijing model, the Jiangsu Civil Affairs Bureau adopted new direct registration procedures making it easier for CBOs to register so as to legalize those groups already active. This corresponds to the consultative authoritarianism model discussed in the preceding chapter that allows independent CBOs to form, but simultaneously uses new tools of state control. These policy changes illustrate the effect of learning on local officials, influencing the transition from the former corporatist model to the new CA model.

LEARNING IN SICHUAN: DEMANDS FOR PUBLIC PARTICIPATION

As seen in Figure 2.1 Sichuan province lies slightly to the west of the middle of the country and borders Qinghai, Gansu, Shaanxi, Chongqing, Yunnan, and Tibet. Rich in mineral resources, Sichuan is the largest agricultural producer in China. As a result of central government investment through the Western Development Plan, Sichuan is increasingly industrialized, producing machinery, pharmaceuticals, and automobile components. In 2012, the province earned a GDP of 2.38 trillion yuan (US$387 billion), which is the eighth largest GDP in country. However, Sichuan also has the fourth largest population and many poor mountainous areas. In 2004, the poverty rate in Sichuan was 11 percent, with 17 counties identified as nationally designated poor counties compared to 24 as provincially designated poor counties in 1986.[13] Sichuan occupies a mountainous terrain, with 90 percent of its area classified as mountains and hills, leaving only a small amount of arable land, approximately 6.4 percent of the total land. As found in other mountainous areas, residents unable to secure access to flat land for agriculture and are more than eight times more prone to poverty.[14] In addition to geographical causes of poverty in Sichuan, the 2008 global economic crisis caused high unemployment for migrant workers, many of whom returned home to Sichuan. In fact, the biggest declines in employment between the end of 2008 and the beginning of 2009 occurred in Zhejiang province, followed by Shanghai and Sichuan. Without remitted wages, many families reentered the ranks of the poor. According to a local official, "the poverty situation in Sichuan province is very bad after the financial crisis."[15]

To address these governance challenges, local officials began to use special investment vehicles to secure additional funding, even though the central government bars provinces from raising extra funds through bonds or other forms of debt. Sichuan is one of the most indebted provinces after Yunnan province, which creates significant challenges for local officials to fight poverty. In response, many poverty-alleviation groups formed or opened a project office in Sichuan, including grassroots organizations, INGOs such as Heifer International, and both domestic and international environmental groups. These environmental groups operate such poverty alleviation pilot programs in Sichuan as testing alternative energy sources in areas not connected to a

[13] These poverty rates are official Chinese rates, but these are difficult to measure as different poverty lines have been used at different time periods, and Chinese rates differ from international ones.

[14] Neil McCulloch and Michele Calandrino, "Vulnerability and Chronic Poverty in Rural Sichuan," *World Development* 31, 2003.

[15] Sara Hsu, Shiyin Jiang, Halcott Heyward, and Jocelyn Lam, "Did the US Financial Crisis Impact China's Rural Poor?" *9th GEM-IWG International Conference*, United Nations Headquarters, New York City, July 13–14, 2009.

main electricity grid and working with farmers to improve water practices for irrigation and reducing fertilizer run off.

As a result of its historical poverty, Sichuan officials initially viewed civil society, in fact all societal actors, as weak compared to the state. This idea about the low capacity of civil society groups versus the government appears to have created concerns among local officials about relative power shifts. Any increase in group capacity, as happened beginning in the mid- to late-1990s, produces a threat perception on the part of local officials that groups will seek to challenge state authority. One local official argued, "Why do Westerners think that civil society can outperform the state? This doesn't make sense. We [local state officials] have been working here for much longer and we are the ones who truly know what the people need."[16] When groups first formed in Sichuan, local officials viewed them as competing for limited resources and public authority. This idea of relative power shifts between civil society and the local state constructed a confrontational relationship between groups and local officials, leading officials to attempt to repress all group activity in the 1990s.

Sichuan initially had fewer independent groups and attempted to have as much state control as Jiangsu province, but it lacked the same level of state capacity to enforce these goals because of the relative poverty of the province. Ineffective attempts at repression led many informal (and unregistered) groups to lead collective protests against government policies when not allowed any other means of voicing dissent. This experience taught local officials that civil society might threaten state authority, whereas other experiences with poverty alleviation groups taught officials that civil society also assists the state in reaching its goals. These contradictory experiences and observations of the neighboring Yunnan province led to the development of CA in Sichuan by the mid-2000s, and the process accelerated after 2008.

[16] Author interview with local official, Chengdu, Sichuan, July 15, 2008.

LEARNING THROUGH EXPERIENCE: COLLECTIVE PROTESTS

Throughout the 1990s and early 2000s, local officials attempted to repress group activity; however, with low state capacity officials used threats of violence instead of the administrative control mechanisms utilized in Jiangsu. Sichuan local officials routinely hired individuals to threaten and use violence against citizens and groups obstructing government goals.[17] Although repression strategies were ultimately ineffective, the strategy in Sichuan had the unintended consequence of radicalizing individuals and groups. For example, Kevin O'Brien and Lianjiang Li conducted interviews with individuals and groups engaged in protests against the local state in China and found that the use of state-sponsored violence or other forms of physical repression radicalize these individuals.[18] They argue that rural officials sometimes attempt to buy off protest leaders but more often turn to repression, which may strengthen the determination of protest leaders and make them more prone to adopt confrontational tactics, partly by enhancing their popular support and partly by increasing the costs of withdrawal.[19] For example, a former village cadre in Xuanhan county (宣汉县) refused to pay a small fee he thought was unlawful, but when the party secretary who came to collect the money humiliated him publicly, he led more than 20 petition drives at the county, city, and province and staged several dozen demonstrations in his village during the next three years.[20] In Sichuan, the use of thugs or "outsourced repression," instead of the techniques of administrative repression used in

[17] Kathy Le Mons Walker, "From Covert to Overt: Everyday Peasant Politics in China and the Implications for Transnational Agrarian Movements," *Journal of Agrarian Change* 8 nos. 2–3, 2008: 462–488; local governments throughout China have used criminal organizations or individuals to enforce tax collection, evictions, and so on.

[18] Lianjiang Li and Kevin J. O'Brien, "Protest Leadership in Rural China," *The China Quarterly* 193, March 2008: 1–23.

[19] Ibid.

[20] Ibid., 15.

Jiangsu, caused disgruntled individuals and groups to simply take to the streets to protest (*jiedao zhengzhi* 街道政治).

In fact, throughout the late 1990s and 2000s, ineffective repression of groups and individuals resulted in increasing numbers of collective protests in Sichuan led by radicalized groups and individuals. As Jae Ho Chung finds, only the five provinces of Henan, Hubei, Anhui, Hunan, and Sichuan recorded protest or incident counts with high frequency and a high number of participants.[21] For example, peasants have protested land ownership rights by squatting on unoccupied land and resisting government attempts to seize land.[22] In urban areas, homeowners protested by collectively taking a walk (集体散步), which circumvents a national law that requires protesters to apply for a permit by saying they were only out for a "stroll." One large protest in 2008 against a proposed petrochemical plant was organized by urban residents through websites, blogs, and mobile phone text messages. About 400 to 500 protesters walked through downtown Chengdu, the capital city of Sichuan, for several hours on a Sunday afternoon and wore white masks to symbolize pollution.[23]

In another example from July 2007, peasants living on the outskirts of Zigong, Sichuan, were being evicted from their homes so the city government could sell the land to private developers. To carry out this forced demolition,

> [A] few hundred or a thousand people attacked the peasant homes and pulled the occupants out by force, they pulled them by their necks and dragged them across the floors, they beat them down the stairwells. Some were from the local police station, some from the court enforcement troupe, but for the most part they were plainclothes people.[24]

[21] Jae Ho Chung, Hongyi Lai, and Ming Xia, "Mounting Challenges to Governance in China: Surveying Collective Protestors, Religious Sects and Criminal Organizations," *The China Journal* 56, 2006: 1–31.

[22] Eva Pils, "Land Disputes, Rights Assertion and Social Unrest: A Case from Sichuan," *Columbia Journal of Asian Law* 19, 2006: 365.

[23] Edward Wong, "In China City, Protesters See Pollution Risk of New Plant," *The New York Times*, May 6, 2008: available at http://www.nytimes.com/2008/05/06/world/asia/06china.html?pagewanted=all

[24] Eva Pils, "Peasant's Struggle for Land in China," *World Justice Forum* conference paper, Vienna, July 2–5, 2008.

Shortly after this raid, these families organized to march downtown with banners and file a collective petition to complain about the eviction by local government.

Although many of these collective protests began as informal and individual actions, the state's attempts at repression caused atomized actions and individuals to coalesce into groups with public policy goals. These groups organized subsequent protests to achieve these goals, such as changing land policies or environmental regulations. As illustrated by these studies and examples, incomplete repression via extralegal methods led to increasing social unrest in Sichuan, which taught officials that groups they viewed as civil society can challenge state authority. In many ways, this lesson merely confirmed in the form of a self-fulfilling prophecy officials' original suspicions about these groups. However, other experiences with groups involved in poverty alleviation and relief efforts contradicted this lesson as explained in the next section.

LEARNING THROUGH EXPERIENCE: POVERTY ALLEVIATION PROJECTS

Sichuan is a geographically large and diverse province, covering an area roughly the size as France, and prior to the division of Chongqing in 1997, it was China's most populous province. More than 90 percent of the province is classified as hilly or mountainous and thus has some of the highest rates of poverty in the country with a per capita GDP of 4,012 yuan (US$590) in 1997 – ranking 22 among 30 provinces in China. Sichuan possesses 7 percent of the 592 counties designated as the poorest counties in China, which ranks it as the third poorest province. Many poverty alleviation and environmental groups operate in Chengdu (成都), the provincial capital of Sichuan province. The Provincial Poverty Alleviation Bureau (PAB), part of the Chengdu local government, conducts poverty alleviation programs. Similar to other local government agencies in Sichuan, the PAB did not collaborate with civil society groups prior to the mid-1990s because of ideas of low group capacity and competition over authority. However, the problem of poverty in Sichuan overwhelmed local resources and funding agencies like the World Bank diverted resources to civil society groups, encouraging new innovative solutions such as public-private partnerships.

In the mid-1990s, a Chinese branch of an INGO operating in Chengdu secured World Bank funding to initiate a pilot program for poverty alleviation based on a model of community participation. After securing international funding for this pilot program, the INGO branch leader, who formerly worked at a different local government agency, used his personal connections to have his former government colleagues introduce him to the relevant officials at the PAB. The group leader offered to assist PAB officials by sharing the group's participation models, technology, and funding to reduce poverty in the mountainous regions. The PAB officials agreed to partner with the group to provisionally pilot this community participation model to achieve anticipated benefits in poverty reduction. As the head of the group stated, "officials risk little in cooperating with us because if they don't like the outcomes or the direction of the project, they simply shut it down. If the project is successful, they take all the credit. So it's really win-win for them."[25]

This community participation or community-driven development (CDD) approach arises from Western models of poverty alleviation focused on empirical findings that different causes of poverty exist and only through community participation in setting poverty alleviation policies can officials understand these different root causes. This CDD model depends on devolution of decision making to the village level, decentralized project implementation, and the control of project funds to allow greater local autonomy and community participation in development activities. More specifically, the international best practices of the CDD approach require promoting the active involvement of villagers in rural community development processes, enabling them to collectively identify and prioritize local needs; prepare and select local

[25] Author interview with head of poverty alleviation INGO, Chengdu, Sichuan, July 3, 2008.

subprojects in a fair, equitable and transparent manner; and develop their own collective capacities for implementation, project management, monitoring, and maintenance.[26]

Following this community participation model, the group conducted training sessions with community leaders and PAB officials on how to discover structural causes of poverty that might differ community to community. Next the PAB met with these local leaders to discuss root causes of poverty in each community in sessions mediated by the INGO and then incorporated that feedback into distinct poverty alleviation plans, rather than imposing a single PAB-developed plan on each community. The poverty alleviation plans were then financed and managed by the government but executed by the local community leaders originally involved in the planning process. As a result of the success of the original pilot in poverty reduction, PAB officials later expanded this program to four additional counties in Sichuan.[27]

In fact, in 2010, the World Bank announced the expansion of this poverty reduction model – the Sustainable Development in Poor Rural Areas Project – through collaboration with the State Council Leading Group Office on Poverty Alleviation and Development of China. This collaborative project involves a total investment of about US$160 million, including a US$100 million loan from the World Bank, a US$5 million grant from the Global Environment Facility (GEF), and about US$55 million of domestic counterpart funding in the 25 poorest counties in Henan, Shaanxi, and Chongqing. As Inger Andersen, World Bank vice president for sustainable development, stated,

> The World Bank has worked with China in poverty alleviation since the mid 1990s and has been successful in assisting the country in its efforts to reduce poverty. With Bank support, China has recently also began to experiment with CDD (community-driven development) approaches and

[26] For more detail on the CDD approach, see the United Nations Economic and Social Commission for Asia and the Pacific's (UNESCAP) report (2009) summarizing these best practices, available at http://www.unescap.org/pdd/publications/poverty_and_development/trends_rural.pdf

[27] Author interview with local PAB official, Chengdu, Sichuan, July 15, 2008.

has implemented its own pilots on CDD and it has developed substantial experience with participation approaches.[28]

Upon its completion by 2015, about 120,000 poor rural households with a total population of 480,000 are expected to have benefited from the project through new or improved village access roads, drinking water supply, rural sanitation, electrification and communication infrastructure, school buildings, water storage, irrigation and drainage systems, and land improvements.

These experiences with collaboration throughout the 1990s and 2000s taught local officials that civil society groups offer benefits such as introducing new solutions to policy problems, external funding, and the ability to connect in different ways with vulnerable populations. An interviewed PAB official, although originally skeptical of this collaboration with the group, now believes partnership to be useful in providing financial and innovation resources not available to the local government, even though he thinks the ability of community leaders to participate at high levels is still constrained.[29] As he argued, "international best practice states that groups should have an 80–20 ratio [80 percent of revenue used for projects and 20 percent used for administration], but groups in China have a 20–80 ratio so clearly they are either incompetent or fraudulent."[30] However, he also expressed interest in collaborating with groups in the future if they supply external funding and new models to fight poverty based on his experiences with the CDD project. The experience with poverty alleviation groups slowly changed PAB officials' relationship with civil society and motivated policy change regarding poverty alleviation in Sichuan. This lesson was reinforced through partnering with civil society after the 2008 earthquake, as I explore in the next section.

[28] See the World Bank press release at http://www.worldbank.org/en/news/2010/10/20/world-bank-support-china-exploring-innovative-approaches-poverty-reduction

[29] Author interview with local PAB official, Chengdu, Sichuan, July 15, 2008.

[30] Ibid.

LEARNING THROUGH EXPERIENCE: WENCHUAN EARTHQUAKE RELIEF EFFORTS

On May 12, 2008, a massive earthquake struck Sichuan province (汶川大地震 *Wenchuan dadizhen*). According to the State Council Information Office, the death toll from the earthquake was approximately 70,000, with a total of 7,000 collapsed classrooms and approximately 10,000 of the nearly 70,000 confirmed deaths were of schoolchildren. Accompanying this tragedy was a significant outpouring of donations and volunteers, leading many analysts to speculate that similar to the SARS crisis in 2003, relief and reconstruction efforts would strengthen the relationship between civil society and the local state in Sichuan. In fact, the experience of civil society's role in relief efforts taught local officials that civil society could amplify the state's relief efforts to more effectively address relief and reconstruction efforts.[31]

Immediately after the extent of earthquake devastation became clear, the Chinese Red Cross, a GONGO, was able to quickly organize an action plan and receive government approval, but many grassroots groups and INGOs were not sure how best to deliver assistance or how to coordinate their activities with those of other groups and the local government. Thus, groups were unable to coherently assist the relief efforts, had difficulty in gaining access to disaster areas, and duplicated other groups' efforts. Although many groups, such as the Western Volunteers Association (*Xibu Zhiyuanzhe*西部志愿者), have extensive networks of volunteers, they did not have the organizational capacity to mobilize and conduct relief efforts.[32]

In addition to capacity and coordination issues on the part of civil society, local government in Sichuan also initially distrusted these groups' intentions. One cadre succinctly summarized the key

[31] Jessica C. Teets, "Post-Earthquake Relief and Reconstruction Efforts: The Emergence of Civil Society in China?" *The China Quarterly* 198, June 2009: 330–347.

[32] Author interview with local civil society group, Chengdu, Sichuan, July 16, 2008.

doubt that many local officials possessed: "if their funding is from overseas, what are the true motives of this group?"[33] Whereas one fear is that these groups intend to ultimately oppose the government, the more immediate fear is that groups want to substitute for government. As expressed also by the interviewed PAB official, this competition might reduce local government's power and authority.[34] Local officials feel threatened that the strengthening of civil society might create social disorder and erode their own power and authority, but also that many in the international community and at the central government might view these groups as a substitute to local government. As one cadre explained,

> Why would people say that local government has low capacity or doesn't understand the needs of our people? We are very professional and are able to accomplish most of our goals. I have worked and lived in this area all of my life, and no one [civil society groups] can do my job better than me or know better than me what the people need.[35]

However, there was tremendous pressure from the public, central government, and foreign governments to allow civil society groups to participate in relief efforts. This led to conflicting attempts to support groups that were deemed politically safe and to control groups that were not well known by the local government. Compounding this distrust was the lack of understanding by local government of the role, capacity, and work processes of civil society groups resulting in local government unwilling to grant permission to enter disaster sites, share information, or partner on relief efforts.[36]

To resolve these capacity and government distrust problems, the founders of the Chengdu Urban Rivers Research Group (*Chengdu Chengshi Heliu Yanjiuhui* 成都城市河流研究会), an environmental group, used personal connections in the government to meet

[33] Author interview with provincial government official, Chengdu, Sichuan, June 23, 2008.
[34] Author interview with local PAB official, Chengdu, Sichuan, July 15, 2008.
[35] Ibid.
[36] Author interview with local journalist, Chengdu, Sichuan, July 10, 2008.

with officials in charge of relief efforts to assess how they might effectively partner with the government. Through this meeting, they convinced the government that they could coordinate the civil society community's activities through organizing a command structure called the Non-Governmental Relief Services Center with approximately 30 groups ranging from environmental to poverty alleviation to rural education groups (*5.12 Minjian Jiuzhu Fuwu Zhongxin* "5.12" 民间救助服务中心).[37] In addition to coordinating relief efforts and communication among civil society groups, this umbrella group served as the bridge between civil society and the local government by providing information, mediation, coordination, and the securing of access.[38]

The group used two methods to mobilize groups, resources, and volunteers. First, the Chengdu Urban Rivers Research Group used its online platform to provide real-time information about relief needs and to coordinate information and efforts among government officials, local NGOs, INGOs, volunteers, and donors. Additionally, the group convened a meeting on May 15, 2008, to plan coordinated relief efforts with other members of the umbrella group and resolved issues such as creating a volunteer database, a training program, and an insurance plan. At the end of this meeting, the members of the umbrella group met with the government to establish relief plans and tour the disaster area together. Through this process, civil society groups organized a relief efforts strategy whereby the Non-Governmental Relief Services Center trained and provided volunteers to government agencies or other groups' relief projects; collected financial and material resources from society and delivered these to the disaster sites; and supported the troops with food, medicine, and water. This assistance greatly supported the government's relief efforts and organized the large amounts of donations and numbers of volunteers that were

[37] Ibid.

[38] Jim Yardley and David Barboza, "Many Hands, Not Held by China, Aid in Quake," *The New York Times*, May 20, 2008: available at http://www.nytimes.com/2008/05/20/world/asia/20citizens.html?pagewanted=all

quickly overwhelming the local government.[39] However, does the fact that civil society played a supporting role to the government provide evidence of corporatism? I argue that two factors differentiate the collaboration between local state and autonomous civil society seen in CA from corporatism. First, the local government did not possess control over the groups' employees, funding, or projects. Second, the umbrella group coordinated actions among groups competing in the same issue areas for funding and advocacy. Both of these factors point to a CA model rather than corporatism.

In fact, partnering to deliver relief efforts created an opportunity for local officials to learn about civil society. Despite initial mutual mistrust, relief efforts allowed both actors to understand more about how to work together to secure mutual goals. For example, civil society organizations supported the government troops with water, medicine, and food, and the troops engaged in the more physical efforts of relief work.[40] In relief efforts, cooperation leads to amplification of efforts, money, resources, reach, and legitimacy.[41] The Wenchuan earthquake served as a catalyst for those who wanted to participate in civic projects, leading to the rapid expansion of the civil society sector that some called the "NGO Spring [*NGO chuntian* NGO 春天]."[42]

However, concerns about possible competition and threats to social order still existed among local officials. This worry was further heightened by legal advocacy groups helping angry parents protest and file lawsuits over school collapses after the earthquake.[43] As social unrest increased, local government

39 Author interview with local journalist, Chengdu, Sichuan, July 10, 2008.

40 Author interview with local civil society group, Chengdu, Sichuan, July 16, 2008.

41 Author interview with local civil society group, Chengdu, Sichuan, July 12, 2008.

42 Author interview with staff member of Yunnan grassroots group, Kunming, June 9, 2010; see also Shawn Shieh and Deng Guosheng, "An Emerging Civil Society: The Impact of the 2008 Sichuan Earthquake on Grass-roots Associations in China," *The China Journal*, no. 65, 2011: 181–194.

43 Jill Drew, "Tangled Blame in Quake Deaths: Chinese Parents Facing Uphill Battle for Redress Over Collapsed Schools," *Washington Post*, June 2, 2008: available at http://www.highbeam.com/doc/1P2-16414794.html

pressured civil society organizations to not interact with parents.[44] Local officials were uncertain if groups would continue to play a social mediation role similar to the one played during relief efforts, or a social mobilization role in opposition to government goals. At the time, groups played both roles and the local government restricted access to the parents rather than risk more social unrest. The local government and military performed relief and reconstruction services effectively and received a great deal of domestic and international acclaim, which strengthened the idea of the state as sole provider of social goods.[45] In this way, post-earthquake relief efforts served to teach local officials' about potential roles for civil society as either a partner or challenger to the state. This was reinforced after the 2008 Tibetan protests spilled over into the Tibetan communities in Sichuan; the local government increasingly worried about groups using international funding to oppose certain government policies and create social unrest.

BUILDING CONSULTATIVE AUTHORITARIANISM: COLLABORATING WITH "TRUSTED" GROUPS

Local officials' concerns about social mobilization against the state led to attempted group repression during the 1990s, but low state capacity meant that this repression was often ineffective and arbitrary. In response, many group leaders and individuals were radicalized and undertook progressively more oppositional activities. As unrest increased, so did officials' fears of social organization and mobilization to challenge state authority. Beginning in the late 1990s, collaboration experiences with civil society groups in poverty alleviation projects and the 2008 earthquake relief efforts created new lessons about the impact of civil

44 Author interview with a staff member of a poverty alleviation group, Beijing, July 21, 2008, and with a staff member of an INGO, Beijing, July 22, 2008.

45 Dennis Lai Hang Hui, "Politics of the Sichuan Earthquake," *Journal of Contingencies and Crisis Management* 17, June 2009; "The Earthquake in Sichuan: China Helps Itself," *The Economist*, May 22, 2008: available at http://www.economist.com/node/11409357

society activity in Sichuan. Collaboration for relief efforts served as a learning process for both groups and government, with civil society learning how to work in a complementary fashion within government processes, coordinate activities among different civil society groups, and transmit information about their activities and needs to a wider audience through extensive use of the Internet and media. Local government officials learned how quickly civil society groups could mobilize resources and how these groups could play a complementary role to government efforts that increased effectiveness and the reach of government resources. Through this learning process, participation in relief efforts created new ideas about potential collaboration between the local state and civil society.

In 2010, Chengdu changed the civil society registration policy to direct registration similar to that used in Beijing and Jiangsu, no longer requiring a supervisory agency. However, local officials still fear erosion of local state authority, so seek to collaborate only with "trusted" groups – those led by former government officials or INGOs with extensive financial resources. In this way, Sichuan also fits the consultative authoritarianism model in that officials allow autonomous civil society groups to form but seek to control this expansion. The model developed in Beijing also taught local officials how to develop a more nuanced toolkit of state control rather than relying on threats and intimidation. Whereas Sichuan and Jiangsu originally shared a more confrontational relationship with civil society than did Beijing or Yunnan, by 2009 a rough convergence around the consultative authoritarianism model developed in both provinces.

CONVERGING ON A CONSULTATIVE AUTHORITARIANISM MODEL

Although both provinces initially attempted to tightly control the emergence of autonomous civil society in the 1990s, learning about the benefits of these groups and the ineffectiveness of corporatist methods of state control through direct experience with civil society led to the creation of a consultative authoritarianism model by the late 2000s.

In the 1990s, Jiangsu officials used administrative tools such as civil society registration to control groups and effectively repress most activity because of concerns about social instability. As a result of a dominant promotion strategy focused on stability and fears of civil society's ability to mobilize against the state, officials emphasized social order and subsequent heavy state supervision. Between the mid-1990s and early 2000s, officials' experiences with groups such as the Amity Foundation and the explosion of unregistered community groups both undermined and reinforced this existing relationship with civil society. Officials responded to community group proliferation and the failure of corporatist tools of control by developing new mechanisms of state control, which illustrates the policy shift away from corporatism and toward consultative authoritarianism by the late 2000s.

Sichuan officials also attempted group repression throughout the 1990s because of fears of social instability and loss of state authority; however, lower state capacity meant officials were unable to totally repress these groups and incomplete repression instead generated the very social protests and unrest feared by local officials. However, beginning in the late 1990s, collaboration experiences with civil society including the 2008 earthquake relief efforts taught local officials about the benefits offered by civil society. These direct experiences with civil society influenced an increasing willingness to collaborate with groups that supply external funding and new models to address development challenges. As found in the cases of Beijing and Yunnan, local officials might be motivated by different reasons to cooperate with civil society groups, ranging from personal beliefs in the efficacy of social intermediaries, the reduced role of the local state under small state–big society reforms, and competition among local cadres for promotion.[46] However, these varying motivations

[46] Series of interviews with an academic from the Civil Society Research Center at Peking University, Beijing, November 27, 2006; December 16, 2006; July 7, 2007; June 1, 2008; and author interviews with local government official, Yunnan, March 9, 2007, and retired Health Bureau cadre, Yunnan, May 6, 2007.

coupled with positive experiences with civil society encourage more collaboration with these groups and increasing pluralism in Chinese public policy.

Although Sichuan and Jiangsu share a more confrontational relationship with civil society than do Beijing or Yunnan, in all of these cases, I find growing convergence on a new model of state-society relationship in China that emphasizes the simultaneous rise of a relatively autonomous civil society with differentiated state control depending on whether groups are perceived to advance state goals or challenge state authority. In the next chapter, I analyze the strategies used by civil society groups in China to create positive learning experiences to influence policy and relationship changes between civil society and local state officials. As illustrated by these cases, learning via direct experience is most effective and amplifies the role of civil society in creating this new relationship.

CHAPTER 4

Civil Society Strategies in China: Creating Opportunities for Learning

In the previous chapters, I focused on the learning experiences of local officials in response to the associational revolution in China beginning in the early 1990s. Many of the cases used in these chapters illustrate the vital role played by civil society groups in creating the opportunities for this learning process to occur, which ultimately led to a shift in the relationship between local officials and civil society from the corporatist model to a new model of consultative authoritarianism. Groups use several strategies to create more cooperative relationships with officials to ultimately influence local policy decisions, including information diffusion, the use of interpersonal connections, the organization of protests, and the use of publicity to shame local governments. As I explain in more detail in the next section, although many options exist on this menu of group strategies, information dissemination and use of interpersonal connections have proven most effective in changing the relationships with local officials and influencing long-term policy change. As evidenced by these and the previous case studies, direct experience is the most powerful learning technique, which amplifies the vital role played by civil society in creating opportunities for positive learning experiences. In this way, civil society is not a passive recipient of the new consultative authoritarianism model as suggested by many scholars, but rather an architect of this model.[1]

[1] Xiaoguang Kang and Heng Han, "Graduated Controls: The State-Society Relationship in Contemporary China," *Modern China* 34, January 2008; Xiaoguang Kang and Heng Han, "Government Absorbing Society: A Further Probe into the State-Society Relationship in Chinese Mainland," *Social Sciences in China* 28, no.2 Summer 2007.

I find that civil society is able to create positive learning experiences for local officials that result in the creation of a new local state–civil society relationship. In this chapter, I focus on analyzing the discrete strategies used by groups by first outlining the menu of strategies used to influence local policy makers and then evaluating which successfully create positive learning experiences that result in relationship change. Finally, I compare the strategies used by three environmental groups to create relationship and policy change with both supervisory agencies and a broader array of local government officials. In two of these cases, I find that the dual strategy of information dissemination through interpersonal networks allows groups to successfully influence relationship and policy change. The third case illustrates the successful use of corporatism to control a civil society organization, which may be viewed as evidence for the continued strength of corporatism and against the emergence of consultative authoritarianism. However, the ability of the group to shop for a new supervisory agency and continue working with provincial officials further demonstrates the failure of corporatism and the emergence of CA as the dominant model of social management.

MENU OF CIVIL SOCIETY STRATEGIES

Many strategies exist for civil society groups to achieve the goal of creating meaningful and lasting change in the community of interest, ranging from purposefully more collaborative to more independent ones. In Figure 4.1, I map out these strategies including a spectrum of independence from the government ranging from more collaborative to more independent. Although all of these strategies are successful in attaining short-term policy goals, the first two strategies have the advantage of also creating relationship change.

The first strategy is the action research strategy that operates with the goal of enshrining an original pilot project in local legislation. This strategy is mostly project based, but several groups also attempt to use information dissemination to influence

More collaborative ↑

Strategy	Description
• Action Research	1. Invite targeted government officials to on-site workshops or conferences to convince of benefits 2. Use partners from lowers levels of government to advocate for policy to higher levels (diffusion) 3. Demonstrate external resource commitment if policy is adopted or expanded, usually in the form of a grant from a foreign foundation or INGO
• Interpersonal Networks	1. Hire retired government cadre from relevant agency or use supervisory agency's connections 2. Receive introduction to targeted official through interpersonal network 3. Collaborate with official on pilot or new policy
• Collective Protest	1. Mobilize affected citizens 2. Select tools for protest - chants, banners, type of activities, and site of protest 3. Contract venues for publicity - media outlets, bloggers, higher-level government officials
• Public Shaming	1. Identify targeted official or agency 2. Collect information on the offense (e.g., pollution) especially pictures and testimony 3. Contract venues for publicity - media outlets, bloggers, higher-level government officials
• Strict Independence	1. Conduct activities only in local community 2. Do not register in any capacity 3. Do not fundraise or hold large events so as not to attract official attention

More independent ↓

FIGURE 4.1. Menu of Civil Society Strategies

government policies by inviting officials to participate in activities and meetings where group leaders share research and policy suggestions derived from international best practices. This strategy aligns with the literature on "epistemic communities," literally translated as "knowledge-society."[2] The epistemic community forms as experts on an issue meet counterparts from other states or organizations, at conferences or as members of an international organization focusing on this particular issue. These experts share a similar language and understanding of the issue and begin to form strong ties with international colleagues, including agreeing on possible solutions to given problems. When a policy maker asks these experts how to go about solving a particular issue, the solution agreed upon by this community will be suggested. Similarly, the goals of the action research strategy are to use expert

[2] Ernst Haas, *When Knowledge Is Power: Three Models of Change in International Organizations* (Berkeley: University of California Press, 1991).

information to influence policy change in two ways: first, policy diffusion or "bubble up" to higher levels of government and second, access to the policy-making process normally closed to participation from parties outside the government.[3] As direct lobbying is still technically an illegal activity in China, most groups indirectly advocate for policy change through government trainings, policy research, and pilot site visits.[4]

As the leader of an environmental NGO explained, this strategy operates in three stages: (1) invite the targeted official to an on-site workshop to convince him/her of the benefits of this policy (2) use local partners from lower levels of government to advocate for this policy on behalf of the group, and (3) demonstrate resource commitment from the group if the policy is adopted or expanded.[5] This indirect advocacy strategy depends on a good demonstration site (i.e., large scale and long operation time), supporting research, and an immediately actionable plan. As described in more detail later, this group was successful in using a partnership with the local Poverty Alleviation Bureau (PAB) to change its policy for creating poverty alleviation plans, which demonstrates the utility of this strategy for both civil society groups seeking long-term policy change and for local government officials desiring additional funding and models to address development problems. This action research strategy aims to create partnerships with the local state to change the long-term relationship and influence the policy process through first changing local government policy and then diffusing upward to the national level.

To trace how this strategy works, I profile a Chinese branch of an INGO dedicated to environmental sustainability. This group began operating in Sichuan in 2004 and by 2007 had 14 employees with funding mostly from international grants. The leader of

[3] Author interview with environmental group, Chengdu, Sichuan, July 16, 2008.

[4] Interview with health-based INGO, Kuming, Yunnan June 6, 2007; See also Jude Howell, "New Directions in Civil Society: Organizing around Marginalized Interests," in *Governance in China*, Jude Howell, ed. Lanham, MD: Rowman & Littlefield Publishers, 2004, 160.

[5] Interview with head of an environmental INGO, Chengdu, Sichuan, July 3, 2008.

this group originally worked at a government bureau and founded his first grassroots group with the bureau as his supervisory agency. However, as a result of conflict between the lead cadre at the supervisory agency and the donor over whether the group should use the funding to achieve the cadre's goals or meet the goals outlined in the grant application, the founder left his government position to work for the INGO.[6] This group uses the action research strategy by organizing pilot projects at the sub-provincial level encouraging the use of alternative energy and sustainable development practices. For example, one program installed bio-fuel stoves in rural villages without electricity. These stoves use organic matter such as pig feces to electrify the whole village without being connected to a central grid. For the first step in the action research strategy, this group held a series of workshops and study tours of these pilot projects for government officials from the PAB and other local agencies.[7]

This project, as with the other pilots run by this group, helps advance the goals of the PAB by using international resources to run programs that, at the least, help the PAB meet its responsibilities of alleviating poverty in rural Sichuan, and at best, create policies that successfully diffuse throughout the country. After seeing the pilot projects, PAB agreed to collaborate with this group to take the lessons learned from the original pilots to implement in other areas. As the group leader explained, "Currently, we are moving from 'pilot to policy,' scaling up the reach of earlier pilot projects and engaging decision makers at all levels of the government to generate support for the replication of successful models."[8] Through this type of collaborative experience, the group creates an opportunity for positive learning through experience.

This initial experience may be reinforced not only through local officials meeting promotion goals but also by advancing personal career success for the official who introduced the policy innovation, such as the former Premier Zhao Ziyang's household

[6] Ibid.
[7] Ibid.
[8] Ibid.

responsibility system (*baochan daohu* 包产到户) in the Sichuan countryside.[9] For example, poverty in rural Sichuan is a large and expensive problem that the PAB struggles to resolve with its limited budget, but through its partnership with the group, PAB has been able to fund new and innovative programs to address rural poverty. In this case, in addition to receiving local publicity arranged by the group, the central government awarded the lead cadre an innovation award that positively impacts future promotion decisions. The group leader contends that participating in conferences and study tours in China and abroad accrues personal benefits to local officials, such as opportunities to network with high-ranking provincial and central officials during conferences and travel to Nepal, Thailand, India, the United States, and all over China on study tours.[10] These experiences generate incentives for continued partnership to secure both agency success and individual advancement. For the third step in the action research strategy, local PAB officials advocated the adoption of similar projects throughout the province and to upper-level government officials. In fact, through a series of upper-level government study tours of the site and press coverage arranged by the group, these pilot programs have subsequently been adopted throughout Sichuan and neighboring provinces and continue to receive international financing.[11]

The advantage of this strategy is that it creates opportunities for two types of learning – observed and experienced. As the literature of epistemic communities finds, INGOs play a vital role in transmitting information (or lessons) through transnational networks of technocrats, practitioners, scientists, activists, and policy makers.[12] This transmitted information serves as a source of local policy maker learning through observed models and best practices. However, the disadvantage to this strategy is

[9] Joseph Fewsmith, "Institutions, Informal Politics, and Political Transition in China," *Asian Survey* 36, no.3, 1996: 230–245.

[10] Interview with head of an environmental INGO, Chengdu, Sichuan, July 3, 2008.

[11] Interview with PAB official, Chengdu, Sichuan, July 10, 2008.

[12] Cornelia Beyer, "Non-Governmental Organizations as Motors of Change," *Government and Opposition* 42, Autumn 2007: 513–535.

that groups must be able to access transnational funding, human resources, and information to start a pilot program and offer trainings and workshops to local officials. Thus, INGOs and large grassroots groups tied into transnational networks will best be positioned to effectively use this strategy.

The second collaborative strategy is the interpersonal networks strategy, which is characterized less by sharing information and more by pursuing collaborative pilot projects or policy change through the use of both formal and informal channels to access decision makers. To establish a collaborative project or influence a policy shift, groups first identify an important issue for both the group and the local government, and then the group leader uses either personal connections (*guanxi wang* 关系网) or past government partners to introduce them to an individual from the correct government agency in that area. These informal channels of access to policy makers usually depend on guanxi (关系), defined as a network of personal reciprocal relationships.[13] Next the group meets with officials from this agency and offers to assist by sharing the group's unique skill set (e.g., conflict resolution skills, participation models, technology, and funding) to solve the problem. Then when the project parameters are decided and a pilot project underway, the group is able to create an opportunity for learning through direct experience with partnering officials.

This strategy depends heavily on both informal and formal access points in government, which results in many groups without access "buying guanxi."[14] One way to buy guanxi is to hire a retired government official: "the directors of most of the [NGO] offices are retired cadres who now hold at least half-time jobs consisting of creating good guanxi connections with the local government (*zhengfu guanxi gongzuo*政府关系工作)."[15]

[13] Author interview with Sichuan University professor, Chengdu, Sichuan, July 12, 2008.

[14] Although this phrase is my own, also see Katherine Xin and Jon L. Pearce, "Guanxi: Connections as Substitutes for Formal Institutional Support," *Academy of Management Journal* 39, 1996: 1641–1658.

[15] Interview with environmental INGO's Chinese staff, Lijiang, Yunnan, March 19, 2007.

As cadres legally must retire in their 60s and are increasingly in good health during retirement, many retired cadres choose to join groups to utilize their ties in the community and government to accomplish tasks they were unable to finish prior to retirement. The group then is able to access the policy process informally via the retired cadre's personal connections in his former agency. This strategy of buying guanxi enables groups without government connections to access the policy process through informal channels.

Many former officials also start grassroots groups. As one retired cadre explains, "When I retired I had the connections and knowledge to make a difference in my community, and the government could not easily provide this service due to lack of resources, so I started a grassroots group."[16] This official retired from the Health Bureau and then formed a grassroots group focusing on sanitation projects in rural communities. This was an area he believed the Health Bureau ignored, and in which he could make a meaningful change in government policy:

> When I retired I felt that I had the connections and knowledge to make a difference in my community and my health was still good . . . my network (*wangluo* 网络) is the most important element for my group's success because I know what the government is thinking and can share my opinions to help improve (*wanshan* 完善) their process.[17]

This group established several sanitation pilot programs and received government permits, funding, and other support for these programs. Although the Health Bureau officials originally agreed to the pilot programs because of personal connections, this collaboration allowed them to learn about the benefits of sanitation projects in rural communities and begin to expand these projects outside of the original scope.

Another strategy for using interpersonal networks to reach policy makers is for group leaders to secure access through formal channels, such as National or Local People's Congress (NPC/LPC) representatives and the Chinese Communist Party (CCP),

[16] Interview with retired Health Bureau cadre, Kunming, Yunnan, May 6, 2007.
[17] Interview with retired Health Bureau cadre, Kunming, Yunnan, May 6, 2007.

often in the form of overlapping memberships in government institutions and civil society. For example, many LPC representatives also form civil society groups around their interests, for example, several prominent LPC members in Beijing who operate groups committed to diverse issues such as migrant and women's rights.[18] In fact, Zhao Meiying finds through survey research that an increasing number of civil society members joined the CCP, from 11.2 percent in 1995 to 23.7 percent in 2004.[19] Also increasingly common are LPC representatives who lead private business associations. As one founder of a private business association who also serves as an LPC representative in Yunnan stated, "the best way to influence policy is through the legislature not the government."[20] However, more commonly, groups use informal channels created through personal connections, which do not depend on accessing the decision-making process through institutional channels such as government agencies or LPCs, but rather through personal relationships with decision makers themselves.

One advantage to this guanxi strategy is that civil society groups can establish opportunities for collaboration with the local state as a practical strategy for accessing the policy process, normally closed to public participation. Therefore, this strategy might be most effective for groups with local officials embedded in group members' guanxi networks, or with the ability to buy guanxi. Although access to the policy process depends in large part on the ability of groups to create interpersonal relationships with government officials, many interviewees pointed out that these connections to government officials help secure access but

[18] Author interview with staff member for grassroots NPO focused on community participation, Beijing, July 3, 2007; and the founder of grassroots NPO focused on rural women, Beijing, July 31, 2007.

[19] 赵美英, "新社会阶层政治诉求的调查与机制研究 [Survey and Causal Mechanism Analysis of the New Social Stratum's Political Demands]," 江苏省社会主义学院学报 [*Journal of Jiangsu Institute of Socialism*] 1, 2006: 35–38.

[20] Author interview with head of private business association and LPC representative, Simao, Yunnan, February 9, 2007; also see Kellee Tsai, *Capitalism without Democracy: The Private Sector in Contemporary China* (Ithaca, NY: Cornell University Press, 2007).

do not guarantee success. In fact, one cadre gave several examples when guanxi was not enough to secure success, but access to resources or services the government could not provide gave a group more influence than one with connections.[21] Thus, personal connections to the local government help secure joint projects, but the same goals of policy and relationship change may also be achieved through collaboration if the group has enough resources or innovative ideas to tempt local officials into working with an unknown group, as seen through the action research strategy.

Groups use three additional independent strategies to influence policy change: collective protest, shaming politics, and complete independence. Both collective protest and shaming politics were used in the Yunnan hydroelectric projects blocked by a coalition of environmental groups described in Chapter 2.[22] Groups pursuing a shaming politics strategy often publicize information via the news media or Internet in an attempt to create public pressure, although this channel is not frequently used by groups other than environmental groups.[23] The final strategy is used by groups that do not want to attract official attention; however, these groups must remain small and not undertake any policy projects.

In comparing these five strategies, the first two more collaborative strategies of action research and guanxi are the most effective in creating the opportunities for observed and experienced learning and thus in gaining long-term relationship and policy change. However, these two strategies also are more effective at lower levels of government where the group may create or have access points; for example, 60 percent of all registered groups operate at the county level and below.[24] The three more independent strategies of collective protest, shaming politics, and

[21] Interviews with head of local biodiversity NPO, March 31, 2007; and government cadre, April 2, 2007 in Lijiang, Yunnan.

[22] Also see Andrew Mertha, *China's Water Warriors: Citizen Action and Policy Change* (Ithaca, NY: Cornell University Press, 2008).

[23] Guobin Yang, "The Co-Evolution of the Internet and Civil Society in China," *Asian Survey* 43, 2003: 405–422.

[24] Hauser Center for Nonprofit Organizations, Harvard University, 2009, available at http://hausercenter.org

full independence are less successful at achieving these long-term goals because the lack of interaction does not offer the same opportunities for officials' learning, and protest and shaming strategies create negative experiences rather than positive ones.

The lack of effective institutional channels for policy participation and the opportunity to influence cadre learning encourages civil society groups to develop more cooperative strategies with local government agencies.[25] This is a purposeful strategy used by successful groups and not simply an inevitable outcome of an authoritarian structure; this means that although the government is unquestionably the stronger party, the relationship between state and civil society is not simply one of coercion but also relies on interaction. This finding differs from Kang Xiaoguang's differentiated control approach in that civil society groups have the motivation and strategies to gain access to the policy process and shape future relationships, rather than simply accepting the current leadership's idea of the role of civil society.[26] Although variation in civil society strategies exists, along with much debate about what these strategies mean for civil society independence in an authoritarian state, the non-collaborative strategies are less successful in achieving long-term relationship and policy change but still are effective for achieving short-term policy goals such as temporarily halting the construction of hydroelectric projects in Yunnan.[27]

This is a similar conclusion to the one that Greenpeace-China drew from its experience in Yunnan in the late 1990s. To protest illegal deforestation, Greenpeace used collective protest and shaming strategies in 2003 against the company involved, APP, and the Yunnan local government. These strategies were successful in 2005 in forcing the local government and APP to halt these

[25] Mary Gallagher, "China: The Limits of Civil Society in a Late Leninist State," *Civil Society and Political Change in Asia*, Muthiah Alagappa, ed. (Stanford, CA: Stanford University Press, 2004), p. 420.

[26] I am indebted to Vivienne Shue for pointing out this important difference.

[27] The use of more collaborative strategies is hotly debated among civil society groups in China, especially concerning the relationship between collaboration and autonomy.

practices, but this negative experience with Greenpeace caused the Yunnan government to force the group out of the province. However, after this experience, Greenpeace used more collaborative strategies with the local Beijing government and was invited to help draft a renewable energy law in 2006. These collaborative strategies were more effective in creating opportunities for two types of learning, both observed and experienced, that ultimately changed the targeted environmental policies but also influenced long-term relationship change with local officials.

As illustrated in the following section, collaborative strategies pursued by civil society generated opportunities for supervisory and local officials to learn about these groups and ultimately undermine the corporatist control system in China to create the new CA model.

THE FAILURE OF CORPORATISM IN CHINA: CREATING LEARNING OPPORTUNITIES FOR LOCAL OFFICIALS

The number and types of Chinese civil society groups have dramatically increased since the mid-1990s, consisting of social organizations, clubs, business and industry associations, charities, foundations, and nonprofits. In fact, the Ministry of Civil Affairs reports that registered social groups have increased from fewer than 5,000 in 1988 to more than 400,000 in 2009, with an estimated additional 2 million to 3 million registered as companies (Figure 4.2).

In addition to the growth in the number of domestic groups, Chinese branches of international nongovernmental organizations proliferated during this time period, with more than 350 groups active in China by 2009, including 700 foreign grantmaking foundations.[28] For example, The Nature Conservancy opened three offices in Western China and Beijing, in addition to multiple project offices, and Greenpeace also opened offices in

[28] Norton Wheeler, *The Role of American NGOs in China's Modernization: Invited Influence* (London: Routledge, 2012).

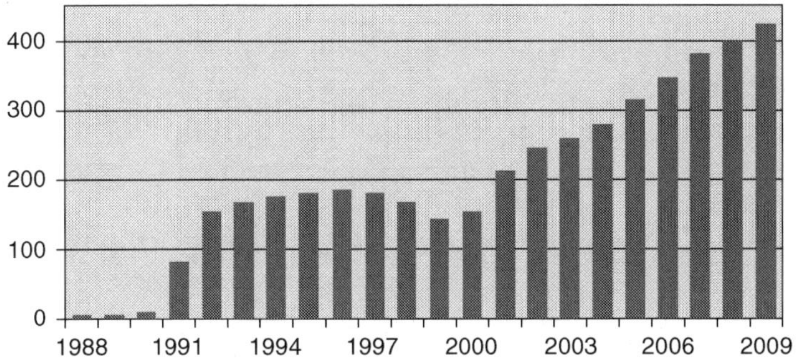

FIGURE 4.2 Growth in Registered Civil Society Groups (in thousands)

Hong Kong, Yunnan, and Beijing. All emerging civil society groups were initially required to register with the Ministry of Civil Affairs through the dual management system (*shuangchong guanli tizhi*), which attempted to incorporate groups through a sponsoring government agency and an annual review with the local Civil Affairs Bureau. This system derived from the revised "Regulation on Registration and Management of NPOs" promulgated by the State Council in October 1998 to standardize and legalize the administration of China's civil society groups.

This system is so expensive and difficult for most groups to navigate that many simply register as a for-profit organization and pay taxes or operate informally without any legal status. The groups that register place themselves under the professional management of a state agency with responsibilities in its area of work (colloquially called a mother-in-law). The professional management agency holds a wide range of responsibilities including supervising the organizations' ideological work, financial and personnel management, research activities, contacts with foreign organizations, and the reception and use of donations from overseas, which are the primary funding source for larger groups.[29] The mother-in-law also takes full responsibility for the activities

29 "Guanyu chongxin queren shehui tuanti yewu zhuguan danwei de tongzhi" [Circular on Reconfirming the Professional Management Units of Social Organizations], *Ministry of Civil Affairs*, 2000.

and finances of its registered groups, which creates a risk and authority-sharing mechanism between the Ministry of Civil Affairs (MoCA) and potential supervisory agencies. This regulation clearly aims to encourage corporatism, whereby the mother-in-law has a regulatory incentive to control group activity to avoid political risk.

Although civil society regulations in China require groups to register with supervisory agencies to control civil society activity through corporatism, these regulations have not been successful. Instead, the changing political economy encourages local officials and supervisory cadres to collude with trusted group leaders, and these experiences gradually subvert the corporatist regulatory structure to build consultative authoritarianism.[30] As I demonstrate in the following comparative cases, civil society plays an important role in this learning process by using collaborative strategies to create opportunities for officials to learn about the benefits offered by these groups. The outcome of this learning process is increasing group participation in policy unintended by either civil society regulations or the single-party system in China and most recently a reevaluation of existing civil society regulations. The fact that civil society groups have begun to fundamentally alter relationships with local officials and influence public policy in a system that legally does not allow for public participation in less than two decades is a remarkable finding, and one that I explore in more detail later.

ENVIRONMENTAL CIVIL SOCIETY IN CHINA: THE SUCCESS OF COLLABORATIVE STRATEGIES

The first formally registered environmental NGO was Friends of Nature (FON) founded in 1994 by Liang Congjie. Although environmental nongovernmental organizations (eNGOs) did not

[30] See Kellee Tsai for an excellent analysis of this process with government agencies regulating private business associations: "Adaptive Informal Institutions and Endogenous Institutional Change in China," *World Politics* 59, no.1, 2006: 116–141.

exist in China prior to 1994, by 2008 the number of registered eNGOs expanded to more than 3,000, with many more unregistered, or informal, NGOs active in this sector. In fact, according to two national surveys, the total number of Chinese eNGOs increased from 2,768 by the end of 2005 to 3,539 by October 2008.[31]

In this section, I compare the strategies used by three grassroots environmental groups to create positive learning opportunities for local officials to influence short-term policy change as well as long-term relationship change. As shown in the case of Yunnan, eNGOs may also create negative learning experiences. Thus, I examine how two groups' strategies led to the desired positive learning experience through the use of both interpersonal networks and action research strategies, whereas a third group was unsuccessful. The three environmental groups are similar in that all employ a mixture of private citizens and government employees, are registered, and receive most of their funding in the form of international grants. However, FON and the Global Environmental Institute (GEI) successfully created positive learning experiences with local and supervisory officials, whereas a third eNGO was unable to replicate its successful relationship with provincial officials with its supervisory agency.[32] Although the successful use of corporatism in this case may be viewed as evidence against the emergence of consultative authoritarianism, I argue that the ability of the group to shop for a new supervisory agency and continue to collaborate with provincial officials further demonstrates the failure of corporatism and the emergence of CA as the dominant model of social management.

The first case analyzes the first formally registered eNGO, Friends of Nature, founded in 1994 by Liang Congjie. Liang Congjie first attempted to register his group with the State

[31] J. Cui, "3500 Environmental NGOs in China," *Xinhua News Agency*, 2008: available at http://news.xinhuanet.com/environment/2008-10/30/content_10282938.htm

[32] Following convention, the group "eNGO" and most interviewee names have been kept anonymous to protect the identity of the sources when requested. However, the group names of FON and GEI are used as much of the information presented is now publicly available, but names of many interviewees are anonymous.

Environment Protection Agency (SEPA); however, after waiting 10 months, the group was ultimately rejected by SEPA unless it was willing to become an umbrella group responsible for representing the interests of all Chinese people sharing environmental concerns.[33] This umbrella type of organization is similar to the federations established under corporatist arrangements such as the All-China Federation of Trade Unions, which was established in 1925 as the umbrella for more than 30 regional trade unions with a total membership of 130 million. Liang believed this was too ambitious in some ways and too limiting in others and sought another supervisory agency. In accordance with the corporatist model, he was also told that each ministry should sponsor only one association or society in each field, and as SEPA already sponsored the China Environmental Science Society, it could not provide sponsorship to another organization.[34] Liang also asked the Environment Protection Bureau of the Beijing Municipal Government, the China Association of Science and Technology, and the Chinese People's Political Consultation Committee to serve as FON's supervisory unit but without success.[35] He ultimately registered as a secondary organization with the Academy of Chinese Culture, a publication house where he was a professor and vice president.[36] The Ministry of Culture in Beijing supervised both the Academy of Chinese Culture and FON. However, despite the intention of these regulations to control the development of civil society, his group went on to found the large environmental movement existing in China today and over time changed many environmental policies and its relationship with several government agencies.

[33] The State Environmental Protection Agency (SEPA) was changed to the Ministry of the Environment (MEP) in 2009.

[34] Interview with Ministry of Civil Affairs employee, Beijing, June 2, 2008.

[35] Song Yang, "Grassroots Nonprofit Organizations in China: Origin and Path," *Public Welfare Times*, March 27, 2009, translation in English available at http://hausercenter.org/chinanpo/2009/03/grassroots-nonprofit-organizations-in-china-origin-and-path/

[36] Tony Saich, "Negotiating the State: The Development of Social Organizations in China," *The China Quarterly* 161, March 2000: 124–141.

FON used a multipronged approach to environmental advocacy composed of the use of interpersonal networks, research action, and shaming via media publicity. These strategies were successful in achieving policy goals and relationship change with MEP; however, the use of a media strategy created challenges for finding a new supervisory agency after the founder's death in 2011. FON formed to work on environmental awareness across China; however, it concentrated many of its projects in Yunnan and the southwestern provinces. The group currently employs approximately 21 employees, many of whom were former government or state-owned media employees. The founder of the group, Liang Congjie, concurrently held a government research position and was well known for environmental activism through FON. Liang's simultaneous employment through a government research academy created high levels of interpersonal trust with his colleagues in the supervisory agency.[37] FON used Liang's interpersonal network to create campaigns encouraging conservation, such as series of widely publicized campaigns to save the snub-nosed monkey and Tibetan antelope and to oppose illegal logging in southwestern China.

Liang played a crucial role by using his position and personal connections as a member of the Chinese Peoples Political Consultative Congress (CPPCC) to bring these issues to the attention of the media and government leaders. In the civil society community, these campaigns are credited with "transforming the environmental movement in China, demonstrating to NGOs and activists that civil society could play a role in shaping policy."[38] The campaigns also demonstrated the success of Friends of Nature's strategy to influence public policy through a multipronged strategy that involved working with government allies, the media,

[37] Peter Ho, "Self-Imposed Censorship and De-Politicized Politics in China: Green Activism or a Color Revolution," in *China's Embedded Activism: Opportunities and Constraints of a Social Movement*, Peter Ho and Richard Edmonds, eds. (New York: Routledge, 2008), pp. 20–43.

[38] Shawn Shieh, "The Passing of Liang Congjie, China's Environmental and Civil Society Pioneer," NGOs in China blog, November 1, 2010, available at http://ngochina.blogspot.com/2010/11/passing-of-liang-congjie-chinas.html

and the public to respectfully pressure government authorities to enforce environmental laws.[39] For example, in September 2008, a FON member in Sichuan accompanied a Chinese Central Television crew to film the widespread logging occurring in Hongya county despite the new central government ban. Liang explained that Prime Minister Zhu Rongji watched the broadcast report, which "made him very angry with the local forestry bureau, and ... made the local officials very, very angry with us."[40] The use of media to highlight local violations of environmental policies and to pressure the central government to enforce these policies was also used to great effect in the snub-nosed monkey campaign in Yunnan. FON's strategy is to first use interpersonal networks to access central government policy makers and then a combination of action research and media shaming tactics to point out violations of existing policies. Even though Liang expressed exasperation at the "uphill struggle involved in the implementation of what is often official central government policy," he also carefully followed this multipronged strategy to "always choose the battlefield that I am quite sure I can win."[41] FON developed this strategy by successfully pursuing prominent environmental campaigns while shielded from repercussions from other government agencies through his connections with his supervisory agency and high-ranking CCP members.

Through this multipronged strategy, FON created opportunities for positive learning experiences for officials working in the area of environmental policy. For example, this learning process is demonstrated by the fact that FON's campaigns were also supported by SEPA, whose leaders originally refused to have a relationship with the group. This change was a result of FON's efforts at "boundary-spanning contention," whereby it

[39] Peter Ho, "Greening without Conflict? Environmentalism, NGOs and Civil Society in China," *Development and Change* 32, no. 5, 2001: 893–921.

[40] Teresa Poole, "China's 'Friends of Nature' Join the Tibetan Antelope on the List of Endangered Species," *The Independent*, November 22, 2008: available at http://www.independent.co.uk/news/chinas-friends-of-nature-join-the-tibetan-antelope-on-the-list-of-endangered-species-1186633.html

[41] Ibid.

undertook activities that skirt the boundaries of what is politically allowed to advance policies by repeatedly pressing the state to include SEPA assessments for any development project that might negatively impact the environment.[42] As a result of the campaign led by this group and continued media pressure, SEPA is now mandated to have greater involvement in developmental projects.[43] In fact, the Environmental Impact Assessment Law of 2002 required public hearings or other forms of public consultation to get community and expert feedback on a project or construction that is likely to have environmental impacts, with the exception of "projects of confidentiality according to national code." After this learning experience, SEPA actively supported FON by encouraging subordinate agencies to allow projects and share resources with the group.[44]

In addition to creating opportunities for environmental officials to directly learn about the benefits of working with civil society groups to push for policy changes, Liang also encouraged learning via observation by winning prominent awards such as the Earth Award established by Friends of the Earth (Hong Kong) and the Conservation and Environment Grants by the Ford Motor Company.[45] His prestige as a result of these numerous international awards helped diffuse the lesson of the benefits of collaborating with civil society to other officials. In these ways, this group creates opportunities for officials throughout the country to learn about civil society. The group's success in achieving policy goals also advocated by cadres in the supervisory agency and bringing international prestige to the supervisory officials

[42] Kevin J. O'Brien, "Neither Transgressive nor Contained: Boundary-Spanning Contention in China," *Mobilization: An International Journal* 8, 2003: 51–64.

[43] Mertha, *China's Water Warriors*; interview with an academic studying eNGOs, Beijing, January 8, 2007.

[44] Elizabeth Economy, "Environmental NGOs in China: Encouraging Action and Addressing Public Grievances," *Roundtable before the Congressional–Executive Commission on China*, February 7, 2005: available at http://www.cecc.gov/events/roundtables/environmental-ngos-in-china-encouraging-action-and-addressing-public-grievances

[45] Guobin Yang, "Environmental NGOs and Institutional Dynamics in China," *The China Quarterly* 2005: 46–66.

created a relationship in which the supervisory agency shielded the group from political pressure, rather than controlling the group as intended by the civil society regulations.

Despite FON's successes in realizing policy and relationship changes, the group's registration status with the Ministry of Culture originally was the result of interpersonal connections, so after Liang Congjie's death, FON was asked by the ministry to locate another supervisory agency. FON's use of a media-shaming strategy taught a negative lesson about the political risks of supervising a group that often embarrasses government officials. Thus, several government agencies refused to supervise FON because of fears of political risk and difficulties in supervising the projects and funding sources.[46] However, other agencies expressed interest in supervising FON because of its advantages – international funding, policy innovation, and prestige. After many discussions, Li Bo, the new director of FON, registered with the Chaoyang District Science and Technology Commission (北京市朝阳区科学技术委员会) as the supervisory unit. The commission shared many environmental policy goals with FON as learned by cadres attending conferences and talks hosted by FON. As illustrated in the following case, some supervisory agencies do not merely shield the group from political repercussions as seen with FON, but also actively use agency resources to promote the group's policy agenda when it corresponds with that of the supervisory agency. If this relationship develops between the commission and FON over the long term remains to be seen; however, FON's strategy has been effective in the past at creating enough positive experiences to lead to policy and relationship change.

The second case examines how the Global Environmental Institute used interpersonal networks and research action to create positive learning opportunities for officials in SEPA, local forestry agencies, and local environmental protection bureaus. GEI is a Chinese nonprofit, nongovernmental organization established in Beijing in 2004, with the mission of designing and

[46] Author interview with China Development Brief staff member, Beijing, June 6, 2011.

implementing market-based models for solving environmental problems to achieve development that is economically, ecologically, and socially sustainable. Jin Jiaman, the founder of GEI, first co-founded another environmental organization, Green Earth Volunteers, in 1996 when civil society groups were just starting to appear in China.

In the mid-1990s, Jin served as director of the Chinese Research Academy of Environmental Science, under the auspices of the Chinese Academy of Science. Her academic research on how ineffective pollution-reducing regulations were when implemented without economic considerations, coupled with her experience at Green Earth Volunteers, convinced her that China's environmental groups should participate in the policy process to advocate innovative approaches to these policy failures: "I felt that by 2002, Chinese NGOs should reach that level of involvement."[47] Committed to forming a research organization with a market-oriented approach to solving environmental problems, Jin founded GEI in 2003 with the support of other members of the Chinese Research Academy of Environmental Science and start-up funding from The Blue Moon Fund, a U.S. foundation. GEI registered as a people-run nonprofit organization (*minban feiqiye danwei*) in Beijing in March 2004, with the Chaoyang District Science and Technology Commission serving as its supervisory agency (*zhuguan danwei*).[48] An international fundraising office was established in the United States, and another is being registered in Brussels. Jin Jiaman retained her affiliation with the government research institute, the Chinese Academy of Sciences, and supervises a team of 12 full-time staff.[49]

The Chaoyang District Science and Technology Commission officials initially were sympathetic to GEI's mission, but to develop a stronger relationship, GEI focused its projects specifically on

[47] Beijing's Global Environment Institute Tests the Boundaries of NGO Activity, WorldWatch Institute, January 2012: available at www.worldwatch.org/node/3961

[48] Interview with GEI employee, Beijing, January 16, 2012.

[49] See GEI's website for staff background information: available at http://www.geichina.org

collaborative approaches involving its supervisory unit. Over time, the group developed such a supportive relationship with the supervisory agency that it shared resources including interpersonal connections to meet mutually agreed-upon policy goals. GEI staff stress that the main goal of the group is to "integrate environmental and economic problem-solving in China by building local and international collaboration between government agencies, research institutions, private enterprises, and nongovernmental organizations."[50] GEI's work covers four program areas: energy and climate change, biodiversity conservation, rural development, and local capacity building. Projects usually follow an action research strategy involving collaboration among GEI staff, academic researchers, other local and international NGOs, and local governments. For example, in GEI's conservation work, the group promotes an innovative approach called "conservation concession" or "conservation incentive agreements," which relies on contractual partnerships between the government and private organizations, such as an institution, private corporation, or community, to help manage state-owned lands with the goals of ecosystem and biodiversity conservation. GEI employees contend that this approach, which has proven successful in the Amazon areas of Peru and Brazil, will help preserve some of China's most ecologically fragile regions in Yunnan, Sichuan, and Guangxi.[51]

Collaborative projects like these create a learning laboratory for cadres in the supervisory agency, local officials, and community members. Not only have county and provincial-level officials who collaborated on the original pilot in Sichuan successfully helped advocate for the expansion of this project, but also GEI won the prestigious protection of the natural environment award

[50] Interview with GEI employee, Yunnan, April 7, 2007.

[51] Ibid.; for analysis of this Conservation International model, see Richard Rice et al., "Conservation Incentive Agreements: An Approach to Linking Conservation and Economic Development on Indigenous Lands in Ecuador," paper presented at *The International Conference on Rural Livelihoods, Forests and Biodiversity*, May 19–23, 2003, Bonn, Germany: available at http://www.cifor.org/publications/corporate/cd-roms/bonn-proc/pdfs/papers/T4_FINAL_Rice.pdf

granted annually by the Ford Motor Company (China) in 2008. The award and its 10,000 yuan (US$1,642) contribution for the further development of the project was presented at the Ford Motor's Environmental Protection Award ceremony at the Great Hall of the People in Beijing, attended by many prominent government officials including the head of the People's Committee for the Protection of the Environment and Natural Resources. Jin Jiaman stated, "I am very excited to learn of the award granted to the Conservation Concessions Agreement project. This, along with the nomination of GEI's Tibet Rural Sustainable Development Project for the Ford Environmental Award last year, shows that GEI's projects are meaningful and are being recognized by the general public."[52] Gaining national prominence for these projects reinforced and diffused the lesson of the benefits of collaboration between civil society and local governments.

Similarly, in its rural development projects, GEI focused on using the action research strategy by promoting a collaborative approach to renewable energy, organic agriculture, and ecotourism. For example, in Chanshui village in western Yunnan, the group established a demonstration project to help local villagers organize a farming cooperative association to connect small organic farmers to markets. This strategy aligns closely with the action research strategy, as Lila Buckley, GEI's assistant executive director, notes: "A lot of our projects have the potential to continue on their own ... once we set up the demonstration project ... What we aim to do in the next few years is help some of our more developed projects connect with investors or establish their own profit-deriving entities."[53] The ultimate goal of the action research strategy is that the project be institutionalized through policy change.

In addition to establishing demonstration sites to promote learning about the benefits of environmental projects with civil

[52] GEI Press Release: available at http://www.geichina.org/index.php?controller=News&action=View&nid=63

[53] Beijing's Global Environment Institute Tests the Boundaries of NGO Activity, 2012: available at http://www.worldwatch.org/node/3961

society, GEI also disseminated its research through trainings and workshops to influence policy makers in multiple government agencies. For example, GEI trained current and future government leaders in an environmental curriculum at the Central Party School of the Chinese Communist Party, focusing on its model for sustainable rural development by helping communities conserve the local ecosystems upon which their livelihoods depend and by establishing market access for rural communities through sustainable rural micro-enterprises.[54] GEI also has facilitated local and international dialogue on climate change among governments, research bodies, and NGOs.[55] The Chaoyang District Science and Technology Commission supports these projects because of common policy goals by using shared resources, including agency leaders' guanxi networks. GEI also created positive learning experiences that changed its relationship with other government partners, including the State Environmental Protection Agency, the State Forestry Agency, the Office of National Coordination Committee for Climate Change, the National Development and Reform Commission, and the National People's Congress Environment and Resources Committee. In fact, GEI intentionally partners with local governments to create opportunities for learning through cost sharing on all collaborative projects, with GEI, the local government, and community each paying one-third of the cost for the project.[56]

GEI's action research and interpersonal network strategy has been very successful in achieving policy and relationship changes. As the World Watch Institute notes, "few fledgling nongovernmental organizations can claim the kind of success that GEI has

[54] Ji-Qiang Zhang and Christine Tsang, "The Global Environmental Institute (GEI)," 2011: available at http://www.bluemoonfund.org/how-we-work/jewels/gei/

[55] "Secretary Clinton Supports Expansion of U.S.-China EcoPartnerships Program," U.S. Department of State Fact Sheet, May 11, 2011: one of the six new EcoPartnerships announced was the Center for Climate Strategies (Washington, D.C.) with Global Environmental Institute (Beijing, China), which was also the only NGO pairing: available at http://www.state.gov/r/pa/prs/ps/2011/05/163178.htm

[56] Interview with GEI employee, Yunnan, April 7, 2007.

enjoyed: an operating budget of half a million dollars, a board comprised of internationally prominent environmental professionals, an impressive portfolio of projects, and even a spin-off organization."[57] This success was enabled by support first from the supervisory agency and then through GEI's collaboration strategy with other local governments and agencies. As Jin explains, "If you want to influence policy, what you say needs to be well researched to be convincing. In China, most of the country's experts work for government research institutions. As an NGO, we do not have the ability yet to keep up with the government."[58] In order to influence policy makers, GEI built long-term cooperative relationships with government officials through the learning laboratory of collaborative projects.

As the GEI case illustrates, the dual management system, intending to use corporatist arrangements to control groups, actually promotes a learning process and gradual alignment of mutual goals between supervisory agencies and civil society. This relationship shift increases the ability of groups to influence public policy in ways not allowed by the political system. As Andrew Mertha notes in the hydropower cases, "The contemporary politics of hydropower have provided an unprecedented degree of political pluralism to the Chinese policy process, in which government agencies in opposition to these hydropower projects seamlessly ally themselves with NGOs."[59] Although it is inaccurate to view groups simply as proxies for the supervisory agency or other local officials, groups are able to advance a mutually desirable policy agenda but one that officials cannot advocate or at least not in the same transparent way.

A more accurate description of the relationship between the group and local officials is one in which interests coincide and each partner contributes to the policy goal in the most appropriate way. For example, groups supply international funding, domestic

[57] Beijing's Global Environment Institute Tests the Boundaries of NGO Activity, 2012.

[58] Ibid.

[59] Mertha, *China's Water Warriors*, p. 3.

and international awareness and prestige, and a demonstration site to provide a model of the desired policy change. The agency directs subordinate agencies to partner with the group, allowing access and resources to successfully run the pilot. Once the pilot is underway, the agency also invites central and provincial cadres on study tours so that they can adopt this model in their localities and diffuse this policy throughout China. The Chinese state consistently engages in a policy process of decentralized experimentation, or "proceeding from point to surface" (*youdian daomian* 由点到面), whereby models are tested regionally and then adopted nationally if successful.[60]

These two cases demonstrate the failure of corporatism through the process of learning enabled by the dual management regulations and the strategies used by civil society groups to create opportunities for positive experiences with local officials. I find that the use of more collaborative strategies such as interpersonal networks and action research are most effective in creating the learning opportunities necessary for relationship change. In fact, many supervisory agencies play a supporting role by accessing resources for groups, arranging pilot sites through subordinate government agencies, and using guanxi networks to set up study tours to diffuse the policy. With guanxi networks throughout the party and state, as well as familiarity with party-state structures and concerns, supervisory agency officials can be important partners for civil society groups, which reside outside of the government administrative system and legal channels for policy participation.

In contradistinction to these two successful cases, many supervisory agencies attempt to tightly control groups as intended by the corporatist regulations. However, as the last case of eNGO illustrates, even when a supervisory agency attempts this control, it is no longer effective with the emergence of autonomous groups. This eNGO worked to preserve ecological and biological diversity in a western province and until 2010 operated with

[60] Sebastian Heilmann, "From Local Experiments to National Policy: The Origins of China's Distinctive Policy Process," *The China Journal* 59, January 2008.

approximately 23 staff members. This group was started in 1995 by individuals from a government agency (the Public Security Bureau) and a government research academy (Chinese Academy of Sciences), who simultaneously ran the organization and continued to hold government research positions. The rest of the staff was mostly composed of private citizens, and the group received the majority of its funding in the form of foreign grants from groups such as the Ford Foundation and the World Wildlife Fund along with limited funding from the provincial government for individual projects.

The group originally registered with the Department of Forestry in 1995. In the beginning, the group brought in significant grants from abroad and applied them to projects that also met the agency's goals. These projects received significant attention from environmental groups abroad as well as from SEPA, which helped raise the profile of the supervisory cadre as the head of the Department of Forestry. However, despite these positive experiences, the relationship between the group leader and the cadre began to suffer by the early 2000s. The supervisory cadre attempted to exert more control over this group to use its foreign funding to advance his personal goals rather than achieve those outlined in the group's grant proposal.[61] As one staff member explained, "the cadre [mother-in-law] doesn't feel that his interests or those of the agency are being met and tried to exert more control which led to conflict between the two men."[62] Over time, this conflict eroded the interpersonal trust between the two, as both believed the other misunderstood the appropriate role of the group. The cadre from the mother-in-law viewed the group and its resources as private sources of finance and prestige, and not as an independent entity with its own agenda. Mutual suspicion over the intentions of the other hindered possible cooperation to advance both the group's and the cadre's goals, and the

[61] Series of interviews with eNGO employee, May 10, 2007; May 14, 2008; and August 11, 2011; interview with environmental INGO employee, March 19, 2007.

[62] Series of interviews with eNGO employee, May 10, 2007; May 14, 2008; and August 11, 2011.

supervisory cadre sought to more tightly control the group's activities and assets.

Although this situation of supervisory cadres exercising power over activities and budgets might be intended by the corporatist regulatory system, the response of the group leader was certainly unintended. Rather than simply allowing for greater control by the mother-in-law, the group leader began shopping for a new mother-in-law: "due to a personal conflict between the leaders of the department and the group, the group will likely change its registration to [the agency] where one of the group leaders still works."[63] The situation of low and deteriorating interpersonal trust led to the supervisory cadre attempting to heavily control the group and the group leader choosing an exit strategy. Although the supervisory cadre learned that the group could bring in additional overseas resources, he did not learn that the group also could implement innovative ideas in collaboration with the agency. The inability of the group leader to teach this lesson via collaborative strategies with the supervisory cadre resulted in this poor relationship, which diverged from the strong relationship he built with provincial officials through using his personal network. However, although the outcome of the interactions between group and supervisory agency resulted in state control predicted by the corporatist regulations, the group simply located a new supervisory unit and then was awarded a large grant from the provincial government to develop programs to protect national endangered plants and wildlife. As this case demonstrates, the incentive for local officials to partner with groups to innovate around policy failures and the mobility of these groups to locate more accommodating supervisory units undermines the corporatist system.

IMPLICATIONS FOR CIVIL SOCIETY DEVELOPMENT AND REGULATORY CHANGE IN CHINA

These cases illustrate how civil society is able to create positive learning opportunities for local officials through collaborative

[63] Ibid.

strategies that serve to change policy and relationships over time. I argue that this finding has important implication for how we understand local state–civil society relationships in China. Structurally, these groups are constrained in legal and financial ways; however, as the case studies illustrate, these constraints may also be opportunities if groups are able to promote learning by officials about the governance benefits of civil society. As Lu Yiyi explains, "the common belief that Chinese NGOs, particularly officially-organised NGOs, suffer from a lack of autonomy is in fact based on two false equations. First, policy is equated with actual practice. Second, government support and commitment of its resources are equated with control."[64] As the empirical evidence from these cases shows, these "equations" are not consistently accurate. Although the dual management system intends to tightly control civil society, groups that skillfully handle the relationship with the supervisory agency are able to maintain autonomy and even enhance policy influence through mother-in-law shielding or support. Similar to my findings, Xueyong Zhan and Shui-Yan Tang contend that environmental NGOs play a much more active role in public policy and have stronger relationships with government agencies than normally thought or allowed by the formally corporatist political system.[65] In fact, based on in-depth research with 28 eNGOs, these authors find that groups with better financial resources and connections to the party-state system are more capable of utilizing opportunities to enhance their policy advocacy capacity.[66] However, whereas a purposeful strategy to influence long-term relationship and policy change is needed, groups also must maintain high interpersonal trust with the supervisory agency and therefore must be sensitive to the political situation into which its activities might put the agency, perhaps leading to

[64] Lu Yiyi, "The Autonomy of Chinese NGOs: A New Perspective," *China: An International Journal* 5, 2007: 173–203.

[65] Xueyong Zhan and Shui-Yan Tang, "Political Opportunities, Resource Constraints and Policy Advocacy of Environmental NGOs in China," *Public Administration* 91, no. 2, 2013, 381–399.

[66] Ibid.

self-censorship.[67] Additionally, many groups find navigating the relationship with supervisory agencies difficult. For example, Ru finds that supervisory agencies sometimes interfere with group operations to use the groups to engage in international cooperation projects, to raise funds, to provide services, and to place excess employees when their agencies are downsized.[68]

In response to the failure of corporatism and learned governance benefits of civil society, local governments are undertaking reform of the civil society regulations regarding both registration and fundraising. For example, in July 2009, Shenzhen signed an Agreement on Promoting a Comprehensive Plan and Making Reform on Civil Affairs with the local Department of Civil Affairs. The department agreed to "establish a system for social organizations to register directly with the Civil Affairs Department instead of finding a competent business unit first." It also authorizes Shenzhen to "adopt the documentation system to develop community social organization." As Karla Simon argues, if it is successful, the experience will spread to all of China, and it can be said to be a starting point for political reform.[69] In fact, as discussed in Chapter 1, this institutional change diffused from pioneers such as Shenzhen and Beijing to other provinces/municipalities including Chengdu, Shanghai, and Nanjing. Many local governments revised the regulations governing charities and other grant-making organizations, easing restrictions on domestic fundraising for many, but not all, groups.[70] At the national level, the proposed Charity Law

[67] See Ho, "Self-Imposed Censorship and De-Politicized Politics in China."

[68] Jiang Ru and Leonard Ortolano, "Corporatist Control of Environmental NGOs: A State Perspective," in *China's Embedded Activism: Opportunities and Constraints of a Social Movement*, Peter Ho and Richard L. Edmonds, eds. (New York: Routledge, 2008), pp. 44–68; Jiang Ru, "Environmental NGOs in China: The Interplay of State Controls, Agency Interests and NGO Strategies," Doctoral dissertation, Stanford University, California (2004).

[69] Karla W. Simon and Hang Gao, "Opening the Space: New Developments for China's Community Organizations," 2010, *CUA Columbus School of Law Legal Studies Research Paper No. 2010–25*: available at http://papers.ssrn.com/sol3/papers.cfm?abstract_id=1581687

[70] Karla Simon, "The Regulation of Civil Society Organizations in China," *International Journal of Civil Society Law* 9, 2011: 55–84.

with similar changes to fundraising regulations was placed on the legislative agenda of the Standing Committee of the National People's Congress beginning in 2013. Civil society played an active role in creating opportunities for positive experiences leading to these regulatory changes at the foundation of the CA model.

CONCLUSION

Illiberal Wave

The International Diffusion of Consultative Authoritarianism

Through the analysis of four regional cases and national regulatory changes in China, I find the relationship between the local state and civil society gradually changes from corporatism in the 1990s to consultative authoritarianism in the 2000s through a process of policy learning by local officials. This process of policy learning occurred through two mechanisms: direct experience with emerging civil society groups and emulating state-society models observed in other provinces and states. I also observe this process of learning about civil society in other authoritarian regimes. In fact, Greenpeace's experience in China is mirrored around the world, with the rise of a fairly autonomous civil society in many authoritarian regimes. In this chapter, I explore how the lessons of local government interactions with an emerging civil society in China diffuse across borders to influence officials in other authoritarian regimes facing similar policy challenges. China, although unique in many ways, has increasingly converged with other nondemocratic regimes in developing a new relationship with civil society – one that allows autonomous civil society more participation in the policy process while creating new tools of state control.

Much of the existing literature on international policy diffusion focuses on the spread of liberalism. As Frank Dobbin, Beth Simmons, and Geoffrey Garrett contend, many types of public policy innovations, from tariff reductions to privatization, have spread around the world in the past half century, mostly framed as part of a project of political and economic liberalization.[1] International policy diffusion is not a new phenomenon; what is distinctive about the late-twentieth-century wave of liberalization is "its rapidity, its wide geographic reach, and its conjoining of political and economic reform."[2] In fact, many scholars argue that the worldwide spread of economic and political liberalism was the defining feature of the late twentieth century, including free-market-oriented economic reforms and a "third wave" of democratization.[3] International policy diffusion illustrates that national policy choices are interdependent, meaning that governments adopt new policies not in isolation but in response to what counterparts in other countries are doing, sometimes mediated by international organizations and private transnational actors.[4] In contradistinction to this wave of liberalism, I contend that an illiberal wave is also occurring. This illiberal wave diffuses ideas among authoritarian regimes, such as effective models of state capitalism and new state–civil society models that allow for better governance under authoritarianism.

Illiberal policy diffusion occurs in many venues where state leaders and staff meet to share policy ideas or resolve international issues, such as international conferences, high-level official meetings, and informally at larger international gatherings such as the Association of Southeast Asian Nations (ASEAN) and United Nations meetings. These events allow state leaders and staff to share best practices and learn new policy solutions to common governance problems such as corruption in single-party states, social unrest, and dealing with international NGOs and media organizations. In this chapter, I trace this process of international

[1] Frank Dobbin, Beth Simmons, and Geoffrey Garrett, "The Global Diffusion of Public Policies: Social Construction, Coercion, Competition, or Learning?" *Annual Review of Sociology* 33, 2007: 449–472.

[2] Ibid., p. 450.

[3] Beth A. Simmons, Frank Dobbin, and Geoffrey Garrett, "Introduction: The International Diffusion of Liberalism," *International Organization* 60, no. 4, 2006: 781–810.

[4] Ibid., p. 782.

authoritarian learning by analyzing interactions between state leaders and staff at these venues, and I find that this new state–civil society model of consultative authoritarianism is slowly diffusing to other authoritarian regimes in a similar fashion to the Chinese economic model of state capitalism. Other leaders view these models from China as successful ways to solve common policy problems shared by these regimes, namely the ability to gain better governance through collaborating with these groups without triggering social mobilization forcing political reform.

This analysis challenges much of the current understanding of civil society in authoritarian regimes. Authoritarian officials learned through initial interactions with civil society that these groups might play a role not in challenging authoritarian governments, as liberal theories predict, but rather in making them more durable. Civil society plays an important role in good governance especially under authoritarianism where states lack formal channels for receiving citizen feedback about policies. By sharing this information, groups improve governance, which might serve to extend authoritarian rule. Although my findings challenge the democratic opposition role ascribed to civil society by liberal theories, the vital role played by these groups in creating better governance should not be overlooked.

My analysis also highlights the role of learning in the changing relationship and policies toward civil society that reveals an endogenous mechanism for authoritarian institutional change. As I find in China, local officials' learning about emerging civil society in the early 1990s led to a new state–civil society relationship that then diffused to other provinces. Civil society plays an important role in this learning process and has created more collaborative relationships with authoritarian regimes than liberal theories predict. These findings do not imply that authoritarian regimes do not still use repression, but rather that repression is not the only or most commonly used tool of control. In fact, a significant part of the consultative authoritarianism model is the creation of varied mechanisms of control, of which repression is the most severe. However, what is more interesting than the presence of repression is the continued growth of autonomous civil society and the process of learning experienced by state officials to balance the governance benefits of these groups with potential dangers.

In this chapter, I first explore the international diffusion of the CA model developed in China by tracing state leaders' exchanges at international venues, followed by domestic policy changes in these states regarding civil society regulation. In some cases, more liberal governments such as that in Bangladesh developed additional tools of state control similar to those used in Yunnan province, and more conservative governments such as that in Syria eased regulations on groups, similar to what occurred in Sichuan province.[5] Next, I examine this process of policy learning in Russia, a state with a similar historical background and political system to China, and I find that officials developed a similar model called "sovereign democracy."

TRANSNATIONAL DIFFUSION OF IDEAS: A NEW AUTHORITARIAN STATE–CIVIL SOCIETY MODEL

Following the China model, authoritarian regimes around the world engaged in the construction of consultative authoritarianism beginning in the late 2000s. The first distinctive characteristic of this CA model is the existence of a more autonomous civil society with varying sources of funding and levels of project independence. Unlike the corporatist model with state-organized federations, more pluralism exists in this model with multiple groups competing inside of one policy space or region.[6] As Bassam Haddad contends in the case of Syria, "The number of

[5] Kareem Fahim, "Doors Start to Open to Activists in Syria," *The New York Times*, August 28, 2010. This easing in Syria of course was prior to the Arab Spring–related protests that engendered a return of government repression for all types of non-state actors, not just civil society, leading to civil war: available at http://www.nytimes.com/2010/08/29/world/middleeast/29syria.html?pagewanted=all&_r=0

[6] Anita Chan and Jonathan Unger, "China, Corporatism, and the East Asian Model," *The Australian Journal of Chinese Affairs* 33, 1995: 29–53; Wolfgang Streeck and Lane Kenworthy, "Theories and Practices of Neocorporatism," in *The Handbook of Political Sociology: States, Civil Societies, and Globalization*, Robert Alford Thomas Janoski, Alexander Hicks, and Mildred Schwartz, eds. (Cambridge, UK: Cambridge University Press, 2005).

associations that are emerging is increasing. The number of concerns that are allowed to become public is also increasing. The whole process is blessed by the government."[7] However, although the proliferation of an autonomous civil society in authoritarian regimes is documented by the Johns Hopkins Comparative Nonprofit Sector Project and NGOs such as Civicus, many Syrian analysts dismiss this as "window dressing" because of continued state control: "It has good intentions but built-in structural limitations," and many rights advocates go further, "dismissing the talk of civil society by the government as window-dressing while it continues to arrest Islamists, Kurds and other political opponents, along with the lawyers who represent them."[8]

Following the CA model, the growth of this autonomous civil society goes hand-in-hand with attempted state control. In fact, the simultaneous existence of an autonomous civil society and the use of multiple, nuanced tools of state control characterize this new consultative authoritarianism model. The second distinctive characteristic is the use of positive and negative incentives to encourage groups to primarily engage in service delivery, not policy advocacy. Although the goal of encouraging groups to work toward meeting state goals is similar in models of corporatism, the mechanisms of government control over civil society are more indirect and increasingly nuanced. Positive incentives consist of allowing groups access to a closed policy process, legal permits to run pilot programs, and financial resources such as project funding. Negative incentives consist of administrative rules and procedures designed to inhibit the growth or functioning of groups, indirect legal challenges over taxation or permit applications, intimidation through excessive supervision and office visits, and temporarily shutting down a group or arresting leaders for questioning.

Positive incentives encourage groups to assist the government with service delivery and other goals to secure access to the policy and legal processes, as well as to receive additional funding. As

[7] Fahim, "Doors Start to Open to Activists in Syria"; Bassam Haddad is the director of the Middle East studies program at George Mason University.

[8] Ibid.

Kelly McMann finds with civic leaders in Kyrgyzstan, "Even adversaries of the local government desire help [assistance from the state]. Overall, 29 percent of the groups view themselves as opponents of local authorities, and more than half of the 29 percent have received state aid or hope for it."[9] In many authoritarian countries, state officials possess a relative wealth of resources and can dispense scarce resources such as office space, utilities, transportation, and funding. This monopoly on resources allows officials to shape civil society through the use of positive incentives, especially access to a policy process normally closed to non-state actors.[10] In short, these positive incentives offer powerful motivations for groups to advance state goals and avoid sensitive areas and methods, such as larger gatherings or assemblies that might threaten social stability.

Negative incentives also play a significant role in guiding group behavior. Many groups complain of administrative rules and procedures designed to inhibit the growth or functioning of the organization, legal challenges over taxation or permit applications, intimidation through excessive supervision and office visits, and temporarily shutting down a group or bringing leaders in to government offices for questioning.[11] Whereas these tools range in severity, they all restrict the operation of the group before the state resorts to outright closure or arrest. For example, in 2006, the Russian Duma considered a draft law barring the participation of foreigners in Russian civil society organizations; prohibiting foreign organizations from operating branches in Russia; and giving the government unchecked powers to intrude in the affairs of civil society organizations, including a requirement that it be

[9] Kelly McMann, "The Civic Realm in Kyrgyzstan: Soviet Economic Legacies and Activists' Expectations," in *The Transformation of Central Asia: States and Societies from Soviet Rule to Independence*, Pauline Jones Luong, ed. (Ithaca, NY: Cornell University Press, 2004).

[10] Jonathan Fox, "How Does Civil Society Thicken? The Political Construction of Social Capital in Rural Mexico," *World Development* 24, no. 6, 1996: 1089–1103.

[11] Arch Puddington, Aili Piano, and Camille Eiss, eds., *Freedom in the World: The Annual Survey of Political Rights and Civil Liberties* (Lanham, MD: Rowman and Littlefield, 2007).

notified of the existence of informal groups such as neighborhood associations.

Protest from Russian civil society leaders, INGOs, and the United States and European Commission led to the elimination of some of the most restrictive features of the draft, but the law ultimately adopted gave the Russian government significantly greater control over NGO activity. Since 2006, a total of 19 countries have introduced similar legislation restricting civil society, joining more than 30 other countries that currently have laws, policies, and practices that control the growth of civil society organizations.[12] Indirect control mechanisms allow the state to guide autonomous groups toward desired goals without using either overt incorporation or repression. These two distinct aspects characterize the consultative authoritarianism model and distinguish it from the corporatist model.

THE PROCESS OF DIFFUSION: AUTHORITARIAN LEARNING ACROSS BORDERS

According to international diffusion scholars, the occurrences of policy transfer have increased; for example, welfare-to-work and workfare programs transferred from the United States to Britain beginning in the early 1980s.[13] Some scholars attribute this increase to globalization, with which transnational corporations and institutions exercise more influence such that the capacity of national policy makers to frame their own agendas is diminished, and others to the ease of travel and communication across borders. This expansion of policy power and increased ease of transnational communications means that public policy now takes place in a transnational system in addition to national political systems.

[12] "Recent Laws and Legislative Proposals to Restrict Civil Society and Civil Society Organizations," *International Journal of Not-for-Profit Law* 8, August 2006: 76–85.

[13] David Dolowitz, "British Employment Policy in the 1980s: Learning from the American Experience," *Governance* 10, no. 1, 1997: 23–42.

Thus, when government officials search for policy solutions, they are increasingly likely to look for them abroad.[14]

The policy transfer literature contends that transfer occurs through several hypothesized mechanisms, some more coercive than others, and results from a rational process by policy makers of gradual imitation, copying, and modification from a common source or point of origin.[15] Policy transfer or diffusion then occurs incrementally through the advancement of knowledge and awareness within a community. This community might consist of state leaders, international policy networks, advocacy coalitions, or epistemic communities meeting in bilateral and multilateral events. Non-state policy transfer entrepreneurs, such as INGOs, assist in this process of transnational lesson drawing by transferring the rhetoric, empirical findings, and scholarly discourse that underpins policies.[16]

Most of the focus of this literature has been the transfer of liberal policies among democracies, but this raises the question of how illiberal ideas are transmitted between authoritarian states. Although much of the convergence might be driven by state actors' reactions to common events such as the transnational spread of color revolutions, I find that learning from other authoritarian regimes in the form of observed lessons or best practices influences

[14] David Marsh and David Dolowitz, "Learning from Abroad: The Role of Policy Transfer in Contemporary Policy-Making," *Governance: An International Journal of Policy and Administration* 13, no. 1, 2000: 5–24.

[15] Diane Stone, "Learning Lessons, Policy Transfer and the International Diffusion of Policy Ideas," Centre for the Study of Globalisation and Regionalisation, CSGR Working Paper No. 69/01, April 2000: available at http://wrap.warwick.ac.uk/2056/; also see the following authors for a discussion of this process with a different label, such as lesson-drawing (Richard Rose, *Lesson-drawing in Public Policy: A Guide to Learning across Time and Space* (Chatham, NJ: Chatham House Publishers, 1993); "policy band-wagoning" (G. John Ikenberry, "The International Spread of Privatization Policies: Inducements, Learning and Policy Bandwagoning." *The Political Economy of Public Sector Reform and Privatization* 1990: 88–110); and "policy borrowing" (Robert Cox, "Ideas, Policy Borrowing and Welfare Reform," Global Trajectories Conference, European University Institute: Florence, Italy, 1999, 25–26).

[16] Dolowitz, David, and David Marsh. "Who Learns What from Whom: A Review of the Policy Transfer Literature." *Political Studies* 44 no. 2, 1996: 343–357; Stone, "Learning Lessons."

policy choices, such as the rise of a successful model of state capitalism from China. As found in the regional case studies in China, regime leaders' domestic experiences with civil society also influence policy choices in that they undermine or reinforce the observed lessons taken from other authoritarian regimes. Thus, this policy convergence on a CA model is not simply a coincidence of common reactions to similar events, but rather the active process of transnational authoritarian learning. In much the same way that the spread of the color revolutions illustrated the process of transnational learning on the part of civil society actors, it also illustrates how authoritarian leaders learn from one another to construct a similar model of authoritarian state–civil society relations.[17] Theories of democratization contend that a successful democratic breakthrough in one location helps shape the timing and strategies of transformation in others, with this interconnectivity of transitions in time and space described as "contagion," "diffusion," and "demonstration effect."[18] Similarly, ideas about achieving authoritarian consolidation in the context of a global associational revolution also spread through analogous transmission mechanisms such as the Internet, global media, and international meetings and visits.

One example of authoritarian learning via the Internet is an animated video created by the Iranian Ministry of Propaganda that was posted on You Tube and broadcast over Khozestan TV in 2008.[19] The video depicts Gene Sharp and George Soros, both of whom fund democracy promotion projects and groups, as "agents of the West" plotting to use a color revolution model to

[17] Larry Diamond, "Authoritarian Learning: Lessons from the Colored Revolutions," *The Brown Journal of World Affairs* 12, Summer/Fall 2005; Vitali Silitski, "Preempting Democracy: The Case of Belarus," *Journal of Democracy* 16, October 2005: 83–97.

[18] Vitali Silitski, "Contagion Deterred: Preemptive Authoritarianism in the Former Soviet Union (The Case of Belarus)," CDDRL Working Papers 66, June 2006: available at http://iis-db.stanford.edu/pubs/21152/Silitski_No_66.pdf; and Samuel Huntington, *The Third Wave: Democratization in the Late Twentieth Century* (Norman: University of Oklahoma Press, 1991).

[19] Iranian propaganda video featuring John McCain, George Soros, and Gene Sharp: available at http://www.youtube.com/watch?v=OTCuBFuhikM

overthrow all nondemocratic leaders, especially the Iranian leadership. In the wake of the color revolution, democracy promotion funding and the groups that receive it are perceived as anti-state agents plotting against many authoritarian governments. In this video, George Soros is introduced as "a Jewish tycoon and the mastermind of ultra-modern colonialism" who uses his wealth to bring "supporters of America" to power under the slogan of democracy and human rights, and Gene Sharp as "one of the CIA agents in charge of America's infiltration into other countries."[20] Gene Sharp, as the head of the Albert Einstein Institution, has been the target of attacks from other governments as a symbol of a democratic revolution advocate. For example, Eva Golinger claimed that the Albert Einstein Institution developed a plan to overthrow Venezuela's democratically elected government through training right-wing paramilitaries to use "widespread civil disobedience and violence throughout the nation [to] provoke repressive reactions by the state that would then justify crises of human right violations and lack of constitutional order."[21] Similarly, Thierry Meyssan, an anti-imperialist scholar and consultant who advises governments of countries such as Syria, Russia, and Cuba, argued that "Gene Sharp and his team led the leaders of [the opposition group] Súmate during the demonstrations of August 2004."[22] In response, Hugo Chávez claimed that "they are the ideologues of the soft coup and it seems like they're here [in Venezuela.] They are laying out the slow fuse ... they'll continue laying it out [with] marches, events, trying to create an explosion."[23]

[20] Sam Sedaei, "New Propaganda Piece Hits Iranian Airwaves," *The Huffington Post*, February 26, 2008; available at http://www.huffingtonpost.com/sam-sedaei/new-propaganda-piece-hits_b_88512.html

[21] Eva Golinger, *Bush vs. Chávez: Washington's War on Venezuela* (New York: Monthly Review Press, 2007).

[22] Thierry Meyssan, "The Albert Einstein Institution: Non-Violence According to the CIA," VoltaireNet.org, June 6, 2007. Meyssan also maintains this website to exchange views between nonaligned states and hosts international conferences between these states.

[23] President Hugo Chávez's public address, June 3, 2007: available at http://www.voltairenet.org/article148932.html. Also see Sharp's response: available at http://aeinstein.org/Chavez.pdf

Similarly, in Myanmar, leaders of the ruling junta accused Sharp of being the "concert-master" for the Saffron Revolution in Burma, claiming that the Albert Einstein Institution is funded by the U.S. government "to foster U.S.-friendly regime change in key spots around the world" and that its staff includes "known CIA operatives."[24] In China, these suspicions were illustrated by an article in the *Global Times* displaying a menacing picture of Karl Rove, former deputy chief of staff to President George Bush on its cover, promoting the feature story entitled "An Investigation of America's Think Tanks: The Black Hands Behind the Scenes of Non-Violent Regime Change."[25] This article discussed four think tanks – the National Endowment for Democracy (called "the Second CIA"), George Soros's Open Society Institute, Freedom House, and the Albert Einstein Foundation – which collectively were identified as "soft daggers" pointing at targets for regime transformation through color revolutions.[26]

In addition to learning through information transmitted via the Internet and global media, authoritarian leaders also use public meetings and visits to learn from one another. In fact, when President Chávez denounced the "CIA-organized velvet coups" attempts around the world on June 3, 2007, he did so in the presence of Daniel Ortega, the president of Nicaragua, and the Cuban Minister for Economic Cooperation Marta Lomas, during a meeting for the signing of the Bolivarian Alternative for the Americas (ALBA), a new Latin American economic and political cooperation pact. Moreover, meetings between China and Venezuela to share ideas about state, market, and society relationships have increased.

[24] F. William Engdahl, "The Geopolitical Stakes of the Saffron Revolution," *Asia Times*, October 17, 2007: available at http://www.atimes.com/atimes/Southeast_Asia/IJ17Ae01.html

[25] "Meiguo wei zhiku diaocha–fei baoli zhengquan gengdiede muhou heishou [Investigation of American Think Tanks–the Black Hands behind the Scene of Non-Violent Regime Change]," *Xinhua News Agency*, December 26, 2007: available at http://news.xinhuanet.com/globe/2007-12/26/content_7315955.htm. An English translation is available at http://chinascope.org/main/content/view/677/92

[26] Engdahl, "The Geopolitical Stakes of the Saffron Revolution."

President Chávez made his first state visit to China in October 1999, where he met with Chinese President Jiang Zemin and Premier Zhu Rongji. His trip marked the first Venezuelan presidential visit to China since 1983, and Chávez proposed 24 cooperative projects with the Chinese. In 1999, Venezuela was the largest single recipient of Chinese investment in Latin America, mainly concentrated in two Venezuelan oil fields under development by the China National Petroleum Corporation. In April 2001, President Jiang Zemin visited Venezuela to promote economic and political cooperation, mainly to generate support for opposition to a UN measure to censure China's human rights practices. President Chávez agreed to both areas of cooperation, including supporting China's bid to host the 2008 Olympics and pledging to oppose the UN resolution: "we don't believe any country in the world has the right to condemn another ... We are going to vote against the resolution."[27] Venezuela increasingly seeks to emulate the Chinese model of state capitalism advocating step-by-step economic modernization with deferred political reform and to emulate the CA model present in both China and Russia by restricting the funding and activities of foreign NGOs.[28]

Since 2001, and in 1996 in the case of the original "Shanghai Five," the creation of the Shanghai Cooperation Organization (SCO) provides a forum for China and Russia to discuss and coordinate resistance to color revolutions and responses to increasing

[27] Alexandra Olson, "Jiang Visits Venezuela, Winning Support against Human Rights Resolution," *Associated Press*, April 16, 2001; see also Daniel Erikson, "Written Evidence Submitted by Daniel P. Erikson, Director, Caribbean Programs, Inter-American Dialogue, "China's Emerging Role in Latin America: Evidence from Cuba, Venezuela, and the Caribbean," Select Committee on Foreign Affairs: available at http://www.publications.parliament.uk/pa/cm200506/cmselect/cmfaff/860/860we17.htm

[28] Thomas Ambrosio, "Insulating Russia from a Colour Revolution: How the Kremlin Resists Regional Democratic Trends," *Democratization* 14, 2007: 232–252; Daniel Erikson, "Cuba, China, Venezuela: New Developments," Conference Paper, Fifteenth Annual Meeting of the Association for the Study of the Cuban Economy (ASCE), Miami Dade College, Miami, Florida, August 4–6, 2005.

NGO activity within the SCO Framework.[29] Participation in the SCO creates opportunities to communicate ideas and experiences with civil society and encourage consensus among most Central Asian Republics toward the Russian and Chinese position.[30] As an example of this consensus, just a few weeks before President Putin approved a new measure restricting foreign NGO activity, he and President Hu Jintao issued a joint declaration in which the imposition of "alien models of social and political systems" was deemed "inadmissible," which was then seconded by the other members of the SCO who stated that "concrete models of social development cannot be exported."[31] These statements signaled common opposition to a perceived model of Western governments and "agents" using domestic civil society groups to push democratization in authoritarian regimes. As Sergei Lebedev, head of the Russian intelligence service, stated, "NGOs are very attractive for [foreign] intelligence services ... as covers, masks, screens."[32]

These examples illustrate how leaders learn from one another about the potential dangers of civil society and how to implement differentiated controls as one part of the consultative authoritarianism model. Additionally, as I describe later, leaders share best practices or lessons about the governance benefits of civil society, which encourages the expansion of autonomous groups as the second pillar of the CA model.

In a similar fashion to the SCO, ASEAN allows for the sharing of ideas among Southeast Asian countries (and China), especially through the Asian Cooperation Dialogue (ACD). The ACD has

[29] Shiping Tang and Yunling Zhang, "Zhongguo de diqu zhanlue (China's Regional Strategy)," *Shijie jingji yu zhengzhi (World Economics and Politics)* no. 6, June 2004.

[30] Michael Rywkin, "Security and Stability in Central Asia: Differing Interests and Perspectives," *American Foreign Policy Interests* 28, no. 3, June 2006: 193–217.

[31] "Putin, Hu Jintao to Say Monopoly in International Affairs Inadmissible," *TASS*, June 28, 2005: available at http://usatoday30.usatoday.com/news/world/2005-07-01-russia-china_x.htm (no longer available on the Russian news service site ITAR TASS).

[32] William Fisher, "Russia: NGO Law Could Strengthen Civil Society," *IPS – Inter Press Service*, January 25, 2006, available at http://www.ipsnews.net/2006/01/russia-ngo-law-could-strengthen-civil-society-group-argues/

held four meetings at the level of foreign ministers to serve as the official dialogue forum on issues of development in Asia, with Premier Wen Jiabao speaking at the Islamabad ACD in April 2005 and attended by 26 foreign ministers of Asian countries. At this meeting, Wen Jiabao and his staff discussed the issue of development with countries such as Bangladesh and learned from the Bangladeshi experience of collaborating with civil society in the 1980s and 1990s, which can be seen by local governments in China increasingly implementing this Bangladeshi model of public-private partnerships to providing services such as health care and basic education.[33]

Although much of this communication between authoritarian regimes is about creating new social controls, it also transmits best practices about how to encourage civil society groups to assist the state with development goals. Over the past several decades, NGOs have become major players in the field of international development, with an estimated 6,000 to 30,000 national NGOs in developing countries. From 1970 to 1985, total development aid disbursed by international NGOs increased tenfold, and in 1992 alone, international NGOs channeled more than $7.6 billion of aid to developing countries.[34] It is estimated that more than 15 percent of total overseas development aid is channeled through NGOs, with some countries passing up to 37 percent of aid through NGOs.[35] International development assistance is composed of approximately 80 percent to 85 percent of government sources as official development assistance (ODA) and 15 percent to 20 percent from NGOs, foundations, and other development

[33] Jason Subler, "China Cautiously Enlists NGO Help in Poverty Fight," *Reuters*, April 9, 2007: available at http://www.reuters.com/article/2007/04/09/idUSPEK14506; Jessica Teets, "Reforming Service Delivery in China: The Emergence of a Social Innovation Model," *Journal of Chinese Political Science* 17, no. 1, 2012: 15–32.

[34] "Nongovernmental Organizations and Civil Society/Overview," *World Bank*, 2001,

[35] Ibid; OECD, *How DAC Members Work with Civil Society Organisations*, 2011: available at http://www.dochas.ie/Shared/Files/4/How_DAC_Members_work_with_CSOs_2011.pdf

charities.[36] This recalibration of development funding is driven in large part by donor governments; in fact, the Organization for Economic Cooperation and Development's (OECD) Development Assistance Committee (DAC), the principal body through which the OECD handles ODA issues, developed the *Development Co-operation Guidelines Series*, which encourages partnership between civil society and governments for development.[37] In response, for example, an increasing share of Finland's ODA is distributed through NGOs, with approximately 15 percent of Finland's ODA currently channeled through national and international NGOs. The World Bank also encourages collaboration between NGOs and developing countries that receive World Bank assistance. Throughout the 1970s and 1980s, most World Bank–NGO collaborations involved international NGOs; in more recent years, this trend has been reversed with an increasing number of projects involving community-based organizations.[38] Many authoritarian governments have responded to shifting donor priorities and favorable development experiences by encouraging the proliferation of a fairly autonomous civil society sector to help provide public goods and services.

However, as Bangladeshi leaders taught Chinese policy makers about the development benefits of civil society, Chinese leaders taught them how to implement China's model of state controls over these groups.[39] This was in response to many officials' fears that by the 1990s Bangladeshi civil society would emerge as a shadow government to provide services that the state was incapable of providing. For example, the civil society share of ODA received by Bangladesh increased from 8 percent in 1991–1992 to

[36] "DAC1 Official and Private Flows," OECD, 2008: available at http://www.oecd.org/dac/stats/47137659.pdf

[37] See DAC's "Ownership and Partnership: The Role of Northern and Southern Civil Society in the Poverty Reduction Strategies," December 2000, available at http://www.ohchr.org/Documents/Publications/GuideMinorities13en.pdf

[38] World Bank, "Nongovernmental Organizations and Civil Society/Overview."

[39] Joshua Kurlantzick, "Asia's Democracy Backlash," *Current History*, November 2008: 375–380.

14 percent in 1994–1995.[40] In response to this trend, the government sought to develop tools of social control to strengthen the state and encourage civil society to move from a role of substitution to one of complementarity with the state. As Deepa Narayan finds in the case of the Bangladesh Rural Advancement Committee (BRAC), the group originally provided an extensive network of schools for the poor without any state involvement and was perceived to be a competitor and threat to the power of the state.[41] In fact, BRAC is one of largest NGOs in the world with 16,000 full-time and 31,000 part-time staff, and an annual budget of US$86 million.[42] However, as a result of state encouragement via positive and negative incentives similar to those in China, BRAC now pursues more collaborative strategies to strengthen the state's leadership role in service provision.[43]

Many scholars of authoritarian regimes interpreted the successful suppression of demonstrators in May 2005 by Uzbek President Islam Karimov, the victory of Nursultan Nazarbayev in presidential elections in Kazakhstan in December 2005, and the reelection of Alexander Lukashenko as the president of Belarus in March 2006, as a challenge to the expansion of autonomous civil society and a reinforcement to more repressive tactics, which might be better able to withstand possible color revolution contagion than more open and liberal counterparts.[44] However, as described in the next section, both the Russian and Chinese leaderships viewed the color revolutions as supporting the development of a consultative

[40] Sarah White, "NGOs, Civil Society, and the State in Bangladesh: The Politics of Representing the Poor," *Development and Change* 30, 1999: 312.

[41] Deepa Narayan, "Social Capital and the State: Complementarity and Substitution," *World Bank Policy Research Working Paper No. 2167*, August 1999: available at http://papers.ssrn.com/sol3/papers.cfm?abstract_id=623906

[42] F.H. Abed and A.M.R. Chowdhury, "The Bangladesh Rural Advancement Committee: How BRAC Learned to Meet Rural People's Needs through Local Action," in *Reasons for Hope: Instructive Experiences in Rural Development*, Anirudh Krishna et al., eds. West Hartford, CT: Kumarian, 1997).

[43] Narayan, "Social Capital and the State."

[44] Peter Rutland, "Russia: Nothing Succeeds Like Autocracy," *Transitions Online*, 2007; Mark Kramer, "Russian Policy toward the Commonwealth of Independent States: Recent Trends and Future Prospects," *Problems of Post-Communism* 55, 2008: 3–19.

authoritarianism model. The color revolutions did serve as a cautionary lesson about potential costs of autonomous civil society; however, at the same time, efforts to tighten control over these groups were viewed as only a short-term response that did not address the more fundamental problem of how to resolve or at least manage the tensions inherent in the process of transition toward a market economy, including increasing political demands for participation in policy making. Thus, the dilemma facing authoritarian leaders after the color revolutions was how to channel potential societal opposition and block the unwelcome intrusion of foreign actors without retreating to measures that would threaten goals of national development.[45] For Presidents Putin and Medvedev in Russia, the solution was found in the "sovereign democracy" or "managed democracy" model, which in China, state leaders were calling "consultative democracy," or as I have labeled it, consultative authoritarianism.[46]

THE RISE OF "SOVEREIGN DEMOCRACY" IN RUSSIA

In this section, I outline the development of the CA model in Russia, influenced by both domestic experiences with civil society and international lessons like the color revolutions and the Chinese model. The development of a CA model in Russia illustrates that this new model of state–civil society relationship is part of a larger illiberal trend in the world, and not simply occurring in China. More importantly, the process of international policy diffusion or authoritarian learning demonstrates that state–civil society relationships are not determined by

[45] Jeanne L. Wilson, "Colour Revolutions: The View from Moscow and Beijing," in The "Coloured" Revolutions: Causes, Processes and Consequences Conference, Cambridge University, 2008: available at https://www.ucl.ac.uk/ceelbas/workshops/Jeanne_Wilson_paper.pdf

[46] Medvedev Address Hints at Change, *Moscow Times*, January 23, 2008: available at http://www.themoscowtimes.com/news/article/medvedev-address-hints-at-change/303224.html

regime type alone, but rather developed over time through different sources of learning. Civil society and international donors play a vital role in this learning process, as seen in the following case study.

In 2006, Vladislav Surkov, a Kremlin advisor and close associate of Vladimir Putin, developed the idea of "sovereign democracy." At a February 2006 meeting of United Russia, the Kremlin-associated political party, Surkov outlined three principal threats to Russian sovereignty: international terrorism, economic non-competitiveness, and the possibility of a color revolution. The youth group leaders who organized the color revolutions in former Soviet republics were perceived by Russian officials to be funded by external actors, who now desired to discredit the Russian state and provoke domestic conflict: "I am not able to say, that this issue is no longer on the agenda, because if they can achieve this in four states, why not do it in a fifth? Our foreign friends will also try in the future to try to repeat this."[47]

In response to this perceived threat emanating from civil society backed by pro-democracies donors, Russian academic and political elites, including Surkov, defined the idea of sovereign democracy as an alternative to the Western liberal democracy model. Similarly to Li Junru's concept of "consultative democracy" developed at the same time in China, sovereign democracy proponents advocate the maintenance of a centralized political system, often referred to as a "vertical of power," and identify the establishment of civil society (*grazhdanskoe obshchestvo*) as an important aspect of sovereign democracy. However, this idea of civil society differs from the pluralist model found in the West, which envisions autonomous groups influencing the policy-making process. In the sovereign democracy model, groups serve to assist and supervise the activities of the civil service and state administration. For example, Putin's speeches often refer to civil society and the

[47] "Suverenitet–eto politicheskii sinonim konkurentosposobnosti [Sovereignty–This is the Political Synonym of Competitiveness]": available at http://www.edinros.ru/primt.html?id=111148, cited in Wilson, "Colour Revolutions."

media as performing a "watchdog" role in fighting corruption among officials.[48]

The sovereign democracy model developed as a result of a process of learning by officials as Russia transitioned from a single-party Communist state to an emerging democracy beginning in the 1990s. After the collapse of the Soviet Union and the first Russian presidential election in 1991, Boris Yeltsin won the presidency of the new Russian Federation and attempted to build an economy with elements of market capitalism, with often painful results.[49] In fact, the "shock therapy" style reforms triggered a severe economic downturn that devastated Russian living standards in the 1990s.[50] In addition to economic crisis, the profusion of small parties and lack of coherent alliances created a chaotic legislature leading to the 1993 constitutional crisis when Yeltsin dissolved the legislature and forced through a new constitution with strong presidential powers. The cohesion of the Russian Federation was further threatened by the formation of separatist groups in the republic of Chechnya, leading to the First and Second Chechen Wars.

By the mid-1990s, economic reforms consolidated an oligarchy with roots in the old Soviet system, with most big enterprises acquired by former state managers.[51] While still in economic depression, Russia's economy was damaged further by the financial crash of 1998, leading to the resignation of Yeltsin. Prime Minister Vladimir Putin, a former KGB official and head of the KGB's post-Soviet successor agency, won the presidential election

[48] See Putin's interview with *Time Magazine*, December 19, 2007: available at http://content.time.com/time/specials/2007/personoftheyear/article/0,28804,1690753_1690757_1690766,00.html and the transcript of his Yearly Large Press Conference, February 14, 2008, available at http://archive.kremlin.ru/eng/speeches/2008/02/14/1011_type82915_160266.shtml

[49] Donald A. Filzer, *Soviet Workers and the Collapse of Perestroika: The Soviet Labour Process and Gorbachev's Reforms, 1985–1991* (Cambridge, UK: Cambridge University Press, 1994).

[50] Peter Nolan, *China's Rise, Russia's Fall* (New York: Macmillan Press, 1995).

[51] Paul Gregory and Robert Stuart, *Russian and Soviet Economic Performance and Structure* (Reading, MA: Addison-Wesley, 2001).

as well as a second term.[52] During his presidency, Putin tightened control over parliament, civil society, and economic oligarchs. Under Putin's leadership from 2000 to 2008, the Russian economy grew through increased oil and gas exports, and executive power expanded and strengthened.

As a result of neoliberal ideas of privatization and liberalization used to reform the Soviet Union under Gorbachev and consolidate reforms under Yeltsin, state–civil society relations until 1999 were fairly neutral, with each side engaged in a learning process about the intentions and capabilities of the other. During this time, group formation and activity increased, especially charity groups to help the losers of economic reform. However, following the chaotic political and economic pressures forcing Yeltsin's resignation, this relationship changed under Putin from first a division of authority between state and society to later a more repressive relationship, whereby Russian officials sought to more actively repress group formation and activity. During Putin's second term, Russian officials maintained a more confrontational relationship with civil society, repressing group development through a variety of regulatory and coercive measures. In the next section, I analyze the changing relationship between the state and civil society in Russia under Putin's leadership and focus on the sources of learning, both domestic and international, leading to this relationship change. Russian officials increasingly sought further centralization and strengthening of the state in response to the negative lessons derived from the policy failures of decentralization under Yeltsin in the 1990s and from threats of further fragmentation from Chechnyan separatist groups.

DEVELOPMENT OF AUTONOMOUS CIVIL SOCIETY IN RUSSIA

The relationship between civil society and the state changed considerably during the time period between the dissolution of the

[52] Roy Medvedev, *Post-Soviet Russia: A Journey Through the Yeltsin Era* (New York: Columbia University Press, 2002).

Soviet Union and Putin's rule. During the Soviet era, the state actively repressed independent civil society and encouraged citizen participation in government federations for labor and other interests. However, under Gorbachev's reforms, there was an explosion of informal group formation. When the Soviet Union fell, this social activism diminished mainly for two reasons – lack of focus for mobilization and economic decline. The dissolution of the Soviet system, which had been "the focus of the explosion of informal groups since 1987, took the wind out of the sails of the informal movement, as individuals and groups faced a changing array of problems and reoriented their activities in the context of a new state structure and the reorganization of politics, the economy, and society."[53] This decline was strengthened by efforts of political elites to discourage activism in the initial phases of post-communist state construction, as well as shock therapy reforms that "not only impoverished a significant portion of the country and inhibited the development of a middle class, it also began to reconfigure the structure of social interests that gives birth to activism."[54]

However, President Yeltsin established the beginnings of the framework necessary for civil society groups by reaching out to social groups, seeking a "social accord" to support his political and economic reforms in 1992 and 1994. Despite little previous experience with these groups, Yeltsin learned that they could assist the state by providing popular support for further economic reforms and helping those injured by market transition. For example, civil society helped halt the 1991 coup attempt against Soviet President Gorbachev launched by the government members opposed to perestroika by organizing mass demonstrations rallying around Russian President Yeltsin and his liberalizing reforms. The new constitution of 1993 written under President Yeltsin guaranteed civil liberties and identified Russia as a "social state," ensuring the legal formation and functioning of civil society groups. In

[53] Marcia Weigle, "On the Road to the Civic Forum: State and Civil Society from Yeltsin to Putin," *Demokratizatsiya* 10, 2002: 119.

[54] Ibid.

1995, President Yeltsin passed several laws creating legal identities for groups and regulating the relationship between government authorities and independent groups, emphasizing equality before the law.[55] However, despite these legal protections, decentralization of state authority meant that federal laws were not always supported by local legislation or enforced by local authorities, restricting group activity and development during the 1990s.

In response to Gorbachev's glasnost policies, 15 percent of NKOs (*nekommercheskie organizatsii*), or civil society, were formed between 1985 and 1991. This trend continued under Yeltsin's rule, with the number of groups in Moscow doubling from 1994 to 1997.[56] The number of registered groups in Russia reached approximately 350,000 by 2003, including more than 70,000 social and noncommercial organizations, many of which are directly or indirectly involved in charitable work. By 2011, 360,000 NKOs registered, but researchers estimate that only around 136,000 of these are active.[57] Charity organizations provide services such as care for orphans and the disabled to an estimated 20 million to 30 million Russians, worth 15 billion rubles a year. Additionally, more than 2,500 groups work on legal protection and education issues. As one survey conducted in the city of Volgograd found, groups receive only 1 percent of their funding from philanthropic sources, 13 percent from the state, 15 percent from the commercial sector, 22 percent from membership dues, and the remaining amount from foreign donors.[58] In fact, foreign organizations play a large role in legal reform organizations, funding approximately 81 percent of all legal reform NKOs. Although the state portion of group funding is small, local governments also contribute in non-monetary ways such as providing office space, subsidized or free transportation, or means of communication, which are all important to group development.

55 Ibid., p. 122.

56 George E. Hudson, "Civil Society in Russia: Models and Prospects for Development," *Russian Review* 62, 2003: 193–332.

57 Russian Civil Society Profile, CIVICUS, 2012: Available at http://socs.civicus.org/CountryCivilSocietyProfiles/Russia.pdf

58 Ibid., p. 221.

Although group formation and activities have expanded, according to a poll conducted with 1,500 urban and rural residents in June 2001, only 5 percent of Russian citizens were active in these groups.[59] By 2012, another survey found that 8 percent were actively involved, with another 27 percent involved with NKOs but not currently active.[60] Low participation rates might manifest as a legacy of mandatory social mobilization under the Soviet Union, as Marc Morjé Howard finds in other post-communist states.[61] The chaos and weak central authority that characterized the early years under Yeltsin ultimately undermined initial lessons about the benefits of collaboration for government officials. The lesson internalized by both officials and civil society groups was that strong state institutions, principally the rule of law, must be established and enforced for state agencies and groups to function effectively:

> Russian civil society activists do not see themselves as a permanent opposition to an authoritarian-oriented state. They adhere to a "strong state–strong society" model: The institutionalization of state power is a prerequisite for civil society development, and a strong civil society is vital to ensuring the state's democratic orientation. The "weak state–weak society" model of the Yeltsin era only exacerbated problems of civil society development.[62]

During Putin's first term from 2000 to 2004, he responded to these lessons by consolidating power through the centralization of administrative power and curbing the economic and political power of some of the Yeltsin-era oligarchs, such as Boris Berezovsky. He also worked to strengthen state institutions by advocating legal reform on land, tax, labor, and commercial statutes.[63] In 2004,

59 Alexander Domrin, "Ten Years Later: Society, 'Civil Society,' and the Russian State," *The Russian Review* 62, 2003: 193–211.

60 CIVICUS, 2012.

61 Marc Morjé Howard, *The Weakness of Civil Society in Post-Communist Europe* (Cambridge, UK: Cambridge University Press, 2003).

62 Weigle, "On the Road to the Civic Forum," p. 127.

63 Robert Sharlet, "In Search of the Rule of Law," in *Developments in Russian Politics*, Stephen White, Zvi Y. Gitelman, and Richard Sakwa, eds. (Durham, NC: Duke University Press, 2005).

Putin was reelected to his second term with 71 percent of the vote, and he continued to recentralize authority and prevent further dissolution of Russia from internal separatist groups and what he perceived as "foreign-funded democratization" attempts. This linkage between the West and Chechnyan groups can be seen following the Beslan school hostage crisis in 2004, when Putin accelerated state recentralization and as some analysts argue "undermined every independent source of political power in Russia, decreasing the degree of pluralism in the Russian society."[64] This process occurred simultaneously in the political, economic, and social realms.[65]

Recentralization generated increasing state capacity, popularity for President Putin, and overall economic growth. In fact, although the Russian's state intervention in the economy was criticized in the West, this intervention improved corporate governance of many companies; under the Putin administration, the economy grew an average 7 percent annually.[66] In opinion polls conducted in 2002, "the restoration of state power" and the "revival of Russia as a mighty global power" were considered the main priorities in Russia by 48.3 percent of respondents.[67] Although recentralization successfully created a stronger state, this practice left little room for social activity. Putin deemed other sources of authority a threat to the recentralization and strengthening of the Russian state, repressing any competing sources of authority, whether religious, ethnic, or interest-based groups. Putin focused on creating a strong

[64] Alfred Evans Jr., "Vladimir Putin's Design for Civil Society," in *Russian Civil Society: Critical Assessment*, Alfred B. Evans, Jr., Laura A. Henry, and Lisa McIntosh Sundstrom, eds. (Armonk, NY: M.E. Sharpe, 2005), pp. 147–158; Dov Lynch, "'The Enemy Is at the Gate': Russia after Beslan," *International Affairs* 81, 2005: 141–161.

[65] Peter Baker, "Putin's Kremlin Asserting More Control of Economy: Yukos Case Reflects Shift on Owning Assets, Notably in Energy," *Washington Post*, July 9, 2004: available at http://www.washingtonpost.com/wp-dyn/articles/A37580-2004Jul8.html

[66] Andrei Yakovlev, *State-Business Relations and Improvement of Corporate Governance in Russia*, Bank of Finland Institute for Economies in Transition, 2008: available at http://ideas.repec.org/p/hhs/bofitp/2008_026.html

[67] Domrin, "Ten Years Later," p. 202.

centralized state in Russia and maintained a cautious relationship with civil society in his first term, neither actively encouraging nor repressing groups as long as they did not challenge state authority; during his second term, increasing conflict in Chechnya and the model of the color revolutions in the former Soviet republics changed this uncertain relationship with groups into an active policy of repression.

Putin's administration increasingly viewed these groups as elements that subverted state authority and allowed foreign elements to play an active role in the potential dissolution of independent states. For example, in 2007, "Dissenters' Marches" were organized by the opposition group Other Russia, led by former chess champion Garry Kasparov and national Bolshevist leader Eduard Limonov. These demonstrations were often met by police action, which included interfering with the travel of the protesters and the arrests of as many as 150 people who attempted to break through police lines.[68] When asked about the Dissenters' Marches and Kasparov's arrest, Putin responded that as Kasparov spoke English rather than Russian during his arrest, he was performing for a Western audience rather than for the benefit of his own people.[69] This view of civil society groups, or any type of social mobilization, suggests that foreign enemies are funding and supporting oppositional groups to create a weaker Russia. In fact, Putin argued, "Those who oppose us don't want us to realize [their] plan! Because they have completely different tasks and views on Russia. They need a weak, sick state! They need a disorganized and disoriented society, a divided society, so that they can do their deeds behind its back and eat cake on our tab!"[70] Increasingly, the dominant lesson of civil society internalized by

[68] "Garry Kasparov Jailed over Rally." *BBC News*, November 24, 2007: available at http://news.bbc.co.uk/2/hi/europe/7110910.stm

[69] Time Magazine, *Person of the Year 2007*, December 17, 2007: available at http://content.time.com/time/specials/2007/personoftheyear/article/0,28804,1690753_1690757_1690766,00.html

[70] Andrey Kolesnikov, "Unity of Forum and Content," *Kommersant*, November 22, 2007, available at http://www.kommersant.com/p828086/election_campaigning/

state officials is one of foreign-funded agents trying to usurp state authority, which led to the creation of a more oppositional relationship with civil society than that under Yeltsin.

As discussed earlier, in 2006, Vladislav Surkov proposed the idea of sovereign democracy and quickly unified many political elites around a political philosophy prohibiting international interference of any kind: "Sovereign democracy is a Kremlin coinage that conveys two messages: first, that Russia's regime is democratic and, second, that this claim must be accepted, period. Any attempt at verification will be regarded as unfriendly and as meddling in Russia's domestic affairs."[71] As Ivan Krastev argues, Russian leaders are suspicious of foreign democratization efforts, which led officials to exercise greater control formally as well as informally over civil society groups and to use anti-Western rhetoric when speaking both of democratization efforts abroad and anti-state groups domestically.[72] This trend is especially visible with civil society groups in Chechnya. Michael Maxwell contends that recent trends show a Russian crackdown on human rights organizations in Chechnya by refusing to register them, arbitrarily closing down existing organizations, or accusing them of extremism.[73] Although a reaction to social unrest in Chechnya, this fear of civil society also derived from the observation of the color revolutions in the former Soviet republics, especially the Orange Revolution in Ukraine. The color revolutions served as a warning to state officials about "people power" and reinforced this fear of how outside forces might interfere or influence internal affairs:

> Because the Soviet system was able to function in a highly autarchic manner, it could largely insulate itself from such flows over a long period of time. This unaccustomed openness to the larger environment now

[71] Maria Lipman, "Putin's 'Sovereign Democracy,'" Carnegie Endowment for International Peace, 2006, available at www.carnegieendowment.org/publications/index.cfm?fa=view&id=18540

[72] Ivan Krastev, "Democracy's Doubles," *Journal of Democracy* 17, no. 2, 2006: 52–62.

[73] Michael Maxwell, "NGOs in Russia: Is the Recent Russian NGO Legislation the End of Civil Society in Russia?" *Tulane Journal of International and Comparative Law* 15, 2006: 247.

> evokes an acute anxiety about the ability of the regime to remain in control of its environment, and a fear of the way in which outside forces might intervene in or influence internal development, or even destabilize the existing political order.[74]

Russian officials blamed foreign political influence and funding for the success of anti-regime groups in Serbia, Georgia, Ukraine, and Kyrgyzstan, which reinforced elite fears of a soft takeover within the context of an expanding European Union and NATO.[75] Many state officials perceived the color revolutions as "another worrying example of Western attempts to 'manufacture democracy' in former Soviet space. Under the guise of mass popularity ...Western-funded international organizations that advocate democracy – such as the OSCE, as well as U.S.-funded NGOs such as Freedom House... – are considered to have underwritten the 'revolution.'"[76] The Russian analysis of the revolutions is that they are linked by a series of common features: (1) the driving force behind each was a youth protest movement that used catchy slogans and symbols (2) groups in one country, such as The Belgrade Center for Nonviolent Resistance, taught activists in other countries how to organize and mobilize; and (3) this chain reaction of revolutions was planned by Western enemies and follows established Western patterns. For example, one Russian official drew parallels between U.S.-sponsored regimes in Latin and South America during the Cold War and U.S. actions in post-Soviet space, arguing that there is a "transfer of a certain continental model to another continent."[77]

In response to fears of further dissolution of the Russian state because of external actors acting through civil society, President Putin formed a department in his executive administration to prevent social mobilization: "In the wake of the Orange Revolution in Ukraine, Modest Kolerov, Pavlovsky's deputy at the Center for

[74] Gail W. Lapidus, "Between Assertiveness and Insecurity: Russian Elite Attitudes and the Russia-Georgia Crisis," *Post-Soviet Affairs* 23, 2007: 139.

[75] Ibid., 140.

[76] Graeme Herd, "Russia and the 'Orange Revolution': Response, Rhetoric, Reality?" *The Quarterly Journal* 2, 2005: 15.

[77] Ibid., p. 18.

Effective Policies, joined the presidential administration as head of the new 'anti-Orange' department dealing with the post- Soviet republics."[78] This new agency sought to protect Russia from a similar event by establishing new regulatory laws for civil society groups that allows the state more control through a regulatory body known as the Public Chamber as well as restricting demonstrations and protests through laws against "extremism." As Gail Lapidus argues, "The main lesson learned from the color revolutions was the danger of a mobilized public coalescing around an attractive opposition figure, and the goal of Russian policy has been to prevent the emergence of either."[79] The government perceived the threat as primarily external in origin but working through domestic groups and responded by repressing civil society and other sources of social power in Russia.

The new civil society legislation passed in 2006 restricted group development by regulating the activities of nongovernmental and noncommercial organizations operating in the Russian Federation, including the establishment of new registration procedures and stricter monitoring of NKO activities, financial contributions, and budgets.[80] Russian officials contend that the law is designed to prevent terrorist activities by ensuring that groups are not created or used to facilitate the planning, organization, or financing of terrorist activities. However, Michael Maxwell argues that "the law comes in the wake of several recent events that seem to indicate this is just another example of President Putin attempting to gain effective control over the entire political system."[81]

Despite the creation of new regulatory tools to control civil society, an important part of sovereign or managed democracy is also the tenet that civil society has proven to be beneficial to governance, so state officials sought not to repress grassroots groups completely but simply to exert more control over these autonomous groups. As with the development of the CA model in

[78] Krastev, "Democracy's Doubles," p. 57.
[79] Lapidus, "Between Assertiveness and Insecurity," p. 140.
[80] Maxwell, "NGOs in Russia," p. 236.
[81] Ibid., p. 237.

China, the establishment of the Public Chamber in 2005 intended to create a system of state control over autonomous civil society to provide a way for the state to encourage the development of a beneficial civil society.[82] The Public Chamber consists of 126 members – one-third selected by the president, one-third nominated by civil society organizations, and one-third chosen by members of the Public Chamber itself – and serves as a forum for the public discussion of societal issues, at least among a selected group of participants. According to President Putin, a key priority for the Public Chamber is to facilitate an exchange of views and dialogue with NGOs as a feedback mechanism between society and the state. The Public Chamber members have thus far discussed human rights, health care, local self-government, military reform, and environmental problems. The Public Chamber represents the implementation of this idea of the government guiding a more collaborative domestic civil society while restricting INGO activity in Russia. In fact, the new regulations and the creation of the Public Chamber embodied in the concept of sovereign democracy illustrate the development in Russia of the model of consultative authoritarianism – the simultaneous rise of a fairly autonomous civil society and new mechanisms of state control.

As William Fisher and several of the groups he interviewed contend, the NKO bill and establishment of the Public Chamber might serve to create a stronger legal framework for civil society by codifying regulations on formation and fundraising.[83] For example, in response to Valery Galchenko's, the coauthor of the 2006 NKO bill, claims that INGOs sought "the gradual destruction of Russia's state structure" and that pro-democracy organizations such as Open Russia and the Soros Foundation were "the greatest threat to our society," the government proposed a strategy of increased funding for groups as part of the Public Chamber

[82] Information about the Public Chamber is available on its website at http://www.oprf.ru

[83] William Fisher, "NGO Law Could Strengthen Civil Society, Group Argues," *Inter Press Service*, January 25, 2006: available at http://www.ipsnews.net/2006/01/russia-ngo-law-could-strengthen-civil-society-group-argues/

legislation.[84] In August 2007, the Russian government announced that it would provide 1.25 billion rubles for funding NKOs. In addition to securing more collaboration from domestic groups, this source of funding should offset the dependence of Russian NKOs on funding from abroad. According to Valery Fadeyev, a member of the Public Chamber, "Against the background of powerful funding by the West, including for political purposes, it is necessary for us to set down our own funding."[85]

In addition to creating funding lines for grassroots groups, Putin sought to collaborate with these groups to provide more social services through state sponsorship. State agencies encouraged grassroots groups to collaborate with the state on service delivery projects, and officials created a series of officially sponsored organizations to undertake similar projects, such as youth organizations that also promote patriotic and pro-Putin views.[86] Although elite disagreement over the role of civil society in Russia still existed in both state and society, increasing numbers of policy makers converged on this model of sovereign democracy. For example, in 2008, Gorbachev criticized Russia's electoral system and channels for citizen participation and called for extensive reforms.[87] However, as Ivan Krastev contends, Putin and ruling officials learned from domestic experiences and the Orange Revolution in Ukraine to return to classic Soviet measures – more repression but also more social services.[88] However, unlike

84 Suzanna Farizova, "They're Destroying Our Citizens from Within," *Kommersant-Vlast*, November 28, 2005: 40, reproduced in "What the Papers Say (Part A)", December 5, 2005, as cited by Thomas Ambrosio, "Insulating Russia from a Colour Revolution: How the Kremlin Resists Regional Democratic Trends." *Democratisation* 14, no. 2, 2007: 232–252.

85 "Nekommercheskie organizatsii nachinayut osvoenie byudzheta [Noncommerical Organzations Begin to Master the Budget]," *Kommersant*, July 8, 2007: available at http://lenta.ru/news/2007/08/08/nko/

86 Lapidus, "Between Assertiveness and Insecurity," p. 148.

87 C. J. Chivers, "Gorbachev, Rebuking Putin, Criticizes Russian Elections," *New York Times*, January 29, 2008: available at http://www.nytimes.com/2008/01/29/world/europe/29russia.html?_r=0

88 Krastev, "Democracy's Doubles," 59.

the Soviet model, these groups are autonomous and receive only part of their overall funding from the state.

This state–civil society model is characterized by scholars as managed democracy, differentiated control, and pluralized authoritarianism in different national contexts, but all consist of a state–civil society relationship whereby a fairly autonomous civil society proliferates and is not indiscriminately repressed but instead is viewed by state officials in a more nuanced fashion and controlled in different ways depending on the group type and issue area.[89]

In the case of developing sovereign democracy in Russia, policy makers learned from both domestic experiences with civil society and the lesson of the color revolutions; Russian leaders also learned from the experience of Chinese officials. For example, the Shanghai Cooperation Organization provided a forum for China and Russia to discuss and coordinate resistance of color revolutions and responses to increasing NGO activity within the SCO Framework.[90] SCO meetings created opportunities to communicate about experiences with civil society and encourage consensus among Central Asian republics toward the Russian and Chinese model.[91] As an example of this transnational learning, just a few weeks before President Putin approved the new legislation restricting foreign NGO activity, he and President Hu Jintao issued a joint declaration in which the imposition of "alien models of social and political systems" was deemed "inadmissible," which was then seconded by the other members of the SCO who stated that "concrete models of social development cannot be

[89] Ibid.; Kang Xiaoguang and Han Heng (康晓光与韩恒), "分类控制：当前中国大陆国家与社会关系研究[Differentiated Control: Current State and Society Relationship Research in Mainland China]," 社会学研究 *[Sociology Research Journal* 6, 2005, available at http://www.chinareform.net/2010/0116/8243.html; Diamond, "Authoritarian Learning"; and Orion Lewis, "Pluralized Authoritarianism: Media Reform and Legitimacy in China," presentation at the 2010 Fudan-IAS Conference on Legitimacy and Governance, July 3–4, 2010, Fudan Institute for Advanced Study in Social Sciences, Fudan University, Shanghai, China.

[90] Shiping and Yunling, "China's Regional Strategy."

[91] Rywkin, "Security and Stability in Central Asia."

exported."[92] These statements signaled common opposition to a perceived model of Western governments and agents using domestic civil society groups to push democratization in authoritarian regimes. Russian domestic experience with civil society mirrored the lessons learned from the Chinese experience and those of the post-Soviet republics, and thus the CA model developed in China appeared to be an effective solution for the policy dilemma of what sort of relationship to maintain with civil society.

In this way, the Russian concept of sovereign democracy created a central role for the state in guiding the development of both the market and civil society and considered the future development of civil society to be dependent on a strong state: "democracy is not a street bazaar."[93] As discussed earlier, sovereign democracy in Russia corresponds to the consultative democracy model advocated by Li Junru, illustrating a process of authoritarian learning across borders. As Li argues, "The United States wants us to adopt multiparty democracy, but our national conditions are different. We cannot copy any country's model of democracy – we must develop our own form. Consultative democracy is our contribution."[94] The ideas of both sovereign democracy in Russia and consultative democracy in China converge on a model of consultative authoritarianism, whereby state officials advocate a simultaneous expansion of autonomous civil society and mechanisms of state control to attain a balance between the governance benefits of civil society and the potential dangers of social mobilization for further political liberalization.

AN ILLIBERAL WAVE: THE IMPLICATIONS OF A CONSULTATIVE AUTHORITARIANISM MODEL

This process of policy diffusion occurring across authoritarian regimes in the late 2000s suggests important implications for

92 "Putin, Hu Jintao to Say Monopoly in International Affairs Inadmissible."

93 Putin, Annual Large Press Conference.

94 David Shambaugh, *China's Communist Party: Atrophy and Adaptation* (Berkeley: University of California Press, 2008).

future democratization or liberalization and the role of civil society in the process of institutional change. As Wolfgang Streeck and Kathleen Thelen note, literature on institutional change tends to rely on a punctuated equilibrium approach whereby long periods of institutional stasis are punctuated with an exogenous shock that results in institutional change.[95] This approach is used in the democratization literature as well, which notes that long periods of authoritarian rule are punctuated with an exogenous shock leading to democratization.[96] However, this punctuated equilibrium approach misses the process of gradual endogenous change. Several scholars have responded to this gap in our understanding of institutional change in authoritarian regimes by researching the increasing use of elections in initiating either greater liberalization or consolidation of authoritarianism.[97]

In a similar fashion to elections, the development of an autonomous civil society is considered to be an important foundation or prerequisite for further democratization by increasing citizen participation in the public sphere.[98] However, in an age of a global associational revolution, does the rise of a fairly autonomous civil society catalyze democratization in authoritarian regimes? My

[95] Wolfgang Streeck and Kathleen Thelen, *Beyond Continuity: Institutional Change in Advanced Political Economies* (Oxford, UK: Oxford University Press, 2005).

[96] Samuel Huntington, *The Third Wave: Democratization in the Late Twentieth Century* (Norman: University of Oklahoma Press, 1991); Stephen Haggard and Robert Kaufman, "The Political Economy of Democratic Transitions," *Comparative Politics*, 1997: 263–283.

[97] Jennifer Gandhi, *Political Institutions under Dictatorship* (Cambridge, UK: Cambridge University Press, 2008); Steven Levitsky and Lucan Way, "Elections Without Democracy: The Rise of Competitive Authoritarianism," *Journal of Democracy* 13, no. 2 (2002): 51–66.

[98] Gabriel Almond and Sydney Verba, *The Civic Culture: Political Attitudes and Democracy in Five Nations* (Princeton, NJ: Princeton University Press, 1963); Larry Diamond, "Rethinking Civil Society: Toward Democratic Consolidation," *Journal of Democracy* 5, 1994: 4–17; Juan Linz and Alfred Stepan, *Problems of Democratic Transitions and Consolidation: Southern Europe, South America and Post-Communist Europe* (Baltimore, MD: Johns Hopkins University Press, 1996); Guillermo O'Donnell, "Horizontal Accountability in New Democracies," in *The Self-Restraining State*, Andreas Schedler, Larry Diamond and Marc F. Plattner, eds. (Boulder, CO: Lynne Rienner, 1999).

analysis of the development of civil society in China and other authoritarian regimes finds that civil society does not have a unidirectional influence on a process of democratization. As Jason Brownlee observes with elections, authoritarian leaders adapt to the rise of civil society in innovative ways that serve to either undermine or reinforce existing institutions.[99] Scholars have found similar processes of adaptation and institutional innovation in China, as seen in the adaptive authoritarianism literature that examines the CCP's capacity to adapt to a changing environment to generate stability and regime legitimacy.[100] The CCP, along with rulers in other authoritarian regimes, has adapted to lessons highlighting the governance benefits of civil society by developing a consultative authoritarian model that attempts to balance the benefits of an autonomous civil society with sophisticated tools of social control. However, although the global associational revolution might not lead directly to a new wave of democratization, increasing civil society activity is initiating better governance in authoritarian states.

Civil society activity improves governance by increasing the amount of information available to the government about citizen needs and suggesting appropriate models to address these needs. By encouraging citizen participation in the policy process, at least at an aggregate level, civil society increases pluralism or the

[99] Jason Brownlee, *Authoritarianism in an Age of Democratization* (Cambridge, UK: Cambridge University Press, 2007).

[100] Andrew Nathan, "China's Changing of the Guard: Authoritarian Resilience," *Journal of Democracy* 14, January 2003: 6–17; also see the following authors: Vivienne Shue, "Legitimacy Crisis in China?" *State and Society* 21, 2004: 24–49; Dali Yang, "Economic Transformation and State Rebuilding in China" in *Holding China Together: Diversity and National Integration in the Post-Deng Era* (New York: Cambridge University Press, 2004), pp. 120–145; Kjeld Erik Brodsgaard and Zheng Yongnian, eds., *The Chinese Communist Party in Reform* (New York: Routledge, 2006); Bruce Gilley, "Legitimacy and Institutional Change: The Case of China" *Comparative Political Studies* 41, no. 3, 2008: 259–284; Andrew G. Walder, "Unruly Stability: Why China's Regime Has Staying Power." *Current History* 108, no. 719, 2009: 257–263; Thomas Heberer and Gunter Schubert, eds., *Regime Legitimacy in Contemporary China: Institutional Change and Stability* (New York: Routledge, 2008); and Holbig and Gilley. "Reclaiming Legitimacy in China."

articulation of many diverse societal interests, which is essential for good governance.[101] Whereas the availability of information affects decision making in both democracies and nondemocracies, in the latter regime type, accessing accurate information is especially difficult because of institutions characterized by a lack of transparency and channels for political participation. In this environment, information becomes a powerful resource of which civil society is uniquely positioned to take advantage. Also, through sharing this information in the form of policy research or pilot projects, civil society creates the opportunity for official learning. Therefore, although I agree with Ivan Krastev that elites allow the development of things such as elections and civil society "for the sole purpose of helping those in power to stay in power," I find evidence that groups are improving governance outcomes through advocacy and service delivery in the areas of health, education, and labor and disability rights.[102] Although civil society might not play a democratizing role in all authoritarian regimes, these groups clearly play an important role in improving governance and human welfare in these countries. The consultative authoritarianism model allows for more space and participation and reflects a more nuanced understanding on the part of authoritarian officials of the diverse roles that groups may play in society to improve governance in political systems characterized by low transparency and accountability.

The cases presented in this book also suggest some interesting policy implications for civil society scholars, practitioners, and donors. As I find in these cases, the actions of domestic and international groups play an important role in creating the learning opportunities leading to different relationships between government officials and groups. Therefore, collaboration with state officials rather than complete autonomy is necessary to create these learning opportunities. Groups that focus on collaborative projects that engage policy makers are more likely to achieve long-term

[101] Omar Encarnacion, *The Myth of Civil Society: Social Capital and Democratic Consolidation in Spain and Brazil* (New York: Palgrave, 2003).
[102] Krastev, "Democracy's 'Doubles.'"

policy and relationship change. This is of course not to suggest that groups seek to be incorporated into authoritarian states, but rather that groups maintain operational autonomy in policy research and pilot programs and then seek to share these experiences with relevant government officials. As seen in the four regional cases in China, the more these officials learn of the governance benefits of civil society, the more space will be created for the autonomous functioning of these groups.

However, one danger is that the explicit intent of democracy promotion held by several donors that fund domestic civil society generates negative lessons that actually undermine the intended liberalization or welfare outcomes. A shift in rhetoric from democracy promotion to better governance on the part of funding agencies and INGOs would likely create higher levels of local government collaboration and greater access to the policy process in authoritarian regimes. Donors must focus more on funding groups with good governance goals and collaborative projects that create important learning opportunities, and less on funding groups with explicit democratization and anti-state rhetoric, if they desire to change authoritarian leaders' relationships with civil society and enable more citizen participation in the policy process. This is not to suggest that organizations committed to democratization collude with dictators, but rather focusing on the fact that democratization is a complex and often long process. However, improving the welfare for the majority of the world's population is an equally important goal, and helping develop a civil society engaged in mostly service delivery might create the social trust and democratic skills to support any future grassroots process of democratization.

Transnational policy diffusion among authoritarian leaders occurs as a result of learning through both experiences with civil society and observed models of color revolutions and practices in other nondemocracies. Motivated by common governance challenges, authoritarian leaders learned from the Chinese experience, and one another, that a CA model effectively balances the benefits of civil society with the need for new tools of state control. Consultative authoritarianism consists of state–civil society relationships in which civil society is not indiscriminately repressed, but instead viewed in a more nuanced fashion and controlled in indirect ways depending on group type and issue area. The CA model allows selected groups limited participation in the policy process, in ways impossible under former corporatist framework. However, while allowing limited pluralism in the policy process, scholars and donors should not view this model as a democratizing trend but rather a method for achieving better governance under the conditions of authoritarian rule. In this way, the growth of autonomous civil society in authoritarian regimes might not lead directly to democratization, but it appears to be making the Chinese government more accountable, more transparent, and ultimately better governed.

Bibliography

Abed, F. H., and A. M. R. Chowdhury, "The Bangladesh Rural Advancement Committee: How BRAC Learned to Meet Rural People's Needs through Local Action," in *Reasons for Hope: Instructive Experiences in Rural Development*, Anirudh Krishna et al., eds. West Hartford, CT: Kumarian, 1997.

Almén, Oscar, "Only the Party Manages Cadres: Limits of Local People's Congress Supervision and Reform in China," *Journal of Contemporary China* 22, 2013: 237–254.

Almond, Gabriel, and Sydney Verba, *The Civic Culture: Political Attitudes and Democracy in Five Nations*. Princeton, NJ: Princeton University Press, 1963.

Ambrosio, Thomas, "Insulating Russia from a Colour Revolution: How the Kremlin Resists Regional Democratic Trends," *Democratization* 14, 2007: 232–252.

Baker, Peter, "Putin's Kremlin Asserting More Control of Economy: Yukos Case Reflects Shift on Owning Assets, Notably in Energy," *Washington Post*, July 9, 2004, available at http://www.washingtonpost.com/wp-dyn/articles/A37580-2004Jul8.html

Barber, Benjamin, *Strong Democracy*. Berkeley: University of California Press, 1984.

Bardhan, Pranab, and Dilip Mookherjee, eds., *Decentralization and Local Governance in Developing Countries*, Cambridge, MA: MIT Press, 2006.

Baum, Richard, "The Limits of Consultative Leninism," *Asia Program* 131, Woodrow Wilson International Center, June 2006: 13–20.

BBC News, "Garry Kasparov Jailed over Rally," November 24, 2007, available at http://news.bbc.co.uk/2/hi/europe/7110910.stm

Bennett, Colin, "What Is Policy Convergence and What Causes It?" *British Journal of Political Science* 21, 1992: 215–233.

Beyer, Cornelia, "Non-Governmental Organizations as Motors of Change," *Government and Opposition* 42, Autumn 2007: 513–535.

Biello, David, "China Sacks Plastic Bags: Ban Could Save 37 Million Barrels of Oil and Alleviate 'White Pollution,'" *Scientific American*, May 23, 2008.

Blyth, Mark, *Great Transformations: Economic Ideas and Institutional Change in the Twentieth Century*. Cambridge, UK: Cambridge University Press, 2002.

Bo, Zhiyue, and Gang Chen, "Global Financial Crisis and the Voice of the New Left in China," *East Asian Institute Background Brief No. 443*, March 26, 2009, available at http://www.eai.nus.edu.sg/BB443.pdf

Booth, J. A., and P. B. Richard, "Civil Society, Political Capital, and Democratization in Central America," *Journal of Politics* 60, 1998: 780–800.

Boulding, Carew, "NGOs and Political Participation in Weak Democracies: Sub-national Evidence on Protest and Voter Turnout from Bolivia," *Journal of Politics* 72, no. 2, 2010: 456–468.

Brook, Timothy, and B. Michael Frolic, "The Ambiguous Challenge of Civil Society," in *Civil Society in China*, Timothy Brook and B. Michael Frolic, eds. New York: M.E. Sharpe, 1997.

Brooks, Sarah, "Interdependent and Domestic Foundations of Policy Change: The Diffusion of Pension Privatization around the World," *International Studies Quarterly* 49, no. 2, 2005: 273–294.

Brownlee, Jason, *Authoritarianism in an Age of Democratization*. New York: Cambridge University Press, 2007.

Buesgen, Michael, "Environmental NGOs' Role in Expanding Social Spaces – Diversification with Chinese Characteristics: A Case Study of ENGOs' Opposition to the Nujiang Dam in China's Yunnan Province," *China Journal of Social Work* 1, 2008: 160–171.

Business Week, "The Stars of Asia–Opinion Shapers," June 9, 2003.

Cai, Hongbin, and Daniel Treisman, "State Corroding Federalism," *Journal of Public Economics* 88, nos. 3–4, 2004: 819–843.

Cao, Yang, and Victor G. Nee, "Comment: Controversies and Evidence in the Market Transition Debate," *American Journal of Sociology* 105, 2000: 1175–1189.

Cao, Yaxue, "Drinking Tea with the State Security Police – Components of a He Cha Session," *Seeing Red in China*, March 1, 2012, available at http://seeingredinchina.com/2012/03/01/drinking-tea-with-the-state-security-police-components-of-a-hecha-session/

Chamberlain, Heath, "Civil Society with Chinese Characteristics?" *The China Journal* 39, 1998: 69–81.

Chamberlain, Heath, "On the Search for Civil Society in China," *Modern China* 19, April 1993: 199–215.

Chan, Anita, and Jonathan Unger, "China, Corporatism, and the East Asian Model," *The Australian Journal of Chinese Affairs* 33, 1995: 49.

Chan, Che-Po, and Gavin Drewry, "The 1998 State Council Organizational Streamlining: Personnel Reduction and Change of Government Function," *Journal of Contemporary China* 10, no. 29, 2001: 553–572.

Chen, Qiao (陈荞), "民政部：公益慈善类等3类社会组织有望直接登记 [Ministry of Civil Affairs: Sees Potential for Three Types of Social Organizations to Register Directly]," 京华时报*[Beijing Times]*, May 24, 2011, available at http://news.sina.com.cn/c/2011-05-24/014022516251.shtml

China Daily, "Beijing's Population Exceeds 22 Million," February 26, 2010, available at http://www.chinadaily.com.cn/china/2010-02/26/content_9511839.htm

Ching, Frank, "No Changing Colors in China," *The Japan Times*, November 2, 2005, available at http://www.japantimes.co.jp/opinion/2005/11/02/commentary/no-changing-colors-in-china/#.Ul3iDFCko_4. -

Chivers, C. J., "Gorbachev, Rebuking Putin, Criticizes Russian Elections," *New York Times*, January 29, 2008, available at http://www.nytimes.com/2008/01/29/world/europe/29russia.html?_r=0

Chung, Jae Ho, Hongyi Lai, and Ming Xia, "Mounting Challenges to Governance in China: Surveying Collective Protestors, Religious Sects and Criminal Organizations," *The China Journal* 56, 2006: 1–31.

Chan, Anita, and Jonathan Unger, "China, Corporatism, and the East Asian Model," *The Australian Journal of Chinese Affairs*, no. 33, January 1995: 29–53.

Chandhoke, Neera, "A Critique of the Notion of Civil Society as the 'Third Sphere,'" in *Does Civil Society Matter? Governance in Contemporary India*, Rajesh Tandon, and Ranjita Mohanty, eds. New Delhi: Sage Publications India Ltd, 2003: 27–58.

Clinton, William Jefferson, "Finding Our Collective Voice," *InterAction Annual Forum*, April 12, 2006.

Cui, J. "3500 Environmental NGOs in China," *Xinhua News Agency*, October 30, 2008, available at http://news.xinhuanet.com/environment/2008-10/30/content_10282938.htm

Cumings, Bruce, "The Origins and Development of the Northeast Asian Political Economy: Industrial Sectors, Product Cycles, and Political Consequences," *International Organization* 38, Winter 1984: 1–40.

Das, Dilip, "The Invisible Hand versus the Visible Hand: The Korean Case," *Seoul Journal of Economics* 5, 1992.

Deng, Guosheng, "An Emerging Civil Society: The Impact of the 2008 Sichuan Earthquake on Grass-roots Associations in China," *The China Journal*, no. 65, 2011: 181–194.

Diamond, Larry, "Rethinking Civil Society," *Journal of Democracy* 5, no. 3, 1994: 4–17,

Diamond, Larry, "Authoritarian Learning: Lessons from the Colored Revolutions," *The Brown Journal of World Affairs* 12, Summer/Fall 2005.

Diamond, Larry, "Rethinking Civil Society: Toward Democratic Consolidation," *Journal of Democracy* 5, July 1994.

Ding, X. L., "Institutional Amphibiousness and the Transition from Communism: The Case of China," *British Journal of Political Science* 24, July 1994: 293–318.

Dobbin, Frank, Beth Simmons, and Geoffrey Garrett, "The Global Diffusion of Public Policies: Social Construction, Coercion, Competition, or Learning?" *Annual Review of Sociology* 33 (2007): 449–472.

Dobbs, Michael, "U.S. Advice Guided Milosevic Opposition: Political Consultants Helped Yugoslav Opposition Topple Authoritarian Leader," *Washington Post*, December 11, 2000, available at. http://www.highbeam.com/doc/1P2-565855.html

Dolowitz, David, "British Employment Policy in the 1980s: Learning from the American Experience," *Governance* 10, no. 1, 1997: 23–42.

Dolowitz, David, and David Marsh, "Who Learns What from Whom? A Review of the Policy Transfer Literature," *Political Studies* 44, 1996: 343–357.

Domrin, Alexander, "Ten Years Later: Society, 'Civil Society,' and the Russian State," *The Russian Review* 62, 2003: 193–211.

Drew, Jill, "Tangled Blame in Quake Deaths: Chinese Parents Facing Uphill Battle for Redress Over Collapsed Schools," *Washington Post*, June 2, 2008.

Eberstadt, Nicholas, "Power and Population in Asia," *Hoover Institute Policy Review* 123, 2010.

Economy, Elizabeth, "Environmental NGOs in China: Encouraging Action and Addressing Public Grievances," *Roundtable before the Congressional-Executive Commission on China*, February 7, 2005.

Edin, Maria, "State Capacity and Local Agent Control in China: CCP Cadre Management from a Township Perspective," *The China Quarterly* 173, 2003.

Encarnacion, Omar, *The Myth of Civil Society: Social Capital and Democratic Consolidation in Spain and Brazil*. New York: Palgrave, 2003.

Engdahl, F. William, "The Geopolitical Stakes of the Saffron Revolution," *Asia Times*, October 17, 2007.

Erikson, Daniel, "Cuba, China, Venezuela: New Developments," Conference Paper, Fifteenth Annual Meeting of the Association for the Study of the Cuban Economy (ASCE), Miami Dade College, Miami, Florida, August 4–6, 2005.
Evans Jr., Alfred, "Vladimir Putin's Design for Civil Society," in *Russian Civil Society: Critical Assessment*, Alfred B. Evans Jr., Laura A. Henry, and Lisa McIntosh Sundstrom, eds. Armonk, NY: M.E. Sharpe, 2005: 147–158.
[sn]Fahim, Kareem, "Doors Start to Open to Activists in Syria," *The New York Times*, August 28, 2010.
Farizova, Suzanna, "They're Destroying Our Citizens from Within," *Kommersant-Vlast*, November 28, 2005.
Fewsmith, Joseph, *The Logic and Limits of Political Reform in China*. New York: Cambridge University Press, 2013.
Fewsmith, Joseph, "Institutions, Informal Politics, and Political Transition in China," *Asian Survey*, 1996.
Filzer, Donald A., *Soviet Workers and the Collapse of Perestroika: The Soviet Labour Process and Gorbachev's Reforms, 1985–1991*. Cambridge, UK: Cambridge University Press, 1994.
Finkel, Steven E., Aníbal Pérez-Liñán, and Mitchell A. Seligson, "The Effects of U.S. Foreign Assistance on Democracy Building, 1990–2003," *World Politics* 59, 2007: 404–440.
Fisher, William, "Russia: NGO Law Could Strengthen Civil Society," *IPS – Inter Press Service*, January 25, 2006, available at http://www.ips.org
Foley, Michael, and Bob Edwards, "The Paradox of Civil Society," *Journal of Democracy* 7, 1996: 38–52.
Food and Agriculture Organization of the United Nations, "Tourism Development in Lijiang County, Yunnan," 1997, available at www.fao.org/.../11718-01dd07a2f01674c455362f75660ca8e86.pdf
Ford, Peter, "China's Ant Tribe: Millions of Unemployed College Grads," *The Christian Science Monitor*, December 21, 2009.
Foster, Kenneth W. "Embedded within State Agencies: Business Associations in Yantai," *The China Journal*, 2002.
Foster, Kenneth W. "Associations in the Embrace of an Authoritarian State: State Domination of Society?" *Studies in Comparative International Development* 35, Winter 2001: 84–109.
Fox, Jonathan, "How Does Civil Society Thicken? The Political Construction of Social Capital in Rural Mexico," *World Development*, 1996.
Frazier, Mark W. *Socialist Insecurity: Pensions and the Politics of Uneven Development in China*. Ithaca, NY: Cornell University Press, 2010.

Frolic, B. Michael. "State-Led Civil Society," in *Civil Society in China*, Timothy Brook and B. Michael Frolic, eds. Armonk, NY: M.E. Sharpe, 1997.

Fu, Tao, "Respite for Yunnan Anti-Dam NGO as Movement Mourns Loss of Key Activist," *The China Development Brief*, January 20, 2005.

Fukuyama, Francis, "Social Capital and the Global Economy: A Redrawn Map of the World," *Foreign Affairs*, September/October 1995.

Gallagher, Mary, "China: The Limits of Civil Society in a Late Leninist State," *Civil Society and Political Change in Asia*, Muthiah Alagappa, ed. Stanford, CA: Stanford University Press, 2004: 420.

Gandhi, Jennifer. *Political Institutions under Dictatorship*. New York: Cambridge University Press, 2008.

Garcia-Guadilla, María Pilar, "Civil Society: Institutionalization, Fragmentation, Autonomy," *Venezuelan Politics in the Chávez Era*, Steve Ellner, ed. Boulder, CO: Lynne Rienner Publishers, 2003: 190.

Geisselmann, Joern, and Christine Warmer, "Public Participation in China's Municipal Affairs," *D+C Development and Cooperation Tribune*, July 2009: 294–296.

George, Alexander, and Andrew Bennett, *Case Studies and Theory Development in the Social Sciences*. Cambridge, MA: MIT Press, 2005: 10.

Golinger, Eva, *Bush vs. Chávez: Washington's War on Venezuela*. New York: Monthly Review Press, 2007.

Gramsci, Antonio, *Letters From Prison*, Raymond Rosenthal, translator, and Frank Rosengarten, editor. New York: Columbia University Press, 1994.

"Greenpeacers in China and Australia Target Illegal Logging," *Research and Environment News from China*, Embassy of Switzerland in Beijing, November 2004, available at http://www.swisstalents.org/enews/documents/200412/ST_NewsC_November_2004.pdf

Gregory, Paul, and Robert Stuart, *Russian and Soviet Economic Performance and Structure*. Reading, MA: Addison-Wesley, 2001.

Greif, Avner, and David Laitin, "A Theory of Endogenous Institutional Change," *American Political Science Review* 98, 2004: 14–48.

Guo, Gang, "Environmental Security and the Lancang Mekong River Basin: Conflicting Interests of Stakeholders in China," *Foundation For Environmental Security and Sustainability*, June 2007.

Haas, Ernst B. *When Knowledge Is Power: Three Models of Change in International Organizations*. Berkeley: University of California Press, 1991.

Haas, Peter, and Ernst Haas, "Learning to Learn: Improving International Governance," *Global Governance* 1, 3, 1995: 255–285.

Habermas, Jürgen, "Three Normative Models of Democracy," *Constellations* 1, 1994: 1–10.

Habermas, Jürgen, *The Structural Transformation of the Public Sphere*. Cambridge, MA: MIT Press, 1989.

Hadenius, A., and F. Uggla, "Making Civil Society Work, Promoting Democratic Development: What Can States and Donors Do?" *World Development*, 1996.

Haggard, Stephen, and Robert Kaufman, "The Political Economy of Democratic Transitions," *Comparative Politics*, 1997.

Hall, Peter, "Policy Paradigms, Social Learning, and the State: The Case of Economic Policymaking in Britain," *Comparative Politics* 25, no. 3, 1993.

He, Baogang, "Civic Engagement Through Participatory Budgeting in China: Three Different Logics at Work," *Public Administration and Development* 31, 2011: 122–133.

He, Baogang, and Stig Thøgersen, "Giving the People a Voice? Experiments with Consultative Authoritarian Institutions in China," *Journal of Contemporary China* 19, 2010: 675–692.

He, Shenjing, and Fulong Wu, "Property-Led Redevelopment in Post-Reform China: A Case Study of Xintiandi Redevelopment Project," *Journal of Urban Affairs*, 2005.

Heberer, Thomas, and Gunter Schubert, "Political Reform and Regime Legitimacy in Contemporary China," *Asien* 99, April 2006: 9–28.

Heilmann, Sebastian, "From Local Experiments to National Policy: The Origins of China's Distinctive Policy Process," *The China Journal* 59, January 2008: 1–30.

Heilman, Sebastian, and Elizabeth Perry, eds., *Mao's Invisible Hand: The Political Foundations of Adaptive Governance in China*. Cambridge, MA: Harvard University Press, 2011.

Herd, Graeme, "Russia and the 'Orange Revolution': Response, Rhetoric, Reality?" *The Quarterly Journal* 2, 2005: 15.

Ho, Peter, "Self-Imposed Censorship and De-Politicized Politics in China: Green Activism or a Color Revolution," in *China's Embedded Activism: Opportunities and Constraints of a Social Movement*, Peter Ho and Richard Edmonds, eds. New York: Routledge, 2008: 20–43.

Ho, Peter, "Greening without Conflict? Environmentalism, NGOs and Civil Society in China," *Development and Change*, 2001.

Howard, Marc Morjé, *The Weakness of Civil Society in Post-Communist Europe*. Cambridge, UK: Cambridge University Press, 2003.

Howell, Jude, "Getting to the Roots: Governance Pathologies and Future Prospects," in *Governance in China*, Jude Howell, ed. Lanham MD: Rowman & Littlefield Publishers, 2004: 231.

Howell, Jude, "New Directions in Civil Society: Organizing around Marginalized Interests," in *Governance in China*, Jude Howell, ed. Lanham, MD: Rowman & Littlefield Publishers, 2004: 157.

Howell, Jude. "Prospects for NGOs in China," *Development in Practice* 5, February 1995: 10.
Hsu, Jennifer, and Reza Hasmath, eds., *The Chinese Corporatist State: Adaption, Survival and Resistance*. London: Routledge, 2013.
Hsu, Sara, Shiyin Jiang, Halcott Heyward, and Jocelyn Lam, "Did the US Financial Crisis Impact China's Rural Poor?" *9th GEM-IWG International Conference*, United Nations Headquarters, New York City, July 13–14, 2009.
Huang, Philip, "'Public Sphere'/'Civil Society' in China?: The Third Realm Between State and Society," *Modern China* 19, April 1993: 216–240.
Huanqiu Shibao [Global Times], "Meiguo wei zhiku diaocha – fei baoli zhengquan gengdiede muhou heishou [Investigation of American Think Tanks–the Black Hands behind the Scene of Non-Violent Regime Change]," December 12, 2007: 39–43.
Huang, Shaojie, "Govt Plans to Spend on Civil Societies: Plan to Financially Assist NGOs Involves Exerting More Influence," *Huanqiu Shibao [Global Times]*, July 13, 2010.
Hudson, George E. "Civil Society in Russia: Models and Prospects for Development," *Russian Review* 62, 2003: 193–332.
Hui, Dennis Lai Hang, "Politics of the Sichuan Earthquake," *Journal of Contingencies and Crisis Management* June 17, 2009.
Huntington, Samuel, *The Third Wave: Democratization in the Late Twentieth Century*. Norman: University of Oklahoma Press, 1991.
Huntington, Samuel, *Political Order in Changing Societies*. New Haven, CT: Yale University Press, 1968.
International Journal of Not-for-Profit Law "Recent Laws and Legislative Proposals to Restrict Civil Society and Civil Society Organizations," 8, August 2006: 76–85.
Jing, Yijia, and E. S. Savas, "Managing Collaborative Service Delivery: Comparing China and the United States," *Public Administration Review*, 2009.
Jorgensen, Lars, "What Are NGOs Doing in Civil Society?" in *NGOs, Civil Society and the State: Building Democracy in Transitional Societies*, Andrew Clayton, ed. Oxford, UK: The International Non-Governmental Organisation Training and Research Centre, 1996: 38.
Kang, Xiaoguang, and Heng Han, "Graduated Controls: The State-Society Relationship in Contemporary China," *Modern China*, 34, January 2008.
Kang, Xiaoguang, and Heng Han, "Government Absorbing Society: A Further Probe into the State-Society Relationship in Chinese Mainland," *Social Sciences in China*, Summer 2007.
Kang, Xiaoguang, and Heng Han (康晓光与韩恒), "分类控制：当前中国大陆国家与社会关 系研究 (Differentiated Control: Current State

and Society Relationship Research in Mainland China)," 社会学研究 *(Sociology Research Journal)* 6, 2005, available at http://www.chinareform.net/2010/0116/8243.html

Ke, Xuedong, "Lijiang's War on 'White Pollution,'" *China Dialogue*, February 28, 2008.

Keck, Margaret, and Kathryn Sikkink, *Activists beyond Borders: Advocacy Networks in International Politics*. Ithaca, NY: Cornell University Press, 1998.

Kennedy, Scott, *The Business of Lobbying in China*. Cambridge, MA: Harvard University Press, 2005.

Knack, Stephen, "Does Foreign Aid Promote Democracy?" *International Studies Quarterly*, 2004.

Kolesnikov, Andrey, "Unity of Forum and Content," *Kommersant*, November 22, 2007, available at http://www.kommersant.com/p828086/election_campaigning/

Kommersant, "Nekommercheskie organizatsii nachinayut osvoenie byudzheta [Noncommerical Organzations Begin to Master the Budget]," July 8, 2007.

Kostka, Genia, and Arthur Mol, "Implementation and Participation in China's Local Environmental Politics: Challenges and Innovations," *Journal of Environmental Policy & Planning* 15, 2013: 3–16.

Kramer, Mark, "Russian Policy toward the Commonwealth of Independent States: Recent Trends and Future Prospects," *Problems of Post-Communism* 55, 2008: 3–19.

Krastev, Ivan, "Democracy's 'Doubles,'" *Journal of Democracy* 17, April 2006: 52–62.

Kudelia, Serhiy, "Revolutionary Bargain: The Unmaking of Ukraine's Autocracy through Pacting," *Journal of Communist Studies and Transition Politics* 23, 2007: 77–100.

Kurlantzick, Joshua, "Asia's Democracy Backlash," *Current History, November* 2008: 375–380.

Kuzio, Taras, "The Opposition's Road to Success," *Journal of Democracy* 16, 2005: 117–130.

Landry, Pierre, "The Political Management of Mayors in Post-Deng China," *The Copenhagen Journal of Asian Studies* 17, 2003.

Lapidus, Gail W., "Between Assertiveness and Insecurity: Russian Elite Attitudes and the Russia-Georgia Crisis," *Post-Soviet Affairs* 23, 2007: 139.

Le, Zou, "NGO Registration Rules to Be Relaxed Nationwide: Civil Affairs Minister," *Global Times*, May 25, 2011.

Lee, Colleen, "Special Political Zones," *The Standard*, September 7, 2010.

Levitisky, Steven, and Lucan Way, "Competitive Authoritarianism in the Post–Cold War Era," *Journal of Democracy*, April 2002.

Levitt, Barbara, and James G. March, "Organizational Learning," *Annual Review of Sociology* 14, 1988: 319–340.

Lewis, Orion. "Net Inclusion: New Media's Impact on Deliberative Politics in China," *Journal of Contemporary Asia*, 2013.

Lewis, Orion, "Pluralized Authoritarianism: Media Reform and Legitimacy in China," presentation at the 2010 Fudan-IAS Conference on Legitimacy and Governance, July 3–4, 2010, Fudan Institute for Advanced Study in Social Sciences, Fudan University, Shanghai, China.

Lewis, Orion, and Sven Steinmo, "How Institutions Evolve: Evolutionary Theory and Institutional Change," *Polity* 44, 2012: 314–339.

Li, David D. "Large Domestic Non-Intermediated Investments and Government Liabilities–Challenges Facing China's Financial Sector Reform," World Bank working paper, 2006.

Li, He, "Debating China's Economic Reform: New Leftists vs. Liberals," *Journal of Chinese Political Science* 15, 2010: 1–23.

Li, Junru (李君如), *Dangdai Zhongguo zhengzhi zouxiang (Trends in Contemporary Chinese Politics)*, Fuzhou: Fuzhou renmin chubanshe, 2007: 143–146.

Li, Lianjiang, and Kevin J. O'Brien, "Protest Leadership in Rural China," *The China Quarterly* 193, March 2008.

Linz, Juan, and Alfred Stepan, *Problems of Democratic Transitions and Consolidation: Southern Europe, South America and Post-Communist Europe*. Baltimore, MD: Johns Hopkins University Press, 1996.

Lipman, Maria, "Putin's 'Sovereign Democracy,'" Carnegie Endowment for International Peace, 2006, available at http://carnegieendowment.org/2006/07/15/putin-s-sovereign-democracy/ujs

Lu, Yiyi. "The Autonomy of Chinese NGOs: A New Perspective," *China: An International Journal*, 2007.

Lynch, Dov, "'The Enemy Is at the Gate': Russia after Beslan," *International Affairs* 81, 2005: 141–161.

Ma, Qiusha, "The Governance of NGOs in China since 1978: How Much Autonomy?" *Nonprofit and Voluntary Sector Quarterly* 3, September 2002: 305–328.

Ma, Shu-Yun, and Chan Wai-Yin, "The Provision of Public Goods by a Local Entrepreneurial State: The Case of Preservation of the Nanyue Relics in China," *The Journal of Development Studies* 41, October 2003: 119–141.

Mackerras, Colin, "Xinjiang at the Turn of the Century: The Causes of Separatism," *Central Asian Survey*, 2001.

Mahoney, James, and Kathleen Thelen, eds., *Explaining Institutional Change: Ambiguity, Agency, and Power*. Cambridge, UK: Cambridge University Press, 2010.

Marsh, David, and David Dolowitz, "Learning from Abroad: The Role of Policy Transfer in Contemporary Policy-Making," *Governance: An International Journal of Policy and Administration* 13, no. 1, 2000: 5–24.

Mathews, Jessica, "Power Shift: The Rise of Global Civil Society," *Foreign Affairs* 76, January/February 1997.

Maxwell, Michael, "NGOs in Russia: Is the Recent Russian NGO Legislation the End of Civil Society in Russia?" *Tulane Journal of International and Comparative Law* 15, 2006: 247.

McCulloch, Neil, and Michele Calandrino, "Vulnerability and Chronic Poverty in Rural Sichuan," *World Development* 31, 2003.

McMann, Kelly, "The Civic Realm in Kyrgyzstan: Soviet Economic Legacies and Activists' Expectations," in *The Transformation of Central Asia: States and Societies from Soviet Rule to Independence*, Pauline Jones Luong, ed. Ithaca, NY: Cornell University Press, 2004.

Medvedev, Roy, *Post-Soviet Russia: A Journey through the Yeltsin Era*. New York: Columbia University Press, 2002.

Meisner, Maurice, *Mao's China and After: A History of the People's Republic*. New York: Free Press, 1999.

Mertha, Andrew, "'Fragmented Authoritarianism 2.0': Political Pluralization in the Chinese Policy Process," *The China Quarterly*, 2009.

Mertha, Andrew, *China's Water Warriors: Citizen Action and Policy Change*. Ithaca, NY: Cornell University Press, 2008.

Meyssan, Thierry, "The Albert Einstein Institution: Non-Violence According to the CIA," VoltaireNet.org, June 6, 2007.

Ministry of Civil Affairs, "Guanyu chongxin queren shehui tuanti yewu zhuguan danwei de tongzhi" (Circular on Reconfirming the Professional Management Units of Social Organizations), 2000.

Ministry of Health, Joint United Nations Program on HIV/AIDS, and World Health Organization, *Update on the HIV/AIDS Epidemic and Response in China*, 2006.

Mishra, Pankaj, "China's New Leftist," *The New York Times Magazine*, October 15, 2006.

Moscow Times, Dmitri Medvedev's remarks, January 25, 2008.

Narayan, Deepa, "Social Capital and the State: Complementarity and Substitution," *World Bank Policy Research Working Paper No. 2167*, August 1999.

Narayan, Deepa, and Lant Pritchett, "Cents and Sociability: Household Income and Social Capital in Rural Tanzania," *World Bank working paper*, May 1997.

Nathan, Andrew, "China's Changing of the Guard: Authoritarian Resilience," *Journal of Democracy* 14, January 2003: 6–17.

Naughton, Barry, *The Chinese Economy: Transitions and Growth*. Cambridge, MA: The MIT Press, 2007.

Nolan, Peter, *China's Rise, Russia's Fall*. New York: Macmillan Press, 1995.
O'Brien, Kevin J. "Neither Transgressive nor Contained: Boundary-Spanning Contention in China," *Mobilization: An International Journal* 8, 2003: 51–64.
O'Donnell, Guillermo, "Horizontal Accountability in New Democracies," in *The Self-Restraining State*, Andreas Schedler, Larry Diamond, and Marc F. Plattner, eds. Boulder, CO: Lynne Rienner, 1999.
OECD, "DAC1 Official and Private Flows," 2008.
Oi, Jean, "Fiscal Reform and the Economic Foundations of Local State Corporatism in China," *World Politics* 45, 1992: 99–126.
Olson, Alexandra, "Jiang Visits Venezuela, Winning Support against Human Rights Resolution," *Associated Press*, April 16, 2001.
Pan, Rulong, and Dai Zhengqin, "'Yanse Gemin' yu Guoji Fei Zhengfu Zuzhi [Color Revolutions and NGOs]," *Dianzi Keji Taxue Xuebao Shekeban* 7, 2005: 78.
Park, Albert, Scott Rozelle, Christine Wong, and Changqing Ren, "Distributional Consequences of Reforming Local Public Finance in China," *The China Quarterly* 147, 1996: 751–778.
Perry, Elizabeth J. "Moving the Masses: Emotion Work in the Chinese Revolution," *Mobilization: An International Quarterly* 7, Summer 2002: 111–128.
Peterson, George E. *Decentralization in Latin America: Learning through Experience*. Washington, DC: World Bank, 1997.
Pils, Eva, "Peasant's Struggle for Land in China," *World Justice Forum* conference paper, Vienna, July 2–5, 2008.
Pils, Eva, "Land Disputes, Rights Assertion and Social Unrest: A Case from Sichuan," *Columbia Journal of Asian Law* 19, 2006: 235–292.
Poole, Teresa, "China's 'Friends of Nature' Join the Tibetan Antelope on the List of Endangered Species," *The Independent*, November 22, 2008.
Puddington, Arch, Aili Piano, and Camille Eiss, eds., *Freedom in the World: The Annual Survey of Political Rights and Civil Liberties*. Lanham, MD: Rowman and Littlefield, 2007.
Putnam, Robert, *Making Democracy Work*. Princeton, NJ: Princeton University Press, 1993.
Qian, Yingyi, and Barry Weingast, "China's Transition to Markets: Market-Preserving Federalism, Chinese Style," *Journal of Economic Policy Reform*, 1996.
Reuters, "China Enlists NGO Help in Poverty Fight," April 9, 2007.
Rodan, Gary, "Theorizing the Political Opposition in East and Southeast Asia," in *Political Opposition in Industrializing Asia*, Gary Rodan ed. London: Routledge, 1996.
Rollet, Vincent, "The Transnational Origin of a Local Response to HIV/AIDS in Henan Province," *China Perspectives*, 2009.

Rose, Richard, "What Is Lesson-Drawing?" *Journal of Public Policy* 11, 1, 1991: 5.

Rowe, William T. "The Problem of 'Civil Society' in Late Imperial China," *Modern China* 19, no. 2, 1993: 139–157.

Ru, Jiang, *Environmental NGOs in China: The Interplay of State Controls, Agency Interests and NGO Strategies*, Doctoral dissertation, Stanford University, California (2004).

Ru, Jiang, and Leonard Ortolano, "Corporatist Control of Environmental NGOs: A State Perspective," in *China's Embedded Activism: Opportunities and Constraints of a Social Movement*, Peter Ho and Richard L. Edmonds, eds. New York: Routledge, 2008: 44–68.

Ru, X. ed., *Xiao zhengfu da shehui de lilun yu shiqian [Theory and Practice of Small Government and Big Society]*. Beijing: Social Sciences Collections Publishing House, 1998.

Rutland, Peter, "Russia: Nothing Succeeds Like Autocracy," *Transitions Online*, 2007.

Rywkin, Michael, "Security and Stability in Central Asia: Differing Interests and Perspectives," *American Foreign Policy Interests*, 2006.

Saich, Tony, "Citizens' Perceptions of Governance in Rural and Urban China," *Journal of Chinese Political Science* 12, 2007: 1–28.

Saich, Tony, "Negotiating the State: The Development of Social Organizations in China," *The China Quarterly* 161, March 2000: 124–141.

Salamon, Lester M., S. Wojciech Sokolowski, and Associates, *Global Civil Society: Dimensions of the Nonprofit Sector, Volume Two* (Bloomfield, CT: Kumarian Press, 2004).

Salamon, Lester, et al., *Global Civil Society: Dimensions of the Nonprofit Sector*, Baltimore: Center for Civil Society Studies, 1999.

Salamon, Lester, and Helmut K. Anheier, *The Emerging Not-For-Profit Sector: An Overview*. Manchester, UK; New York: Manchester University Press, 1996.

Sanyal, Bishwapriya, "Cooperative Autonomy: The Dialectic of State-NGOs Relationship in Developing Countries," *International Institute for Labour Studies*, 1994.

Schmitter, Philippe, "Still the Century of Corporatism?" *The Review of Politics* 36, 1974: 85–131.

Schwartz, Jonathan, and Shawn Shieh, eds., *State and Society Responses to Social Welfare Needs in China: Serving the People*. London: Routledge, 2009.

Sedaei, Sam, "New Propaganda Piece Hits Iranian Airwaves," *The Huffington Post*, February 26, 2008.

Shambaugh, David, *China's Communist Party: Atrophy and Adaptation*. Berkeley: University of California Press, 2009.

Sharlet, Robert, "In Search of the Rule of Law," in *Developments in Russian Politics*, Stepehn White, Zvi Y. Gitelman, and Richard Sakwa, eds. Durham, NC: Duke University Press, 2005.

Shieh, Shawn, "The Passing of Liang Congjie, China's Environmental and Civil Society Pioneer," NGOs in China blog, November 1, 2010, available at http://ngochina.blogspot.com/2010/11/passing-of-liang-congjie-chinas.html

Shih, Victor, "China's 8,000 Credit Risks," *Asian Wall Street Journal*, February 8, 2010.

Silitski, Vitali, "Contagion Deterred: Preemptive Authoritarianism in the Former Soviet Union (The Case of Belarus)," CDDRL Working Papers 66, June 2006, available at http://iis-db.stanford.edu/pubs/21152/Silitski_No_66.pdf

Silitski, Vitali, "Preempting Democracy: The Case of Belarus," *Journal of Democracy* 16, October 2005: 83–97.

Simmons, Beth A., Frank Dobbin, and Geoffrey Garrett, "Introduction: The International Diffusion of Liberalism," *International Organization* 60, no. 4, 2006: 781–810.

Simon, Herbert A. "Rational Decision Making in Business Organizations," *American Economic Review* 69, 4, 1979: 493–513.

Simon, Karla, "The Regulation of Civil Society Organizations in China," *International Journal of Civil Society Law* 9, 2011: 55–84.

Simon, Karla, and Hang Gao, "Opening the Space: New Developments for China's Community Organizations," Columbus School of Law Legal Studies Series, Accepted Paper No. 2010–25, 2010.

Spires, Anthony, Lin Tao, and Kin-man Chan, "Societal Support for China's Grassroots NGOs: Evidence from Yunnan, Guangdong, and Beijing." *The China Journal*, 2013.

Stiglitz, Joseph, "Some Lessons from the East Asian Miracle," *The World Bank Research Observer*, 1996.

Stone, Diane, "Learning Lessons, Policy Transfer and the International Diffusion of Policy Ideas," *Centre for the Study of Globalisation and Regionalisation*, 2000.

Stone, Diane, "Non-Governmental Policy Transfer: The Strategies of Independent Policy Institutes," *Governance* 13, no. 1, 2000: 45–70.

Strang, David, and Chang Kil Lee, "The International Diffusion of Public-Sector Downsizing: Network Emulation and Theory-Driven Learning." *International Organization* 60, no. 4, 2006: 883–909.

Streeck, Wolfgang, and Lane Kenworthy, "Theories and Practices of Neocorporatism," in *The Handbook of Political Sociology: States, Civil Societies, and Globalization*, Robert Alford Thomas Janoski, Alexander Hicks, and Mildred Schwartz, eds. Cambridge, UK: Cambridge University Press, 2005.

Swain, Margaret Byrne, "Developing Ethnic Tourism in Yunnan, China: Shilin Sani," *Tourism Recreation Research* 14, 1998: 33–40.

Tang, Shiping, and Zhang Yunling, "China's Regional Strategy," *World Economics and Politics*, June 2004.

Tanner, Murray Scot, "China Rethinks Unrest," *The Washington Quarterly* 27, Summer 2004: 137–156.

TASS, "Putin, Hu Jintao to Say Monopoly in International Affairs Inadmissible," June 28, 2005.

Teets, Jessica C. "Let Many Civil Societies Bloom: The Rise of Consultative Authoritarianism in China," *The China Quarterly*, January 2013: 1 20.

Teets, Jessica C. "Reforming Service Delivery in China: The Emergence of a Social Innovation Model," *Journal of Chinese Political Science*, 2012.

Teets, Jessica C. "Post-Earthquake Relief and Reconstruction Efforts: The Emergence of Civil Society in China?" *The China Quarterly* 198, June 2009: 330–347.

Teets, Jessica C., and Orion A. Lewis, "A China Model? – Understanding the Evolution of a 'Socialist Market Economy,'" 2009: http://www.glasshouseforum.org/newsletter_3-2009_newpublications.html

The Economist, "The Earthquake in Sichuan: China Helps Itself," May 22, 2008.

Time Magazine, "Person of the Year 2007," December 17, 2007.

Tismaneanu, Vladimir, *Reinventing Politics: Eastern Europe from Stalin to Havel*. New York: Free Press, 1992.

Tochkov, Kiril, "Interregional Transfers and the Smoothing of Provincial Expenditure in China," *China Economic Review* 18, 2007: 54–65.

Tocqueville, Alexis de, *Democracy in America*. New York: Harper & Row, 1969.

Tsai, Kellee, "Adaptive Informal Institutions and Endogenous Institutional Change in China," *World Politics* 2004.

Unger, Jonathan, and Anita Chan, "Corporatism in China: A Developmental State in an East Asian Context," in *China after Socialism: In the Footsteps of Eastern Europe or East Asia?* Barrett McCormic and Jonathan Unger, eds. Armonk, NY: ME Sharpe, 1995.

Vladimir Putin Remarks, Annual Large Press Conference, February 14, 2008, available at www.kremlin.ru/eng/text/speeches; http://usatoday30.usatoday.com/news/world/2008-02-14-3007602571_x.htm

Walder, Andrew, "Factory and Manager in an Era of Reform," *The China Quarterly*, 1989.

Walker, Kathy Le Mons, "From Covert to Overt: Everyday Peasant Politics in China and the Implications for Transnational Agrarian Movements," *Journal of Agrarian Change*, 2008.

Wang, Hui, "Grassroots NGOs Use Special Accounts to Raise Funds," *China Development Brief*, no. 48, Winter 2010.
Wang, Hui, "New Trends in Philanthropy and Civil Society in China: International Donors and NGOs Need to Establish an Equal Partnership," *China Development Brief*, no.45, Spring 2010.
Wang, Hui, "Contemporary Chinese Thought and the Question of Modernity," in *Whither China? Intellectual Politics in Contemporary China*, Xudong Zhang, ed. Durham NC: Duke University Press, 2001: 185.
Wang, Ming (王名), "China's NGO and Civil Society Development," *Caijing (Finance and Economy Magazine)*, 2002: 350–352.
Wang, Shaogang, "Money and Autonomy: Patterns of Civil Society Finance and Their Implications," *Studies in Comparative International Development* 40, 2006: 3–29.
Wang, Shaoguang, and Angang Hu, *The Chinese Economy in Crisis: State Capacity, and Tax Reform*. Armonk, NY: M.E. Sharpe, 2001.
Wei, Wei, and Zhao Wenjing (魏巍 and 赵文婧), "城市连线 南京的社区组织要备案 [City Connection: Nanjing's social groups want to register]," 东方今报, February 6, 2007.
Weigle, Marcia, "On the Road to the Civic Forum: State and Civil Society from Yeltsin to Putin," *Demokratizatsiya* 10, 2002: 119.
Wen, Ru温儒 [], "北京公务员等将逐步退出社会组织 [Beijing Officials Will Progressively Withdraw from Civil Society Groups]," 新京报 *[Beijing Times]*, 27 February 2011.
West, Loraine, and Christine Wong, "Fiscal Decentralization and Growing Regional Disparities in Rural China: Some Evidence in the Provision of Social Services," *Oxford Review of Economic Policy* 11, 1995: 70–84.
Wheeler, Norton, *The Role of American NGOs in China's Modernization: Invited Influence*. New York: Routledge, 2013.
White, Gordon, Jude A. Howell, and Shang Xiaoyuan, *In Search of Civil Society: Market Reform, and Social Change in Contemporary China*. Oxford, UK: Clarendon Press, 1996.
White, Sarah, "NGOs, Civil Society, and the State in Bangladesh: The Politics of Representing the Poor," *Development and Change* 30, 1999: 312.
Whiting, Susan, *Power and Wealth in Rural China: The Political Economy of Institutional Change*. Cambridge, UK: Cambridge University Press, 2001
Wilson, Jeanne L. "Colour Revolutions: The View from Moscow and Beijing," *Journal of Communist Studies and Transition Politics* 25, June 2009: 369–395.
Wilson, Jeanne L. "Colour Revolutions: The View from Moscow and Beijing," in The "Coloured" Revolutions: Causes, Processes and Consequences Conference, Cambridge University, 2008.

Wong, Christine, "Budget Reform in China," *OECD Journal on Budgeting* 2007: 33–56.

Wong, Christine, "Central-Local Relations in an Era of Fiscal Decline: The Paradox of Fiscal Decentralization in Post-Mao China," *The China Quarterly* 128, 1991: 691–715.

Wong, Edward, "In China City, Protesters See Pollution Risk of New Plant," *The New York Times*, May 6, 2008.

World Bank, "Nongovernmental Organizations and Civil Society/ Overview," 2001.

Xia, Rui, "Illegal Logging Goes on in Yunnan," *Asia Times*, August 9, 2005.

Xinhua News Agency, "Ten-fold subsidy increase for Henan AIDS patients, December 17, 2012, available at http://news.xinhuanet.com/english/china/2012-12/17/c_132045931.htm.

Xinhua News Agency, "Guojia linyeju zecheng tingzhi yinni jinguang jituan binggou guoyou senlin [State Forestry Bureau demands end to purchase of state-owned forest by Indonesian APP Corporation]," 2007, available at http://news.xinhuanet.com/politics/2007-02/07/content_5711370.htm.

Xiong, Wei (熊伟) and 秦梦 (Qin Meng), "论中国NGO本土能力的困境和出路 (An Analysis of Chinese NGO's Weak Capacity and Solution to this Predicament)," 中国思想网 *(Chinese Thought Network)*, June 17, 2008.

Xu, Xibai, "Neoliberalism and Governance in China," unpublished working paper, 2011.

Xu, Youyu, "The Debates between Liberalism and the New Left in China since the 1990s," *Contemporary Chinese Thought* 34, 2003: 6–17.

Yakovlev, Andrei, *State-Business Relations and Improvement of Corporate Governance in Russia*, Bank of Finland Institute for Economies in Transition, 2008.

Yang, Dali, "Economic Transformation and Its Political Discontents in China: Authoritarianism, Unequal Growth, and the Dilemmas of Political Development," *Annual Review of Political Science* 9, 2006: 143–164.

Yang, Dali, *Remaking the Chinese Leviathan*. Stanford, CA: Stanford University Press, 2004.

Yang, Dali, "State Capacity on the Rebound," *Journal of Democracy*, 2003.

Yang, Dali, "Rationalizing the Chinese State: The Political Economy of Government Reform," in *Remaking the Chinese State: Strategies, Society, and Security*, Chao Chien-min and Bruce J. Dickson, eds. London: Routledge, 2001.

Yang, Guobin, "Environmental NGOs and Institutional Dynamics in China," *The China Quarterly* 2005: 46–66.

Yang, Guobin, "The Co-Evolution of the Internet and Civil Society in China," *Asian Survey* 43, 2003: 405–422.

Yang, Song, "Grassroots Nonprofit Organizations in China: Origin and Path," *Public Welfare Times*, March 27, 2009, available at http://hausercenter.org/chinanpo/2009/03/grassroots-nonprofit-organizations-in-china-origin-and-path/

Yardley, Jim, "Chinese City Emerges as Model in AIDS Fight," *New York Times*, June 16, 2005.

Yardley, Jim, and David Barboza, "Many Hands, Not Held by China, Aid in Quake," *New York Times*, May 20, 2008.

Yin, Deyong, "China's Attitude toward Foreign NGOs," *Washington University Global Studies Law Review* 8, 2009.

Young, Nick, "NGOs and Civil Society in China," in *Berkshire Encyclopedia of China*, Linsun Cheng, ed. Barrington, MA: Berkshire Publishing, 2009.

Young, Nick, "Why China Cracked Down on My Nonprofit," *Christian Science Monitor*, December 4, 2007.

Young, Nick, and Tina Qian, "Listening to the Community Is the Main Ingredient in Chinese NGO Recipe for City Governments," *China Development Brief*, March 2, 2006.

Yu, Keping, "Moving toward Shared Governance by the Government and the Public," *Southern Metropolis Daily*, May 8, 2011.

Yu, Keping, *Innovations and Excellence in Local Chinese Governance*. Beijing: Social Science Literature Press, 2002.

Yu, Keping, "The Emerging of China's Civil Society and Its Significance to Governance," *Focus Asien* 8, April 11, 2001.

Zhan, Xueyong, and Shui-Yan Tang, "Political Opportunities, Resource Constraints and Policy Advocacy of Environmental NGOs in China," *Public Administration*, 2011.

Zhang, Chun, "Civil Society's Changing Role in the Chinese Political System," *Dialogue*, March 18, 2013, available at https://www.chinadialogue.net/article/show/single/en/5804-Civil-society-s-changing-role-in-the-Chinese-political-system.

Zhao, Suisheng, "Deng Xiaoping's Southern Tour: Elite Politics in Post-Tiananmen China," *Asian Survey*, 1993.

Zhou, Benshun (周本顺), "Social Management of Innovation with Chinese Characteristics [走中 国特色社会管理创新之路]," *Qiushi Magazine [求是杂志]* 10, 2011.

Zhou, Meiying (赵美英), "新社会阶层政治诉求的调查与机制研究 [Survey and Causal Mechanism Analysis of the New Social Stratum's Political Demands]," 江苏省社会主义学院学报 *[Journal of Jiangsu Institute of Socialism]*, 2005: 35.

Zhou, Shi (周师), "国内学术界关于私营企业主: 政治参与研究综述," 甘肃理论学刊 *Gansu Theory Research*, 2006.

Zhuang, Pinghui, "Guangdong to Allow Some NGOs off the Leash," *South China Morning Post*, November 25, 2011.

Zweig, David, *Freeing China's Farmers: Rural Restructuring in the Reform Era*, Armonk, NY: M.E. Sharpe, 1997.

Index

72386570R00139

Made in the USA
Columbia, SC
27 June 2017